FOREWORD

기억.기록.기표 (신은진) p.010
Recollections.Archives. Symbols
(Eunjin Regina Shin) p.011

WORKS

p.012

ANTHOLOGY & NOTES

p.043

ESSAY

미디어 아트는 X-예술이다
(박영욱) p.334
Media Art is X-Art
(Young-wook Park) p.338

태싯그룹의 소리가 암시하는 것들:
알고리듬 역사의 시작 (이영준) p.342
Tacit Group's Sounds Imply: The
Beginning of Algorithm History
(Youngjun Lee) p.348

INTERVIEW

모호하고 뾰족한 예술의 경계를 향해
(인터뷰: 장재호 + 가재발) p.356
Toward the borders of ambiguous and
pointed art (Interview: JAEHO CHANG
+ GAZAEBAL) p.365

2008

p. 043

p. 047

2008년 9월 8일
쌈지스페이스 10주년
자료전
쌈지스페이스

p. 049

2008년 10월 4일
헤이리 판 아트
페스티벌
헤이리 야외무대

2009
p.051

2010
p.073

p.055

2009년 5월 30일
OVER MUSIC
SERIES
백남준 아트센터

p.077

2010년 6월 11일
이승조 추모전
일주&선화갤러리

p.056

2009년 7월 7일
SPACE 500
공간

p.057

2009년 7월 31일
전자오락관 소년 –
딱 한판만!
상상마당

p.058

2009년 8월 21일
tacit.perform[0]
두산아트센터

p.079

2010년 10월 9일 – 17일
tacit.install[0]_
neighbors[i] – "당신의
이웃은 안녕하십니까?"
송원아트센터

p.08

2010년 10월 15일
PAMS CHOICE
국립극장 달오름극장

p.068

2009년 11월 20일
Artificial Linearity
아트센터 나비

p.08

2010년 12월 17일
tacit.perform[1]
LIG아트홀

2011
p.097

p.101

2011년 2월 18일
S.U.N. SHOWCASE
몽펠리에, 프랑스

p.102

2011년 8월 26일
Aarhus Festival
Musikhuset, Aarhus,
Denmark

p.104

2011년 11월 3일
Face Puzzle
금천예술공장

p.105

2011년 12월 22일 – 23일
tacit.perform[2] -
"Structural Sounds"
LIG아트홀

2012
p.117

p.121

2012년 2월 15일
S.U.N. @ Agora
Monpellier, France

p.122

2012년 9월 17일
tacit.perform[3]
_ SHOWCASE
GWANGJU
광주 아시아예술극장

p.124

2012년 11월 23일 –
12월 6일
US Tour
Legion Arts (Cedar
Rapids), MCA
(Chicago), Lincoln
Center (New York)

2013

p.135

2013년 8월 19일
Residency @
Gwangju Asia Art
Center
광주 아시아예술극장

p.139

2013년 12월 21일
tacit.perform[3]
국립현대미술관 서울관

p.143

2014

p.167

2014년 2월 8일
DISTORTION
FIELD 14
이화여대 ECC

p.171

2014년 8월 16일
FESTIVAL MORPH
프리버드2

p.173

2014년 9월 21일
WeSA Festival
2014
신사장

p.176

2014년 10월 31일
Goethe Institut
Platoon Kunsthalle

p.178

2014년 12월 20일
tacit.perform[4]
Platoon Kunsthalle

p.18

2015 p.197   2016 p.227

p.201
2015년 5월 18일
HIFI@SEMA
서울시립미술관

p.203
2015년 5월 29일
LECTURE
PERFORMANCE,
BRUSSELS
한국문화원, 브뤼셀,
벨기에

p.204
2015년 10월 30일
tacit.perform[5]
예술의전당 자유소극장

p.212
2015년 11월 11일 –
12일
ABU DHABI
NYU 아부다비
콘서트 홀

p.216
2015년 11월 28일
ACT Festival
공연국립아시아문화전당
The Circle

p.231
2016년 10월 22일
KT Meshup Giga
SJ Kunsthalle

p.233
2016년 11월 26일
WeSA Festival
2016 in DAEGU
대구 예술발전소

2 0 1 7   p.241

2 0 1 8   p.249

p.245

2017년 9월 30일
ARTIENCE
DAEJEON
대전예술가의집 누리홀

p.253

2018년 11월 17일
tacit.perform[6]
_10th anniversary
플랫폼엘

p.265

2018년 11월 30일
Gwangju Media Art
Festival
아시아문화전당
복합2관

p.247

2017년 12월 2일
PLUMS FESTIVAL
Digital Centre in
Moscow

2019
p.267

2020
p.293

p.297
2020년 1월 17일 – 2월 2일
tacit.install[1]_op.sound
[piknic]
갤러리 피크닉

p.271
2019년 5월 10일 – 11일
Festival de Música
Asiática Avanzada
Naves Matadero,
Madrid, Spain

p.276
2019년 6월 24일
ISEA 2019
국립아시아문화전당
예술극장1

p.278
2019년 6월 27일
NORDTALKS
문화비축기지

p.279
2019년 8월 31일 –
10월 20일
NO LIVE
코스모40

2019년 9월 26일
Zer01ne Day
(구) 원효로서비스센터

p.286
2019년 9월 28일
WeSA Festival 2019
플랫폼엘

p.287
2020년 10월 24일
2020 PARADISE
ART LAB FESTIVAL
파라다이스 아트랩

p.302
2019년 10월 5일 –
10월 31일
세종대왕과 음악,
치화평
대통령기록관

p.290
2020년 11월 12일 –
2021년 2월 28일
ㄱ의 순간 (The Moment
of Gieok)
예술의전당 서예박물관

p.307
2020년 12월 11일 –15일
tacit.install[2]_tacit
group@church
TINC

p.315

기억.기록.기표

신은진, 큐레이터

«tacit.print[0]_Anthology 2008-2020»은 국내 오디오 비주얼 예술의
선구자이자 세계적으로 그 영역을 꾸준히 넓히고 있는 태싯그룹의 2008년
부터 2020년까지의 활동을 연대별로 조망하는 출판 프로젝트이다.

21세기 새로운 예술을 만든다는 비전 아래 결성한 태싯그룹은 기간 동안
디지털 테크놀로지에서 예술적 영감을 발견하고 이를 통해 멀티미디어 공연,
인터랙티브 설치, 그리고 컴퓨터 프로그래밍에 의한 알고리즘 아트까지
확장하여 다양한 작업을 선보여 왔다. 사뭇 다른 음악적 배경을 가진 두
뮤지션은 2008년 공연을 기점으로 전자음악을 매개로 예술성과 대중성을
실험하는 태싯그룹으로 본격적인 활동을 시작했다. 당시 척박했던 국내
오디오 비주얼 아트신(scene)의 개척자로 활동해온 이들은 여기에 그치지
않고 2014년부터 지금까지 ‹WeSA(We are Sound Artists)›라는 워크숍 및
공연의 플랫폼을 통해 인재를 양성하고 등용시킴으로써 오디오 비주얼의
제한적인 신을 확장하고자 노력해왔다.

이번 출판 프로젝트에서는 그들의 활동 중 2008년부터 현재까지 꾸준히
발전시켜온 ‹tacit.perform›연작을 중심으로 그동안 전 세계를 오가며
선보여온 주요 공연의 사진과 악보, 코딩 알고리즘 등 다양한 아카이브
푸티지를 시간 순으로 나열하여 보여준다. 특히 퍼포먼스 중심으로 남아있는
시청각 아카이브를 편집하고 재조합하는 과정을 통해 이 책을 접하는
독자들이 지난 10여 년간 태싯그룹의 예술적 여정을 마치 한 편의 다큐멘터리
영화를 관람하는 것과 같은 체험을 할 수 있게 준비단계에서 부터 기획되었다.

«tacit.print[0]_Anthology 2008-2020»은 비록 과거의 시간을 기록하고
기념하는 것에 목적을 두고 있지만 주목해야 할 사실은 이들의 예술적 여정이
이곳에 멈추어 있지 않다는 점이다. 공연장을 목적으로 한 퍼포먼스에서 한 발
나아가 조금 더 수평적인 공간에서 다양한 층위의 관객을 만나기 위한 챕터를
여는 태싯그룹의 새로운 출발점이자 향후 새롭게 변화할 이들의 예술적
방향을 모색하는 기표로 작동하길 기원하며 이 기록물을 세상에 내놓는
바이다.

Recollections.Archives.Symbols

Eunjin Regina Shin, Curator

tacit.print[o]_ Anthology 2008-2020 is a publication project overlooking Tacit Group's creative endeavors between 2008 and 2020. Tacit Group, since its formation, has not only established itself as one of Korea's audiovisual art pioneers, but also expanded its presence globally throughout the years.

Set on a mission to create new and original art in the 21st century, Tacit Group spent well over the past decade drawing artistic inspirations from digital technologies and channeling them to different forms of art, from multimedia performance and interactive installation to programming-based algorithmic art. Beginning with their 2008 performance, the Group's two members, each coming from rather contrasting musical backgrounds, have spared no effort in taking electronic music as the medium to experiment with fine and popular art. It was a time when there wasn't so much as a scene for audiovisual art in Korea, and they had to practically establish the field as we now know. Tacit Group's journey to expand the somewhat narrow boundaries of Korea's audiovisual scene was also accompanied by *WeSA(We are Sound Artists)*, a platform established in 2014 specifically to hold workshops and performances that could in turn develop and promote new talents.

Building on *tacit.perform*, a live performance series running since 2008, this publication project presents a timeline of Tacit Group's vast archive footage—pictures, scores, coding algorithms—taken from selected performances in and out of Korea. Right from the early planning stage, this project aimed to offer readers an experience equivalent to watching a documentary film about the Group's artistic journey for the past decade or so, and audiovisual archives went through editing and recombination in a way that could best contribute to the narrative.

While *tacit.print[o]_ Anthology 2008-2020* indeed sets out to document and celebrate the past, it should be equally noted that this in no way concludes Tacit Group's artistic journey. Rather, it is to be hoped that this publication marks the beginning of a new chapter in which the Group takes a step further from auditorium-based performances and shifts toward a more horizontal space to reach a wider audience, and also functions as a symbol of the Group's inquiry into a new and changed artistic direction.

Analytical

2011 tacit.preform[2] - "Structural Sounds" Audio Visual Performance

사운드를 보여주고 비주얼을 들려주는 작품이다. 사운드는 고속 푸리에 변환(Fast Fourier Transform)이라는 분석 툴을 통해 그래픽으로 변환되며, 이 그래픽을 이용해 사운드의 기본 골격인 웨이브폼(waveform)을 만들어낸다. 공연은 태싯그룹의 연주로 시작된다. 그 사운드가 실시간으로 변환돼 그래픽으로 나타나고 그 그래픽이 다시 사운드가 된다. 결국 사운드가 그래픽이 되고 그래픽이 사운드가 되는 순환구조에 의해 오디오비주얼 작품이 실시간으로 구현된다.

2011 tacit.perform[2] - "Structural Sounds" Audio Visual Performance

This work visualizes sound and sonifies visuals by analyzing them. The sound is transformed into a graphic through an analysis anointed the Fast Fourier Transform, with the graphic then being used to create a waveform, which is the basic armature of the sound. The performance begins with Tacit Group converting sound in real time and displays it as a graphic, at which point the graphic becomes sound again. This audiovisual rendition creates a circuitous route in which sound becomes graphic and graphic becomes sound, realized in real time.

Bilateral Feedback

2020 PAL Audio Visual Performance

아날로그와 디지털의 융합은 예술과 산업이 지속해서 시도해온 이슈다. 하지만, 무한한 아날로그의 정보를 유한한 디지털 영역으로 이식하는 것은 간단치 않다. 이 작품은, 디지털 내부의 상호작용을 탐구해온 태싯그룹이 아날로그와 디지털의 융합에 본격적으로 도전하는 시발점이다. ‹Bilateral Feedback›은 모듈라 신시사이저에서 발생하는 아날로그 신호와 컴퓨터에서 발생하는 디지털 신호가 상호 작용한다. 아날로그 장비들의 신호(Audio 신호와 Control Voltage 신호)와 컴퓨터의 디지털 신호는 태싯그룹이 만든 프로그램을 통해 아날로그에서 디지털로, 디지털에서 아날로그로 계속 변환되며 끊임없이 서로에게 영향을 미친다. 궁극적으로는 어느 신호가 아날로그인지 어느 신호가 디지털인지를 구분하는 게 무의미해진다. 이를 통해 아날로그 사운드의 극히 미세한 움직임과 디지털 컴퓨터 그래픽의 픽셀 하나하나는 유기적인 관계 속에 작품을 형성해 간다.

2021 PAL Audio Visual Performance

The convergence of analog and digital is an important issue that art and industry continue to debate and attempt. However, it is not easy to transpose infinite analogical information into the digital domain. Until now, the Tacit Group has focused on exploring interactions within the digital world. In this project, Tacit Group explores the fusion of analog and digital.

Bilateral Feedback is a work of interaction between analog signals generated by modular synthesizers and digital signals generated by computers. Signals from analog devices (audio signals and control voltage signals) and digital signals generated by computers are continuously converted from analog to digital and vice versa - through a program created by Tacit Group - constantly affecting each other. Ultimately, distinguishing which is analog and which is digital, becomes inconsequential. Through this process, the minute migrations of analog sound and pixel motions of digitally generated graphics form an organic relationship.

Composition One

2010 tacit.install[0]_neighbors[i] - "당신의 이웃은 안녕하십니까?" Audio Visual Installation
2 × 2 × 2m 공간
프로젝터, 적외선 센서, 적외선 펜, 테이블, 2채널 스피커, 컴퓨터

텅 빈 듯 보이는 화면에 관객이 점을 찍음으로써 숨겨져 있던 본래의 이미지를 찾아내는 작품이다. 기본적인 개념은 보로노이 다이어그램(voronoi diagram)에서 시작한다. 한 공간에 여러 개의 점이 있다고 하자. 그중 서로 이웃한 점을 두 개씩 골라 수직 이등분선을 그어 연결하면 하나의 도형이 나타난다. 삐뚤삐뚤한 모습이 마치 벌집 같은 이 도형이 바로 보로노이 다이어그램이다. 우크라이나의 수학자 보로노이의 이름을 딴 이 다이어그램은 공간을 여러 셀(cell)로 분리하는데, 하나의 셀 내부의 모든 점은 이웃 셀의 중심점보다 자기 셀의 중심점에 더 가깝다. 관객이 점을 찍으면 보로노이 다이어그램이 생성되며 공간이 분할되는데, 이때 각 셀은 본래 이미지가 가지고 있는 색들의 평균 색을 띠게 된다. 결국, 셀을 잘게 분해할수록 본래의 색에 가까워진다. 이런 관점에서 보면 점을 찍어 셀을 분할하는 것은, 공간을 해체하는 것이기도 하지만 이미지를 구축하는 것이기도 하다.

2010 tacit.install[0]_neighbors[i] - "How are your neighbors?" Audio Visual Installation
2 × 2 × 2m space
Projector, Infrared sensor, Infrared pen, Table, Two channel speaker, Computer

This is a work in which the audience places dots on a screen that appears to be empty, in order to locate a hidden image. The basic concept begins with a voronoi diagram. Supposing there are several dots in one space, if you select two points among them that are adjacent to each other and connect them by drawing a vertical bisector, a figure appears. This meandering figure, similar to a honeycomb in appearance, is a Voronoi diagram. The diagram, named for the Ukrainian mathematician, Voronoi, divides the space into cells, where all points inside the cell are closer to the center of the cell than to the center of the neighboring cell. Through this process, Voronoi diagrams are created. Space is divided when the audience appoints the dots, where each cell assumes the average color of the combined colors of the original image. Eventually, the more the cell is divided, the closer it resembles its original color. From this viewpoint, dividing cells by drawing dots is not only dissolving the space, but also constructing a visible image.

Convex Composer

2010 tacit.install[0]_neighbors[i] - "당신의 이웃은 안녕하십니까?" Audio Visual Installation
2 × 1 × 1m
프로젝터, 카메라, 2채널 스피커, 컴퓨터

관객이 테이블 위에 물체를 놓음으로써 음악이 만들어지는 작품. 테이블에 물체를 놓으면 그 위치에 상응하는 사운드가 생성되며, 이웃해 있는 물체들이 그룹을 이루어 차례로 사운드를 발생시킨다. 위치와 거리, 다른 개체와의 관계를 이용해 작곡이 이루어지는 것이다. 흩어져 있는 물체들의 볼록 외곽선을 찾아내는 데에는 대표적인 기하학 알고리듬인 컨벡스 헐(convex hull)이, 가까운 점끼리 그룹을 짓는 데는 클러스터링 (clustering)이 사용됐다.

2010 tacit.install[0]_neighbors[i] - "How are you, your neighbors?" Audio Visual Installation
2 × 1 × 1 m
Projector, Camera, Two channel speaker, Computer

Music is created by the audience by placing objects on a table. When an object is placed on the table, a predetermined sound is generated at that location, and neighboring objects form a group to generate sequential sounds. The composition is formed employing location, distance, and relationship to other objects. A Convex hull, a standard geometric algorithm, is used to locate convex outlines of scattered objects, while clustering is used to group points in proximity.

Dance Composition No.1

2009 tacit.perform[1] Audio Visual Performance

여러 장르의 예술을 결합하는 통합예술은 대부분 아티스트들이 생각을 교환한 후 각자의 방식대로 작품을 만든다. 그리고 결과물로써 개별 작품들의 합체를 보여준다. 하지만 이 작품은 컴퓨터의 디지털 테크놀로지를 이용해 무용수가 직접 음악과 영상을 제어한다. 음악과 영상이 어떤 식으로 표현되어 나올지는 아무도 예측할 수 없으며 작품은 오로지 무용수의 몸짓과 음악/영상 아티스트들에 의해 프로그래밍된 알고리듬에 따라 결정된다.

2009 tacit.perform[1] Audio Visual Performance

Using an integrated artform combining dance, music, and video, each artist exchanges ideas and creates work through their own form of expression, exhibiting the union of individual works as a result. However, in this work, the dancer directly controls the music and video using digital technology provided by a computer. How music and video will be expressed is unpredictable, and is determined solely by the movements of the dancers and the algorithm programmed by the music/video artists.

Drumming

2015 Hi-Fi Audio Visual Spectacular Audio Visual Performance

스티브 라이히(Steve Reich)의 1970년 작품 ‹Drumming›을 태싯그룹 스타일로
재탄생시켰다. 타악기와 인성을 이용하는 원곡과 달리 태싯그룹은 전자음을 사용하고
악보를 기하학적으로 시각화했다. 컴퓨터는 기계적으로 연주를 하고, 연주자들은 리듬과
음색을 즉흥적으로 변화시킨다. 관객은 이러한 변화를 영상을 통해 직관적으로 인지하게
된다. 즉, 스크린의 상단에 막대기(bar)가 떨어지는 순간, 그것에 해당하는 사운드가
연주되는데, 그 막대기의 질감, 크기와 떨어지는 속도가 정확하게 사운드에 일치하는
것이다. 컴퓨터의 기계음, 연주자들의 즉흥성 그리고 현장성이 결합하여 태싯그룹
특유의 스타일이 만들어진다.

2015 Hi-Fi Audio Visual Spectacular Audio Visual Performance

Steve Reich's *Drumming*, composed in 1970, was reconstituted through a Tacit
Group interpretation. The original song was for percussion instruments and
voices, however the Tacit Group converted the piece into electronic sound
and visualized the score geometrically. The notes are played by the computer
mechanically, and the players improvised with the rhythm and tone. The audience
intuitively perceives this change through video. Essentially, the moment a bar falls
at the top of the screen, a corresponding sound is played, and the texture, size, and
descending rate of the stick precisely correspond to the sound. The mechanical
sound generated by the computer combined with the improvisational nature of the
performance, create a patina unique to the Tacit Group.

Drumming for Monome Ensemble

2009 tacit.perform[1] Audio Visual Performance

사람들은 악기라고 하면 피아노, 바이올린, 기타 등을 떠올린다. 그리고 그 악기들을 이용해 음악을 만드는 것을 작곡이라 생각한다. 하지만 음악인들은 항상 새로운 형태의 악기와 새로운 작곡 방법을 모색해왔다. 이 작품에서는 연주자가 8×8, 64개의 버튼만 장착된 '모노메(Monome)'라는 악기를 이용해 즉흥연주를 한다. 각각의 버튼은 미리 프로그래밍된 알고리듬에 의해 사운드를 생성한다. 그뿐이 아니다. 연주자들은 모노메를 통해 사운드뿐 아니라 영상을 제어할 수도 있다. 태싯그룹은 이 작품을 통해 새로운 음악/영상의 표현과 그 한계를 실험했다.

2009 tacit.perform[1] Audio Visual Performance

When we discuss instruments, we often think of the piano, violin, and guitar. We consider creating music using those instruments to be compositions. However, musicians have always sought out new types of instruments and new ways of composing. In this work, the performer improvises using an instrument called a Monome, equipped with only 8 by 8 or 64 buttons. Each button is preprogrammed with an algorithm. Additionally, performers utilize this instrument not only for playing music, but to control a multitude of images. Using this format, Tacit Group experimented with new musical/image inspired expressions and their inherent limitations.

Game Over

2009 tacit.perform[0] Audio Visual Performance

여섯 명의 연주자가 서로를 상대로 테트리스 게임을 벌인다. 테트리스 블록이 하나씩 내려오고 블록이 쌓이는 과정과 모양이 음악이 된다. 연주자들은 기본적으로 각기 다른 음색을 부여받는다. 그리고 랜덤하게 떨어지는 블록을 연주자들이 어떻게 움직이는지, 얼마나 오래 살아남는지에 따라 작품은 매우 즉흥적이고 우연하게 흘러간다.

2009 tacit.perform[0] Audio Visual Performance

Onstage, six performers compete against each other in a game of Tetris. Tetris blocks fall one by one, and the sound adjusts commensurate with the shape of blocks stacked in the game. Players produce sounds with different tones, resulting in tunes that are both spontaneous and haphazard. The final outcome depends on the randomly placed blocks, the player's game process, and the game time length.

Gesture & Texture

2015 tacit.perform[5] Audio Visual Performance

우리의 인생은 무한히 작은 찰나의 연속이다. 소리의 삶 역시 다르지 않다. 소리에 있어 그런 찰나는 움직임(gesture)으로 인식되기도 하고, 질감(texture)으로 보이기도 한다. 이 둘 즉, 움직임과 질감은 미시적 관점과 거시적 관점에서 유기적인 관계를 맺으며 소리의 삶을 채운다.

2015 tacit.perform[5] Audio Visual Performance moments

Our life is a series of seemingly infinite minutiae. Sound life is no different and can at times be perceived as an instant gesture, or it can appear as a texture. Gesture and texture, fill the life of sound by forming an organic relationship stemming from both the micro and macro perspectives.

Hun-min-jeong-ak

2009 tacit.perform[0] Audio Visual Performance

연주자가 타이핑하는 자음과 모음들의 조합이 음악을 만들어 가는 작품으로, 한글의 창제 원리에 바탕을 두었다. 한글의 원리는 크게 두 가지다. 하나는 글자가 그 요소들의 수평적, 수직적 조합에 의해 만들어진다는 것. 그리고 다른 하나는 글자의 요소들이 언어의 실제 소리를 바탕으로 만들어졌다는 것이다. 태싯그룹은 이 원리를 바탕으로 한글의 요소와 소리를 매칭했다. 연주자가 타이핑을 하면 그에 상응하는 소리가 생성되는 것이다. 연주자들은 자음과 모음을 조합하여 추상적 모양을 만들기도 하고, 의미 있는 글자를 타이핑해 대화를 할 수도 있다. 이런 과정이 모두 즉흥적 퍼포먼스가 된다.

2009 tacit.perform[0] Audio Visual Performance

The combination of typing consonants and vowels entered by a performer creates music, based on the Hangul alphabetical system. There are two main principles involved in the creation of Hangul. One is that letters are created by a horizontal and vertical combination of elements; the other being the constitution of letters are based upon the actual sounds of language. These two principles are embodied in a computer program, and when the performer types, each element of the letter transitions into a corresponding sound. The performers create abstract shapes by combining consonants and vowels, also improvising performances in which they communicate with other performers and/or the audience through meaningful letters.

Improvision

2009 tacit.perform[0] Audio Visual Performance

'Improvision'은 즉흥연주(improvisation)와 시각(vision)을 붙여 만든 단어다. 작품을 구상하던 당시에는 음악과 이미지를 미리 정해놓고 오디오비주얼 작업을 하는 것이 일반적이었다. 태싯그룹은 이 작품을 통해 즉흥성을 실험하고자 했다. 연주자는 정교하게 만들어진 연주 시스템을 즉흥적으로 컨트롤 하고, 이에 상응하는 그래픽이 프로젝션 매핑(projection mapping) 기법을 통해 실시간으로 보인다.

2009 tacit.perform[0] Audio Visual Performance

'Improvision' is a portmanteau combining the words improvisation and vision. Audiovisual works at the time generally programmed music and images in advance. Through this Tacit Group project, we experimented with improvisation where the performer improvised control of an elaborate performance system. The corresponding graphic was displayed simultaneously, utilizing a projection mapping technique.

In C

2009 tacit.perform[0] Audio Visual Performance

‹In C›는 미니멀 음악의 선구자로 알려진 테리 라일리의 작품이다. 라일리의 악보에는 53개의 짧은 악구가 그려져 있다. 연주자들은 이 악구들을 순서대로 연주해야 하지만 개별 악구를 몇 번 반복해야 하는지는 정해져 있지 않다. 연주자는 자신이 원하는 만큼 악구를 반복할 수 있는 것이다. 연주자에 따라 반복 횟수가 달라지면, 결과적으로 화성과 리듬을 예측하기 힘든 다양한 조합이 나타난다. 라일리의 작품은 어쿠스틱 악기를 위한 것이지만, 태싯그룹은 디지털 영상과 전자음을 결합한 새로운 형태의 퍼포먼스로 재탄생시켰다.

2009 tacit.perform[0] Audio Visual Performance

In C is a piece composed by Terry Riley, who is regarded as a pioneer in the field of minimalist music. There are 53 short phrases written on sheet music, and players must perform these phrases in order. However, the number of times individual phrases should be repeated is not predetermined, and the performer can repeat the phrase as many times as he or she wishes. As the number of repetitions varies from player to player, various and unpredictable combinations of harmony and rhythm result. This specific piece is meant primarily for acoustic instruments, but the Tacit Group reconstituted Riley's work with a fresh interpretation that combines both digital images and electronic sounds.

LOSS

2013 tacit.perform[3] Audio Visual Performance

이 작품에는 연주자가 없다. 태싯그룹이 만든 시스템(우주)만이 존재한다. 6명의
연주자는 여러 유전자가 결합된 사운드를 하나씩 창조하고 무대에서 내려간다. 이렇게
탄생한 사운드들은 원칙에 의해 살아간다. 먹이를 먹고 이성을 만나 결혼을 하며
새로운 사운드를 탄생시키기도 한다. 그리고 일정한 시간이 흐르면 조금씩 늙어가다가
소멸한다. 빠른 유전자를 가진 사운드는 많은 먹이를 먹고 크게 성장하고 자주 이성을
만나 여러 자손을 남긴다. 이런 거대한 사운드와 그의 자손들이 시스템(우주)을 점령하면,
왜소한 사운드들은 상대적으로 기회를 박탈당하고 주변을 떠돌다 조용히 소멸한다.
반면, 거대한 사운드가 나타나지 않아 평화롭지만 조금은 단조로운 세상을 여러
사운드가 사이좋게 살아갈 수도 있다. ‹LOSS›의 세계에서 음악은 연주되는 것이 아니라
사운드의 탄생, 성장, 번식, 소멸하는 과정이 전개되는 과정이다.

2013 tacit.perform[3] Audio Visual Performance

There is no designated performer in this particular work. There is only a system
(space) created by Tacit Group in which six performers come down from the stage
after creating six sounds that combine several strands of sonic DNA. The sounds
created operate by the principles of life: which is to say they consume nutrients,
meet members of the opposite sex, marry, and through this process a new sound is
born. After a certain period of time, it grows old little by little and then disappears.
Sounds with rapid genes consume large amounts of food, grow strong, and often
meet the opposite sex leaving behind multiple offspring. When these outsized
sounds and resultant descendants occupy the system (space), other dwarfed
sounds wander around being comparatively deprived of opportunities, and are
quietly extinguished. Consequently, there is no cacophonous sound, hence many
sounds can live in a peaceful but somewhat monotonous world. In the realm of
LOSS, music is not played insomuch as the process of birth, growth, reproduction,
and extinction of sound unfolds into music.

Maze Scoring

2010 tacit.install[0]_neighbors[i] - "당신의 이웃은 안녕하십니까?" Audio Visual Installation
5 × 5 × 3m 공간
스크린, 프로젝터, 2채널 스피커, 컴퓨터, Wii 컨트롤러

미로 생성 알고리듬(maze generating algorithm)을 이용한 작품. 관객이 입력한 점이 알고리듬으로 생성된 미로를 빠져나가는 과정이 음악으로 플레이된다. 점이 제대로 된 길로 향하는지, 벽에 부딪히는지에 따라 사운드가 달라지는 것. 사실 알고리듬이 미로를 만드는 과정은 인간이 미로를 풀어가는 과정과 매우 흡사하다. 앞, 뒤, 좌, 우 중 하나의 길을 선택한 후 막다른 곳에 다다르면 최근의 갈림길로 되돌아가 다른 길을 탐험하는 것이다.

2010 tacit.install[0]_neighbors[i] - "How are you, your neighbors?" Audio Visual Installation
5 × 5 × 3m space
Screen, Projector, Two channel speaker, Computer, Nintendo Wii controller

This work employs a maze generating algorithm. After creating a maze utilizing an algorithm, music is created in the process of designating a path through audience input points and participation. Notes generated depend on whether the point is a road or a wall. In fact, the process by which the maze generating algorithm operates is very similar to the thought process involved when humans navigate a maze. When one encounters a dead end after choosing one of several paths, they return to the fork from whence they diverged and explore an alternate route.

Morse ㅋung ㅋung

2015 tacit.perform[5] Audio Visual Performance

사운드의 세계는 우리가 사는 세상과 마찬가지로 우연과 필연의 경계가 흐릿하고 모호하다. ‹Morse ㅋung ㅋung›은 이러한 모호성을 모르스 부호와 한글의 규칙을 결합해 만든 새로운 규칙을 통해 시각, 청각화한 작품이다. 연주자가 입력한 한글 텍스트는 컴퓨터를 통해 특정한 리듬의 사운드로 변환된다. 이러한 규칙은 일견 당연한 결과인 것으로 보이지만 조금만 자세히 들여다보면 연주자의 예상치 못한 텍스트 입력이라는 우연성이 개입돼 있다. 이렇듯 필연과 우연이 부딪치며 사운드의 세계는 생명력을 갖게 된다.

2015 tacit.perform[5] Audio Visual Performance

Similar to the world in which we live, the boundaries between random chance and the inevitable are blurred and ambiguous. *Morse ㅋung ㅋung* is a work that visually and audibly transforms this ambiguity into a completely new ordinance by coupling the system of Morse code with that of Hangul. The Hangul text entered by the performer is converted into a specific rhythmic sound through a computer. Upon initial examination, rules inherent to Hangul appear to produce a natural result. But if one looks closely, there is an aberrant input of text entered by the performer. The inevitable and coincidental then collide, and a world of sound comes to life.

Morse ㅋung ㅋung (Installation 2020)

2020 ㄱ의 순간(조선일보 창간 100주년 기념 특별전) Audio Visual Installation
1660 × 1660 × 500mm 3개
LED, 철판, 컴퓨터, 5채널 스피커
프로듀서: 신은진, 서체 디자인: 홍은주 김형재, 구조물 제작: 팀에이든, 테크니션: 정창균

한글은 태싯그룹이 지속해서 탐구해 온 테마 중 하나다. 한글이 다른 문자 체계와 달리 인체의 발음 기관에서 나오는 소리를 바탕으로 하고 있다는 점은 큰 영감이었다. 이를 통해 최소한의 요소로 최대한의 음악적 표현을 구현해 보고자 했다. 한글 획의 길고 짧음은 리듬을 표현하는 음표에 대입했다. 초성, 중성, 종성의 조합과 사람의 입과 혀의 모양이 만들어내는 음색의 관계는 소리로 재창조했다. 이를 짧은소리와 긴소리, 쉼표의 세 요소로 언어를 부호화하는 모르스 부호와 합쳤다. 컴퓨터는 한글을 소리로 바꾸는 동시에 글자에 할당된 길고 짧은 음가를 합치고, 여기에 다시 박자에 따른 쉼표를 추가함으로써 음악을 만들게 된다. 초기 오디오비주얼 공연 작품으로 시작된 ‹Morse ㅋung ㅋung›은 프로젝션을 통한 설치작품 단계를 거쳐 LED를 사용한 3차원 큐브로 발전했다. 관객의 움직임과 시선에 따라 독해가 가능한 글자로 보일 수도 있고 추상적인 도형으로 보일 수도 있다. 소리에서 글자로, 글자에서 소리로 변환되는 일련의 분해와 재창조의 과정을 통해 한글이 단지 언어를 전달하는 매개체가 아닌, 추상성과 조형성을 눈과 귀로 동시에 알려주는 예술의 매개체가 될 수 있음을 보여주려 했다.

2020 The Moment of Gieok (Chosun Ilbo 100th Anniversary Special Exhibition) Audio Visual Installation
1660 × 1660 × 500mm 3
LEDs, Iron plating, Computer, Five channel speaker
Producer: Regina Shin, Type design: Hong Eunjoo, Kim Hyungjae, Fabrication: team Aidan, Technician: Changgyun Jung

Hangul is one of the themes that Tacit Group has constantly explored. Hangul is a great source of inspiration in that, unlike other writing systems, it is based on sounds pronounced using organs in the human body. Through this, we attempt to seize upon maximum musical expression with a minimum of external elements. Extended and abbreviated lines used in the stroke of Hangul were substituted for the notes denoting rhythm. Additionally, the relationship between the onset, the nucleus, and the coda of a letter and the tone created by the shape of a person's mouth and tongue was recreated with sound. This is then again combined with Morse code that encodes the language with three elements: a short sound, a long sound, and a comma. The computer creates music by converting Hangul into sound, simultaneously combining the long and short notes assigned to the letters, whilst adding a rest according to the meter. *Morse ㅋung ㅋung*, which began as an audiovisual performance work, evolved into a three-dimensional cube employing LEDs whose light travels through an installation using projection. Depending on the movement and angle of orientation in the audience, it can be seen as letters that can be read, or appear as abstract shapes. Through a process of decomposition and re-creation morphing from sound to letter and the reverse, Hangul becomes a medium of art that not only conveys language, but serves to abstract and form through the eyes and ears. This is how we wished to present it.

Neighbors
Interact

2010 tacit.install[0]_neighbors[i] - "당신의 이웃은 안녕하십니까?" Audio Visual Installation
2 × 2 × 2m 공간
LED 모니터, 헤드폰, 테이블, 센서, 컴퓨터

‹네이버스 인터랙트(Neighbors Interact)›는 현실 세계를 시뮬레이션한다. 생명체의
원칙은 단순하다. 랜덤한 위치, 움직임, 무게로 태어나며 서로를 끌어당긴다. 무게가
무거우면 더 세게 끌어당기고, 너무 가까워져 충돌하면 가벼운 쪽이 죽는다. 생명체들은
소리도 만들어낸다. 혼자 있을 때의 소리는 아주 작지만 다른 생명체에 다가가면 커진다.
단순한 원칙이지만 시뮬레이션이 진행됨에 따라 소리와 이미지는 복잡한 양상으로
나타난다. 디지털 테크놀러지의 발달과 함께 현실 세계를 시뮬레이션하려는 많은 시도가
이루어져 왔다. 인공생명(artificial life) 이론은 그 대표적 예로, 생명체가 태어나고
죽으며 상호작용을 하는 것을 비교적 간단한 알고리듬으로 시뮬레이션한다. 이러한
알고리듬은 문제의 해답을 찾는 것이 아니라 새로운 세계를 탐구하는 실험성에 목적을
둔다.

2010 tacit.install[0]_neighbors[i] - "How are your neighbors?" Audio Visual Installation
2 × 2 × 2m space
LED monitor, Headphones, Table, Sensor, Computer

Neighbors Interact attempts to simulate the actual world. The principles of life are
simple. Sentient beings are born in and with random positions, movements, and
weights all attracting and repelling each other. If the weight of the being is heavier,
its center of gravity pulls harder, and if it gets too close to another and collides,
the lighter one perishes. Living things also emit sound. The sound of being alone
is extremely slight, but the sound increases with proximity to other creatures. It is
a seemingly straightforward principle, but as the simulation proceeds, the sound
and the image appear in increasingly complex patterns. As digital technology
advances, several attempts have been made to simulate the real world. The
concept of artificial life is a representative example of this, which simulates the
interaction between living things from birth to death, using a relatively simple
algorithm. These algorithms are not aimed at finding answers to specific problems,
but for experimentation in exploring new worlds.

Operational

2011 tacit.preform[2] - "Structural Sounds" Audio Visual Performance

연주자들은 작품에 필요한 악기를 직접 제작하고 개발하기도 한다. 오픈 소스 하드웨어라고 불리는 이런 악기들은, 몇 개의 현, 건반, 울림판으로 정의된 전통 악기와 달리 연주자 스스로 구상하고, 제작하고, 그때그때의 필요에 따라 재구성할 수도 있다. 악기의 버튼이나 노브(knob) 같은 구성을 바꿈으로써 전혀 다른 작곡법도 가능해진다. 이는 영상 분야에도 동일하게 적용 가능해서 작가의 의도에 따라 다양하고 즉흥적으로 비주얼을 제어할 수 있다. ‹Operational›은 음악과 영상을 같은 방식으로 제어하는 '모노메'와 '아크'라는 악기를 사용한다. 사운드와 비주얼이라는 서로 다른 두 개의 영역이 동일한 의도 아래 연결되는 새로운 공연을 보여준다.

2011 tacit.perform[2] - "Structural Sounds" Audio Visual Performance

Performers create and develop instruments for, and in, their work. These instruments, known as open source hardware, can be conceived, produced, and reconfigured according to specific requirements unlike traditional instruments, which are defined and often limited by strings, keys, and soundboards. By changing the composition and configuration of the instrument's buttons and knobs, a completely different method of composition becomes possible. These adaptations can also find equal application in the medium of video. Hence, it is possible to control visuals in a variety of ways according to the intent of the artist using *Operational* instruments such as the 'monome' and 'arc' that control music and video in the same way. It demonstrates a new method of performance in which two different areas of sound and visual are connected with the same intention.

OP SOUND II

2010 tacit.install[0]_neighbors[i] - "당신의 이웃은 안녕하십니까?" Audio Visual Installation
2 × 2 × 5m 공간
프로젝터, 스피커 16개, 컴퓨터

16개의 스피커가 서로 다른 속도로 소리를 뿜어낸다. 동시에 시작된 소리는 시간이
지남에 따라 조금씩 흩어지며 다양한 음높이와 리듬으로 변화하고 결과적으로
복합박자(poly-meter)의 사운드가 생성된다. 그리고 오랜 시간 후에 결국 다시 하나의
소리로 다시 뭉친다. ‹OP SOUND II›는 시계의 시침이 12시간마다 원점으로 돌아가는
것과 같은 모듈로 연산(modular arithmetic 또는 modulo operation)과 최대공약수,
최소공배수 등 유클리드 알고리듬 (Euclid's algorithm)에 근거한다. 간단히 말해 서로
다른 속도로 움직이는 16개의 시계가 있는 셈이다. 제목인 'op sound'는 옵아트(op art;
optical art)를 응용한 것으로 두 가지 의미가 있다. 하나는 옵아트의 주요 특성 중 하나인
착시(illusion)를 청각적으로 풀어냈다는 것이며, 다른 하나는 옵사운드의 옵(op)을
'operational'로 해석해 소리가 연산자(operator)의 역할을 하여 음악을 만들어낸다는
것이다.

2010 tacit.install[0]_neighbors[i] - "How are your neighbors?" Audio Visual Installation
2 × 2 × 5 m space
Projector,16 speakers, Computer

16 speakers emit sound at different speeds. Sounds commencing in tandem
dispense little by little over time and transform into various pitches and rhythms,
resulting in a poly-meteric composition. After a period of extended time, a
reunification into one sound occurs. *OP SOUND II* is based on a modular
arithmetic or modulo operation - such as when a clock's hour hand returns to
its origin every 12 hours - and Euclid's algorithm which is related to the greatest
common factor and least common multiple. Basically, there are 16 clocks moving
at differing speeds. The title 'op sound' is derivative of op art (optical art) and
consists of two meanings. One is that the optical illusion, which is one of the main
characteristics of op-art, is addressed aurally. The other being that the op-sound's
op is interpreted as 'operational', so that the sound acts as an operator.

op.sound
[cosmo40]

2019 No Live Audio Visual Installation
3 × 30 × 2m 공간
LED, 스피커 3개, 컴퓨터

‹op.sound[cosmo40]›는 태싯그룹이 최초로 선보인 '장소 특정적 설치 작품'이다. 2010년 발표했던 ‹OP SOUND II›가 복합박자로 생성되는 알고리듬을 이용한 오디오비주얼 설치 작품이라면, 이번 작품은 산업 공장 리노베이션 건축물인 코스모40의 벙커라는 특수한 공간 특성(어두컴컴하고 소리가 많이 울리는)을 고려해 사운드와 조명을 사용한 장소 특정적 설치 작품이다. 30미터 길이를 달하는 배수구의 트렌치 아래 설치된 LED 조명은 태싯그룹 특유의 공연 시스템을 전시용 포맷으로 변형하는 방식으로 사운드와 함께 디자인되었으며, 벙커의 육중하고 폐쇄적인 공간과 맞물려 관람객에게 몰입적 경험을 제공한다.

2019 No Live Audio Visual Installation
3 × 30 × 2m Space
LED, 3 speakers, computer

op.sound[cosmo40] is the first 'site-specific installation work' presented by Tacit Group. While *OP SOUND II*, released in 2010, is an audio visual installation employing an algorithm generated by complex beats, this is a site-specific installation using sound and lighting within a special venue, a bunker named Cosmo 40. The LED lighting installed below the trench of a drainage canal 30 meters in length, is paired with sound in a way that transforms Tacit Group's singular performance system into an exhibition format, integrating the cavernous yet restricted space of the bunker into an immersive experience for the audience.

op.sound
[piknic]

2020 tacit.install[1]_op.sound[piknic] Audio Visual Installation
10 × 8 × 5m 공간
LED바 16개, 스피커 16개, 컴퓨터

2010년부터 선보여온 ‹op.sound› 연작 중 하나. 복합적인 박자에 의해 생성되는
알고리듬을 이용했던 ‹OP SOUND II›와 코스모40이라는 산업 공장 리노베이션
건축물의 특수한 공간 특성을 이용한 장소 특정 설치작품 ‹op.sound[cosmo40]›에
이은 네 번째 버전이다. '피크닉'이라는 이름의 장소에서 선보인 이 작품은 5미터
높이의 보이드한 공간에 열여섯 개의 LED 조명 기둥이 열여섯 개의 스피커와 연동되어
작동한다. 기존의 공연용 시스템을 전시용으로 변형했으며, 정돈된 화이트 큐브 안에서
소리와 빛에 집중할 수 있도록 했다.

2020 tacit.install[1]_op.sound[piknic] Audio Visual Installation
10 × 8 × 5m space
16 LED light bars, 16 speakers, Computer

op.sound[piknic] is one of the op.sound series that have been released since
2010, which used an algorithm generated by complex beats, and a site-specific
installation using the unique environment of an renovated industrial factory
space, Cosmo 40, in 2019. This is the fourth version following op.sound. This
work, presented at a location dubbed 'Piknic', works in an open space five meters
high, with sixteen LED light poles paired with sixteen speakers. The existing
performance system was transformed for exhibition, making it possible to focus
on sound and light in an orderly white cube.

op. sound
[3671240]

2020 tacit.install[2]_tacit group@Church Audio Visual Installation
size variable
혼합재료, 5.1채널 사운드
프로듀서: 신은진, 구조물 디자인 및 제작: 팀에이든, 테크니션: 정창균

다섯 숫자를 내포한 다섯 개의 조형물이 서로 감응하며 교회 공간 안에서 사운드와
라이트를 뿜어내는 작품. 숫자와 옵티컬 사운드를 매칭하는 작업인 ‹op. sound› 시리즈
중 가장 최근의 작품으로, 교회라는 공간적 특수성이 영감으로 작용했다. 작품의 기반인
3, 6, 7, 12, 40의 다섯 숫자는 성서에서 중요한 의미를 가지는 것들로 완전함과 부정,
신의 권위와 시련 등을 의미한다. 이런 숫자들이 옵티컬 사운드로 변환돼 교회라는
공간과 공명하는 작품은, 성서가 우리에게 제시하고자 했던 의미를 시각적으로 또
청각적으로 상기한다.

2020 tacit.install[2]_tacit group@Church Audio Visual Installation
size variable
Mixed materials, 5.1-channel sound
Producer: Regina Shin, Design & fabrication: team Aidan, Technician: Changgyun Jung

Five sculptures containing five numbers connected to each other, radiate sound
and light in a former church venue. This is the latest work in the *op. sound* series;
a work that weds numbers with optical sound. The spatial thematics of the
church served as an inspiration. The five numbers, 3, 6, 7, 12, and 40, which are
the basis for the work, occupy important significance in the Bible. They denote
perfection, denial, divine authority and trial. These numerals are transmuted
into optical sound, resonating within the space of the church, visually and aurally
communicating the spiritual message intended for us.

Organ

2015 Hi-Fi Audio Visual Spectacular Audio Visual Performance

사운드를 생명체로 보고 그 내면을 들여다보면, 인체가 수많은 세포로 구성돼 있듯 사운드 역시 아주 작은 알갱이들로 이루어져 있다. ‹Organ›은 소리의 알갱이들이 상호 작용을 통해서 모이고 흩어지는 과정을 시스템으로 구현했다. 연주자들은 사운드의 내면으로 들어가서 작은 알갱이들의 움직임을 조정하여 하나의 완성된 사운드가 탄생하는 과정을 영상을 통해 보여준다.

2015 Hi-Fi Audio Visual Spectacular Audio Visual Performance

Let us view sound as a living organism and look inside it. Just as the human body is made up of numerous cells, sound is also made up of minute particles. *Organ* implemented the process of gathering and dispersing sound particles through interaction as a system. The performers venture inside the sound, adjusting movement of the small particles in order to demonstrate the process of creating a complete sound through video.

Puzzle 15

2011 Aarhus Festival Audio Visual Performance

'Fifteen Puzzle'이라고 불리는 고전적인 퍼즐 게임을 이용한 작품. 퍼즐은 가로 네 칸, 세로 네 칸, 총 16개의 칸으로 나뉘어 있고, 1–15까지 넘버링된 15개의 타일과 하나의 빈칸으로 이루어져 있다. 게임의 목적은 임의로 섞여 있는 넘버 타일들을 빈칸을 이용해 제자리로 맞추는 것. 연주자가 퍼즐을 푸는 과정에서 서로 이웃한 타일이 맞았을 때 그에 상응하는 선율이 연주된다. 따라서 게임이 진행되는 동안 여러 개의 선율이 우연적으로 섞이면서 다양한 화성과 리듬의 진행이 나타나게 된다. 또한 타일들은 1–15라는 숫자 대신 실시간으로 촬영되는 연주자의 얼굴이 쪼개진 영상을 담는다. 공연이 진행되는 동안 연주자의 얼굴 파편들이 다양한 영상으로 재조합되기도 한다.

2011 Aarhus Festival Audio Visual Performance

This work employs a puzzle game, 'Fifteen Puzzle'. This classic puzzle is a game in which there are 15 tiles with four horizontal and four vertical spaces, each with a numerical value ranging from 1 to 15 out of a cumulative total of 16 spaces. The remaining space is used to push randomly mixed tiles into place. In the process of solving the puzzle, when the tiles sitting adjacent to each other meet, the corresponding melody is played. As a result, while the game is in progress, several melodies are randomly mixed, and the progression of the various harmonies and rhythms appear. Additionally, instead of the numbers 1-15, the tiles contain a split image of the player's face, which is taken in real time. In the course of performance, fragments of the performer's face are reconstituted into various images.

Six Pacmen

2013 tacit.perform[3] Audio Visual Performance

1980년 출시된 비디오게임 ‹팩맨(Pacman)›과 1973년 작곡된 스티브 라이히(Steve Reich)의 ‹Six Pianos›를 이용해 만든 작품이다. 연주자들은 각자의 팩맨을 조종해 주어진 아이템을 먹어야 한다. 6명의 연주자가 모두 아이템을 먹으면 비로소 한 레벨이 완성되고 새로운 마디로 악곡이 넘어가게 된다. 어떤 레벨(혹은 마디)에는 연주자를 방해하는 고스트가 나타나기도 한다. 모든 마디를 무사히 연주하면 음악은 끝나고 게임도 끝난다.

2013 tacit.perform[3] Audio Visual Performance

This work was created using the video game Pacman released in 1980 and the *Six Pianos* by Steve Reich composed in 1973. The performers must navigate their Pac-Man character and consume the obstructing item. When all six performer's respective pacmans have eaten the item, one level is completed and the music is transferred to the next bar. At some levels (or bars), ghosts appear to distract and disturb the player. If all the levels are navigated safely, the music ends and the game is complete.

Space
(Intellectual)

2009 tacit.perform[1] Audio Visual Performance

‹Space›는 소리가 사는 세계이다. 이곳에 사는 소리는 마치 생명체와 같이 태어나서 살다가 죽는다. 연주자들은 소리를 창조하고 이들의 기본 특성 중 일부분만 컨트롤할 수 있다. 이후 소리는 정해진 원칙에 의해 상호작용한다. 결국 예측하기 힘든 결과가 만들어지는 것이다. 결정론적인 시스템과 연주자의 즉흥적 입력이 알고리듬 음악의 특성을 극대화하여 보여준다.

2009 tacit.perform[1] Audio Visual Performance

Space is a world where sound lives. The sounds living here are born and die like living things. Performers can create sounds and control some aspects of their existence. Sounds interact according to a set principle, and players can control only a portion of the traits they are born with, making results difficult to predict. This system of partial predetermination paired with the undetermined input of the performer, enhances and accentuates the characteristics of the algorithmic music.

Structural

2011 tacit.preform[2] - "Structural Sounds" Audio Visual Performance

테트리스 게임의 블록이 쌓이는 구조를 이용해 사운드와 영상을 만든다. ‹Game Over›의 후속작으로, 전작이 게임의 알고리듬과 진행에 의존한 수동적인 대결 구도였다면, ‹Structural›은 블록과 게임의 법칙을 활용하는 연주자들의 능동적인 태도가 관건이 된다. 연주자는 블록을 움직이고, 부수고, 쌓는 게임의 법칙 자체를 작품 속으로 끌어들임으로써 자유롭게 자신의 의도를 펼쳐 보이고 작품을 제어할 수 있다.

2011 tacit.perform[2] - "Structural Sounds" Audio Visual Performance

This performance creates sound and video utilizing the building block structure of a Tetris game. As the sequel to *Game Over*, which was a work that was a passively confrontational structure, dependent on the algorithm and progress of the game, Structural sounds allows for the proactive nature of players who more actively execute directives using blocks and the rules of the game. Players can more freely pursue their intentions and control the work while actively moving, breaking, and stacking blocks into the work.

System 1

2014 Morph Festival Audio Visual Performance

작곡의 재료를 극단적으로 제한하는 것은 의외로 매력적이다. 이 작품에서 연주자는 세 가지 소리와 여덟 가지 변형 방식만으로 음악을 만들어 가야 한다. 화면에 보이는 선은 소리의 정보를 담고 있다. 선의 여덟 가지 길이와 세 가지 모양이 서로 다른 소리를 나타내는데, 관객이 소리의 움직임을 눈으로 볼 수 있게 한다.

2014 Morph Festival Audio Visual Performance

Imposing limitations upon the material which is accessible to composition is surprisingly attractive. In this work, the performer must create music with only three sounds and eight variations. The lines displayed on the screen contain sound information. The eight lengths and three shapes of lines represent different sounds, allowing the audience to track the movement of sound with their own eyes.

System 2

2015 tacit.perform[4] Audio Visual Performance

인간과 컴퓨터가 함께 만드는 작품이다. 연주자는 컴퓨터에 초깃값들을 주고 컴퓨터는
프랙탈, 베타 펑션 등의 알고리듬을 이용하여 초깃값을 변형시킴으로써 작품을 만든다.
이 시스템을 통하여 연주자와 컴퓨터가 연주를 하면 소리와 영상이 화면에 그림 악보로
구현된다. 각 연주자는 화면 안에서 그림 악보를 구현할 제한된 공간을 배정받는다. 여섯
명의 연주자가 제한된 공간과 실시간 연주라는 한계 안에서 서로 호흡을 맞춰 나가며
즉흥적으로 연주를 한다.

2015 tacit.perform[4] Audio Visual Performance

This is a collaboration created by both humans and computers. The performer
provides the computer with initial values, whereby the computer then generates
a work by transforming these values using algorithms such as fractal and beta
functions. Through this system, when the player and the computer execute tasks,
sound and video are utilized as a graphic score on the screen. Each performer is
assigned a limited space to create the score within the screen. Performers perform
improvisation, moving together within the limited space and the constraints of
real-time performance.

61/6 Speakers

2020 tacit.install[2]_tacit group@Church Audio Visual Installation
1600 × 1600 × 400mm
알루미늄 아노다이징, 스피커 61개, 앰프 11개
프로듀서: 신은진, 구조물 디자인 및 제작: 정성윤, 테크니션: 정창균

61개의 스피커가 설치돼 있지만 아무 소리도 재생되지 않는다. 감지할 수 있는 것은 스피커의 움직임과 진동뿐이다. 시간의 흐름으로만 인지되던 음악을 설치 작업을 통해 공간 예술로 구현함으로써 소리와 진동의 경계에 대한 질문을 던진다. 작품은 스피커의 진동 속도를 제어하는 방식으로 진행된다. 아주 느린 진동은 가청 주파수를 벗어나 귀로는 들을 수 없지만 눈으로 볼 수 있는 진동이 되고, 점차 빨라지는 진동은 가청 범위 안에 들어와 귀로는 들을 수 있지만 눈으로 보기 어려운 진동이 된다. 61개의 스피커는 조형 작가 정성윤이 제작한 거대한 조형물에 설치됐다. 조형물 아래 서면 다양한 방향에서 감지되는 진동의 전자음을 몸으로 감지할 수 있으며 새로운 공감각적 경험을 하게 된다.

2020 tacit.install[2]_tacit group@Church Audio Visual Installation
1600 × 1600 × 400mm
Aluminum anodizing, 61 speakers, 11 amplifiers
Producer: Regina Shin, Design & fabrication: Jung Sungyoon, Technician: Changgyun Jung

In this work 61 speakers are installed, yet no sound is generated. All one can detect is the movement and vibration of the speaker. Music that was once perceived only as a passage of time is realized as spatial art through an installation work, where questions concerning the boundary between sound and vibration are posited. The work is conducted controlling the speaker's speed of vibration. Extremely slow vibrations generated by an audible frequency become vibrations undetectable to the ears, yet can be seen by the eyes. With the rate of vibration gradually increasing, an audible range is reached but then becomes difficult to see. 61 speakers were arranged on a massive sculpture created by sculptor Sungyoon Jeong. Standing under the sculpture, the body can sense the electronic sound of vibration detected from various directions, allowing you to experience a new synesthesia.

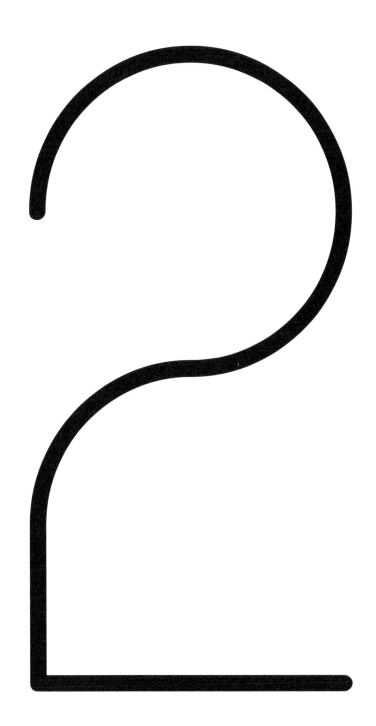

045

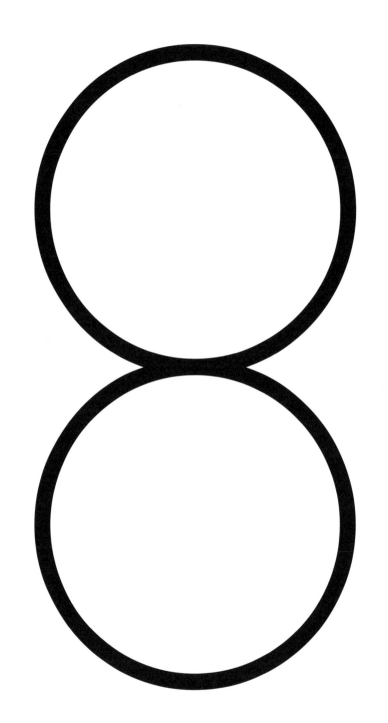

8 SEP, 2008

10TH ANNIVERSARY OF SSAMZIE SPACE

태싯그룹의 첫 공연. 쌈지
스페이스의 10주년 기념
행사이자 폐관 기념 행사에
초청되어 결성 이후 첫 공연을
펼쳤다.

Tacit Group's first
performance. Tacit Group
was invited to the 10th
anniversary of Ssamzie
Space and the closing
ceremony, and gave
the first performance,
following the inauguration
of Ssamzie Space.

2008 HEYRI PAN ART FESTIVAL

헤이리에서 매년 개최되는 문화 페스티벌의 폐막 공연으로 초청받았다. ‹훈민정악›, ‹Music Game Music› 등을 선보였다.

Tacit Group was invited to perform at the closing of the annual cultural festival held in Heyri. Tacit Group presented *Hunminjeongak* and *Music Game Music*.

일시: 10월 4일 금요일 저녁 7시 ‖ 소요시간: 90분
장소: 갈대광장 야외무대 ‖ 장르: 전자음악공연
단체: **Tacit Group** (장재호, 가재발(이진원), 최수환, 배미령, 박재록, 김민강, 윤제호, 조은희)

+++

▶ 공연 소개

개요: 폐막공연에서 선보여지는 작품들은 Tacit Group이 오랜 기간 동안 심혈을 기울여 만든 본격적인 디지털 아트들이다. 기본적으로는 사람들이 자유롭게 먹고 마시고 춤 출 수 있는 장을 마련하는 것이나, 공연의 본래 의도는 예술, 디지털 테크놀러지, 대중적 문화의 만남에 대한 새로운 감각과 정신을 발견하는 것이다.

훈민정악: 연주자들이 한글을 타이핑하면 각 자모들이 미리 할당된 소리를 만들어낸다. 이러한 단순한 원리로 4명의 연주자가 타이핑에 의해 음악을 만들어간다. 매우 즉흥적인 요소가 강한 작품이다.

Terry Riley "In C": 미니멀음악의 선구자인 Terry Riley의 작품 "In C"를 연주한다. 보통 전통적 악기로 연주되는 이 곡은, 이번 공연에서는 컴퓨터가 만들어내는 소리와 음들, 그리고 영상에 의해 연주될 예정이다. 디지털 기술에 의해 재해석될 이번 연주는, 20세기 음악사의 획을 그었던 이 작품에 21세기적 생명을 새롭게 붙어넣을 것이다.

Music Game Music: 사다리나 팩맨 같은 저통적 게임의 요소들이 영상을 통해 보여지고, 이 요소들의

과학기술진흥 ‖ 미디어후원 네이버 ‖ 협찬: 한국영상자료원, 환경재단, 웹시쿠, 나른이미징코리아, 풀로덕트 집, 더 스텝

rks   Window   Help

2008 헤이리 판 페스티벌

8/content/#/stage6

MUG   audio▾   visual▾   news▾   comunity▾   torrents▾   엡하드   designflux   Wikipedia

‹청춘의 십자로›, 김태용 감독

‹리어카, 뒤집어지다›, 극단 몸꼴

‹금빛소리-세계음악여행›, 코리아 브라스 콰이어

‹Digital Music, DigitalDance›, Tacit Group

위 이미지를 클릭하시면, 자세한 내용을 보실 수 있습니다.

일시: 10월 4일 금요일 저녁 7시 ‖ 소요시간: 90분
장소: 갈대광장 야외무대 ‖ 장르: 전자음악공연
단체: **Tacit Group** (장재호, 가재발(이진원), 최수환, 배미령, 박재록, 김민강, 윤제호, 조은희)

+++

▶ 공연 소개

개요: 폐막공연에서 선보여지는 작품들은 Tacit Group이 오랜 기간 동안 심혈을 기울여 만든 본격적인 디지털 아트들이다. 기본적으로는 사람들이 자유롭게 먹고 마시고 춤 출 수 있는 장을 마련하는 것이나, 공연의 본래 의도는 예술, 디지털 테크놀러지, 대중적 문화의 만남에 대한 새로운 감각과 정신을 발견하는 것이다.

훈민정악: 연주자들이 한글을 타이핑하면 각 자모들이 미리 할당된 소리를 만들어낸다. 이러한 단순한 원리로 4명의 연주자가 타이핑에 의해 음악을 만들어간다. 매우 즉흥적인 요소가 강한 작품이다.

Terry Riley "In C": 미니멀음악의 선구자인 Terry Riley의 작품 "In C"를 연주한다. 보통 전통적 악기로 연주되는 이 곡은, 이번 공연에서는 컴퓨터가 만들어내는 소리와 음들, 그리고 영상에 의해 연주될 예정이다. 디지털 기술에 의해 재해석될 이번 연주는, 20세기 음악사의 획을 그었던 이 작품에 21세기적 생명을 새롭게 붙어넣을 것이다.

Music Game Music: 사다리나 팩맨 같은 전통적 게임의 요소들이 영상을 통해 보여지고, 이 요소들의 움직임이 음악을 생성해 낸다. 관중들의 움직임이나 아이들이 내는 목소리가 영상에 나타나는 게임의 요소들을 움직일 수 있는데, 이에 따라 음악도 반응하게 된다.

▶ 단체 소개

Tacit Group은 다양한 개성을 가진 아티스트들로 이루어진 집단이다. 주로 디지털 테크놀러지에서 예술적 영감을 발견하고, 이를 통해 멀티미디어적 공연과 인터렉티브한 설치, 그리고 컴퓨터 프로그래밍에 의한 알고리즘적 ... 한 작업을 하고 있다.

▶ 단체 프로필

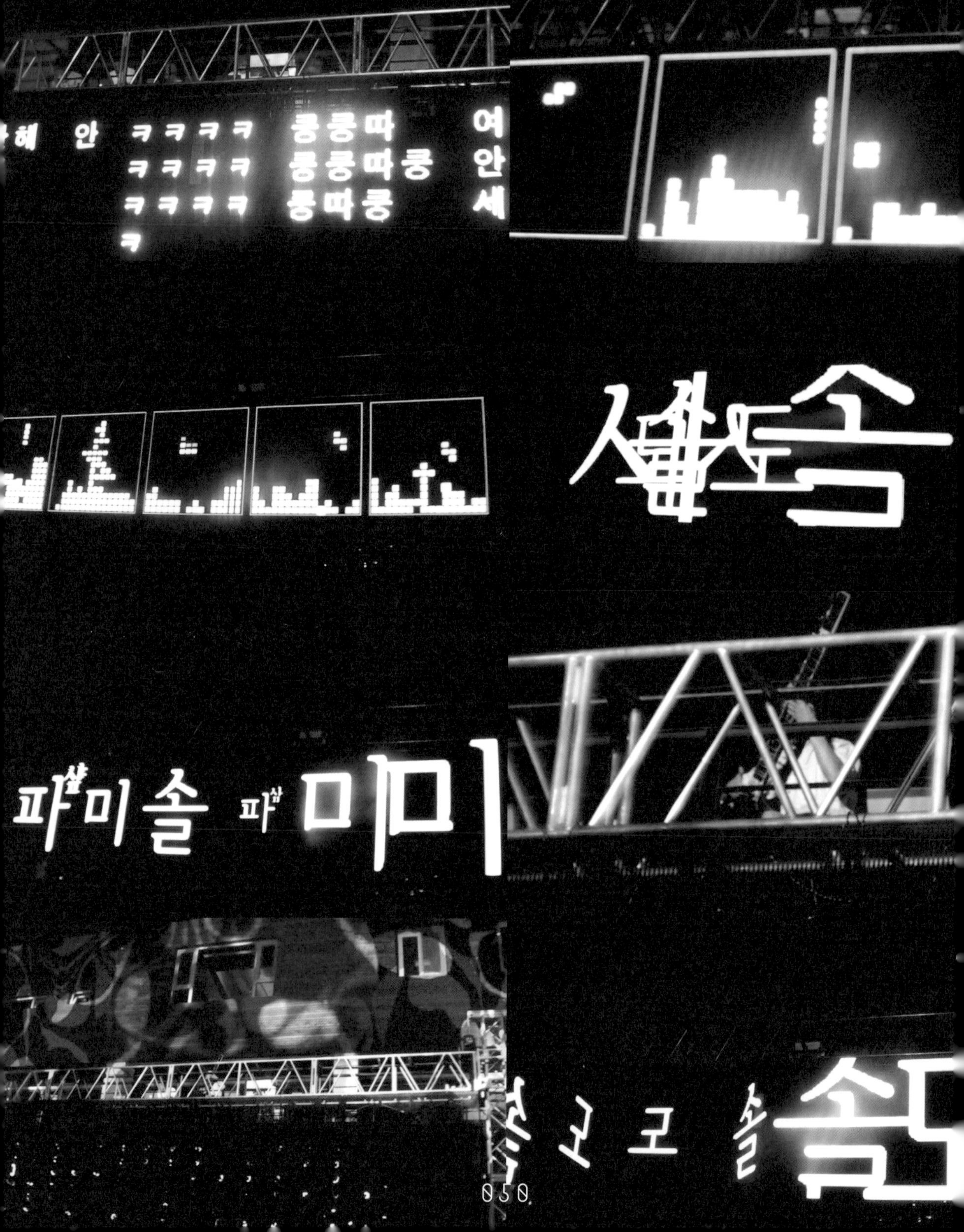
안 ㅋㅋㅋㅋ 쿵쿵따 여
ㅋㅋㅋㅋ 쿵쿵따쿵 안
ㅋㅋㅋㅋ 쿵따쿵 세
ㅋ
파미솔 파 미
고 고 솔

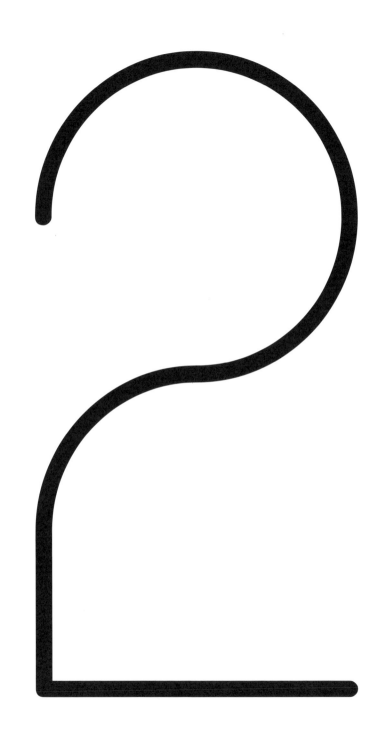

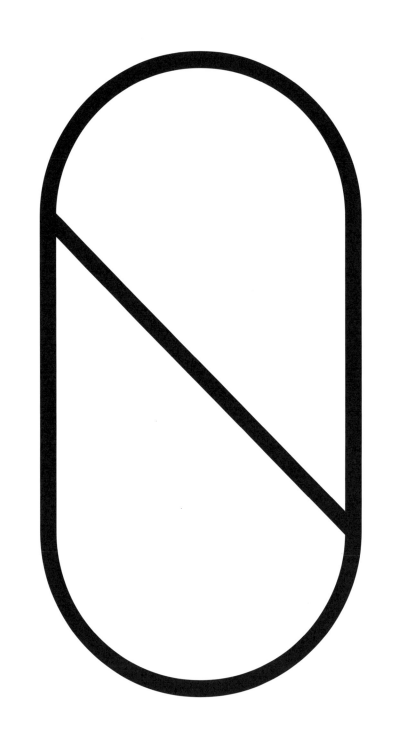

052

053

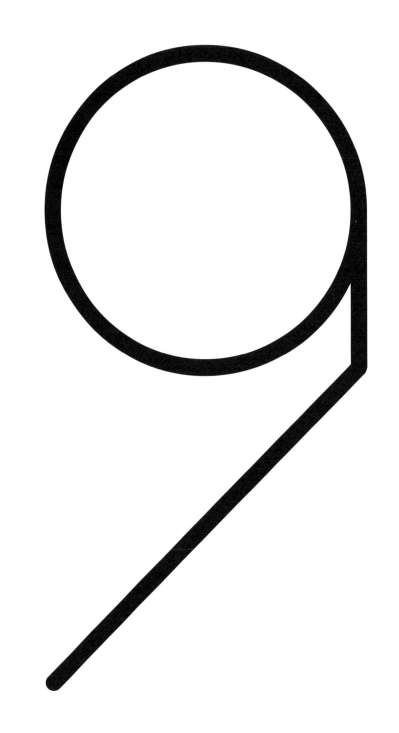

30 MAY, 2009

**OVER MUSIC
SERIES**

백남준 아트센터 초청 공연.
백남준과 플럭서스 그룹에
대한 경의를 담은 '청중에
대한 오마주(Homage to the
Audience)'를 선보였다.

Special invitation to
perform at the Nam June
Paik Art Center. Presented
'Homage to the Audience',
which imparted a tribute
to Nam June Paik and
Fluxus Group.

SPACE 500

1966년 창간된 건축 및
종합문화예술잡지 ‹SPACE›
통권 500호 기념식의
오프닝 공연. 공간 신사옥
벽면을 대형 스크린으로 삼아
실시간으로 오디오비주얼
공연을 펼쳤다.

The opening performance
at the commemoration
ceremony for Volume
500 of *SPACE*, a
comprehensive culture,
arts, and architecture
periodical, established
in 1966. The wall of the
new space was used as
a large display screen to
exhibit an audiovisual
performance in real time.

31 JUL, 2009

GAME CENTER
BOY

고전 게임과 전자오락실을
테마로 진행된 게임 전시회의
오프닝 공연을 펼쳤다.

Tacit gave the opening
performance of the game
exhibition. The theme was
classic games and video
arcades.

tacit.perform[0]

tac
perf
[0]

두산아트센터에서 열린
태싯그룹의 첫 단독 공연.
국내 최초의 본격적인 오디오
비주얼 퍼포먼스 그룹,
디지털 테크놀로지에서
예술적 영감을 발견하는
그룹, 게임으로 음악을 하는
그룹 등으로 호칭됐으며,
20세기 예술의 실험성과
혁신성을 잃지 않으면서도
일상에서 익숙하게 경험하는

아날로그와 디지털의
재료를 예술적 원천으로
삼아 대중적 재미 역시
살린다는 평가를 받았다.
〈Game Over〉 〈훈민정악〉
등 초기의 대표작과 더불어
프로젝션 매핑을 이용한
〈Improvision〉, 테리
라일리의 〈In C〉를 디지털
영상과 음향으로 재해석한
작품을 선보였다.

Tacit Group's first solo
performance was held at
the Doosan Art Center.
Tacit was called Korea's
first full-fledged audio
visual performance
group, a group that
explores artistic
inspiration through
digital technology, in
addition to playing music
through games. It was
noted for sourcing digital

materials in order to
incorporate popular fun
as well. In addition to
their major early works
such as *Game Over*
and *Hunminjeongak*,
Improvision which used
projection mapping, and
Terry Riley's *In C*, were
reinterpreted with digital
images and sound.

tacit.perform[0]

21 Aug, 2009   Seoul

063

tacit
GROUP
TACIT.PERFORM [0]

IMPROVISATION   ALGORITHM   AUDIO VISUAL   LIVE PERFORMANCE   GAME

Tacit Group의 첫 번째 단독 공연 tacit.perform[0]은 '게임'이라는 형식과 주제를 가지고 펼쳐지는 Tacit Group만의 독특한 오디오-비주얼 퍼포먼스입니다. 알고리듬 작곡과 전자음악 연주가 출신 Tacit Group은 지난 해부터 컴퓨터 그래픽이라는 시각적 요소를 공연에 접목한 총체적인 21세기 새로운 공연예술이라는 모토를 내걸고 디지털 멀티미디어 공연을 선보여 왔습니다. 이번 공연은 이들의 활동이 본격적으로 시작됨을 알리는 Tacit Group의 첫 번째 단독공연으로 '게임'이라는 주제와 형식은 예술, 디지털 테크놀로지, 대중적 문화가 아우러지는 새로운 미학적 즐거움을 갈망하는 동시대의 요구이자 이들의 지향점을 보여주고 있습니다.

■ 주요프로그램

1. 훈민정악

<훈민정악>은 채팅이라는 한글 언어 사용 환경이 음악으로 전환되는 작품입니다. 공연 초반부에 연주자가 한글의 자음과 모음을 타이핑을 하면 이에 반응한 사운드가 발생합니다. 단순한 음조로 시작되었던 본 악곡은 곡이 진전될 수록 공연자 사이에 나누는 대화, 그리고 관객과 나누는 시적인 대화를 문학적인 맥락이 음악으로 재해석되는 복잡한 음악으로 발전되는 과정을 볼 수 있습니다. 동시에 공연자들 사이의 채팅 그리고 공연자와 관객과의 대화 내용은 이미지로 무대에 그려서서 언어의 음악으로의 전환이라는 개념을 감성적으로 감상하도록 합니다. 관객과의 의사소통과정이 공연에 즉흥으로 반영되는 이번 공연은 관객 참여적 작업이자 음악과 시각예술, 그리고 문학을 오가는 총체적 공연으로의 새로운 도전이 될 것입니다.

2. Puzzle 15

게임이 음악이 되는 <Puzzle 15>는 Tacit Group이 선보이는 작품입니다. 이 공연에서는 2인의 공연자가 15개의 이미지로 잘려진 퍼즐을 앞다투어 맞추어 가는 게임을 벌입니다. 서로가 짝이 맞는 2개의 퍼즐조각이 만나거나 2개, 3개 이상의 퍼즐 조각들이 줄지어 연결되면 좀더 복잡하고 아름다운 조합의 음악으로 업그레이드되는 시스템을 기본으로 하는 악곡입니다. 이 시스템을 알고리듬 작곡으로 완성된 곡이라고 하고 게임에 이기고자 하는 즉 경기자의 다이내믹이 곧 곡의 연주 과정이 되는 작업입니다. 이러한 방식의 작곡 방법과 곡을 통틀어 생성음악이라고 합니다. 여기서 공연자가 플레이하는 게임은 연주이며, 게임의 화면이 관중에게 실시간으로 보여집니다. 그럼으로써 관객은 음이 만들어져 가는 과정에 몰입하게 되고 어떤 그림이 완성될까 하는 기대감과 그리고 누가 이길까 가슴 졸이는 작업의 감상에 빠지게 됩니다.

3. in C

이 곡은 미니멀 음악의 선구자 테리 라일리(Terry Riley) 의 작품으로 원래는 어쿠스틱 악기 여러 대로 연주하도록 의도된 악곡입니다. 53개의 짧은 악구(phrase) 로 이루어진 이 곡은 연주자들이 주어진 53개의 악구를 차례로 연주해야 하지만 저마다 악구를 원하는 대로 반복 연주 할 수 있어 연주될 때마다 화성과 리듬의 조합에 다양한 변형이 일어나는 작업입니다. 그러나 합주곡으로서 같은 번호의 악구에서 만나야 하는 등의 악보에 기록된 작곡가의 지시를 따라야 하는 곡입니다. 이 작품을 Tacit Group은 네트워크를 활용하여 영상과 전자음악을 결합한 멀티미디어 퍼포먼스로 재탄생 시킵니다.

■ 예술계의 다빈치, 태싯그룹

장재호_현 한국예술종합학교 음악테크놀로지과
교수, 미디어 아티스트
가재발_바나나걸 프로듀서, 미디어 아티스트

Tacit Group은 장재호, 가재발이 주도하는 오디오-
비주얼 퍼포먼스 그룹이다. 이들은 인터랙티브
설치, 전자음악, 컴퓨터 그래픽, 그리고 컴퓨터
프로그래밍에 의한 알고리즘 작곡, 이미지 맵핑
등 여러 장르를 크로스오버하는 총체적인 미디어
아트 공연을 만들면서 총체적인 현대 예술과
우리의 삶을 좀더 가까이 연결한다는 목표를
추구합니다. 쌈지스페이스, 헤이리 판 페스티벌,
백남준 아트센터, 공간사 등에서 작품을 발표하며
음악계/미술계에 신선한 충격을 던진바 있으며,
AES(Audio Engineering Society) 컨퍼런스
공연에서는 국내외 오디오 전문가들에게도 찬사를
받은바 있습니다. 이들은 20세기에 이루어졌던
예술의 혁신성을 본받고 있으나, 예술이 혁신과
실험에서 끝나는 것을 원치 않습니다. 대신에
디지털 테크놀로지에서 발견한 예술적 영감과
대중적 재미를 관객과 더불어 함께 추구합니다.

4. Improvision
Improvision은 즉흥연주와 시각(improvisation +
vision) 이라는 단어를 조합해서 만든 제목입니다.
제목이 제시하듯이 즉흥연주 음악이 연주되는 동안
다양한 이미지가 접목된 표현매체를 소개하는
작업입니다. 음악이 연주되는 동안 그 악곡의
순서에 따라 미리 정해진 이미지가 제시되었던
이전의 시/청각예술을 접목하는 시도와는 달리
3인의 즉흥연주자의 음악적 시각예술적인 감성이
라이브로 보여지는 이 작업은 특히 무대가 가진
굴곡에 맞추어 이미지를 프로젝션하는 '프로젝션
매핑 기법'을 선보이는데 이 때의 즉흥작곡/연주에
해당되는 연주자들의 live coding에 조응하는
이미지들이 보여지는 독특한 오디오-비주얼
공연입니다.

5. Game Over
무대위에는 여섯 명의 연주자들이 서로를 상대로
테트리스 게임을 벌입니다. 하나씩 내려오는
테트리스 블록과 이 블록이 쌓여져 만드는 블록
모양에 따라 들려지는 결과물이 달라지며 함께
게임하는 다른 연주자의 결과물에 따라 서로
다른 변주곡이 만들어 집니다. 랜덤하게 주어진
블럭들과 연주자들의 게임 과정과 경기 시간의
길이에 따라 음악의 결과는 매우 즉흥적이고
우연적으로 흘러갑니다.

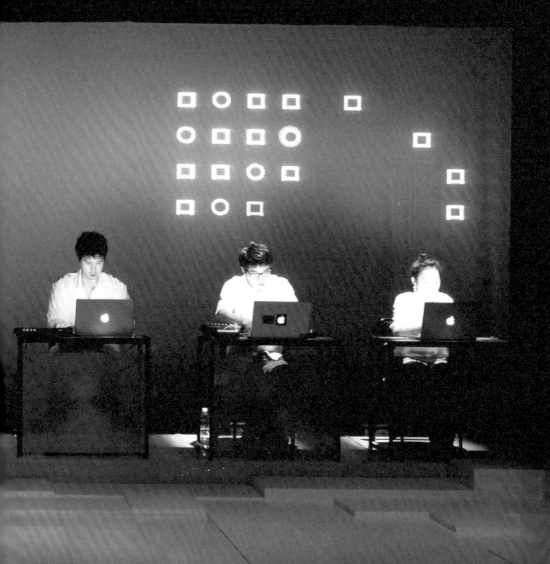

ARTIFICIAL LINEARITY

아트센터 나비에서 진행한 김태은 작가와의 공동 공연. 제목인 '인공적 선형성'은 선형성과 비선형성의 애매한 개념을 함축하는 말로, 비선형적 시스템, 인식과 시간의 흐름이라는 선형성, 컴퓨터의 계산성 등의 요소를 담았다.

A joint performance with artist Tae-eun Kim was held at the Art Center Nabi. The title 'Artificial Linearity' suggests the ambiguous concepts of linearity and nonlinearity, and contains elements such as nonlinear systems, the linearity of recognition and time flow, and computational functions of the computer.

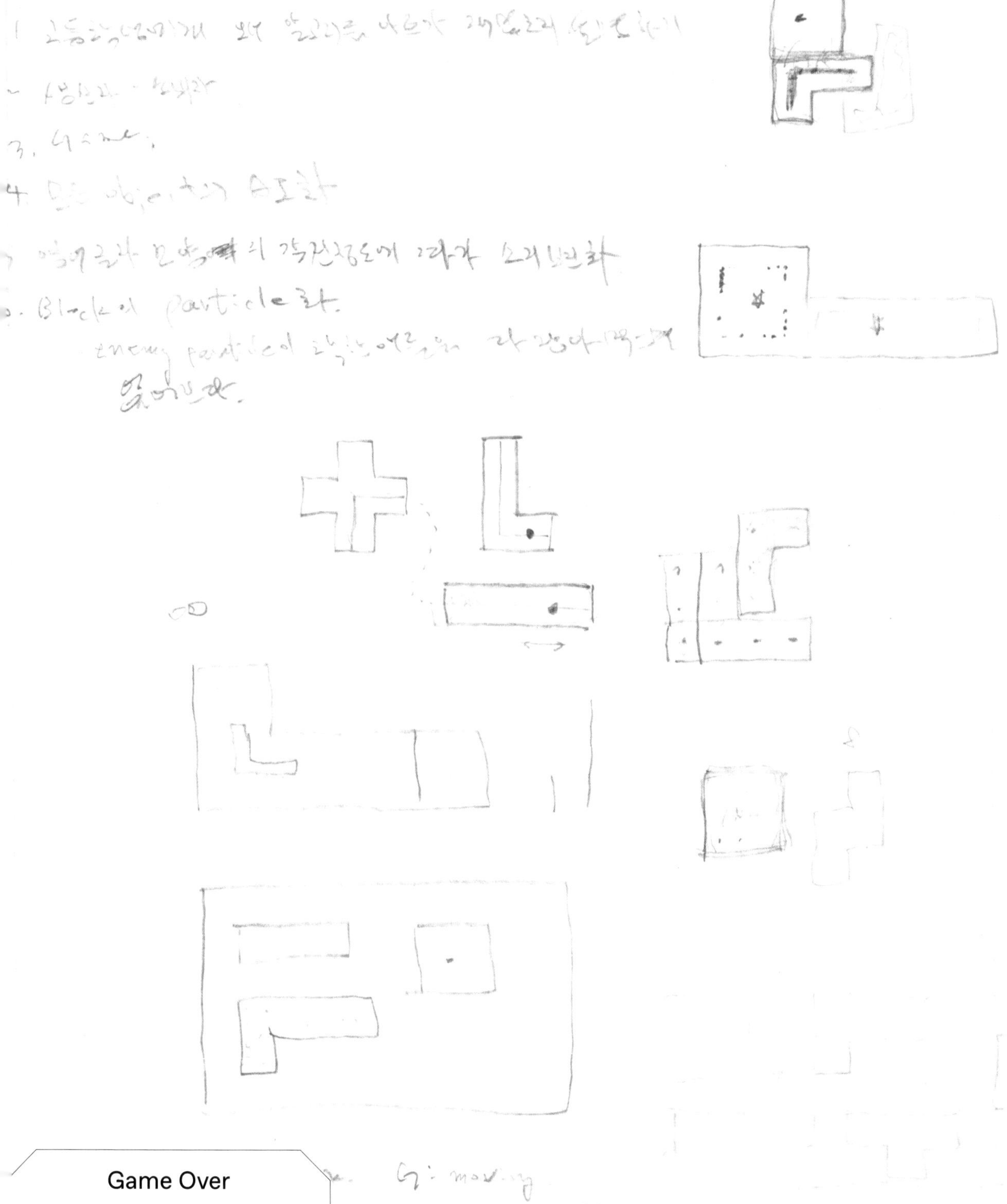

1. 고등학교까지 외 알리고 나라 개발으리 (됐던)

2. 1방법 - 1해결

3. Game.

4. 모든 object에 AI화

5. 엔겨과 모습의 각건경도에 겨가 소리변화

6. Block의 particle화.
    enemy particle 그냥 엔겨가 라겅다망-X
    뭐하꼬.

G: moving

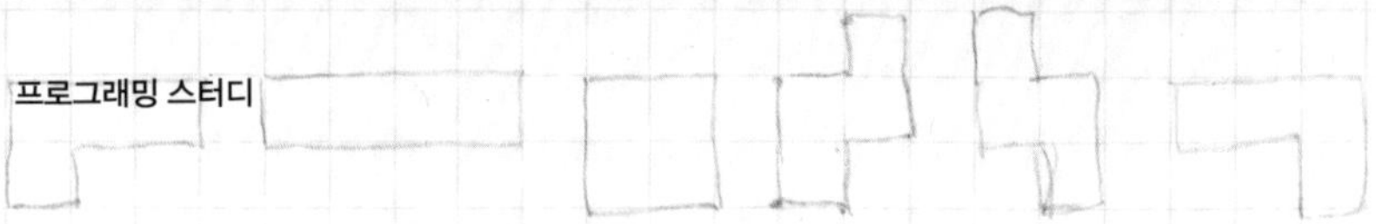

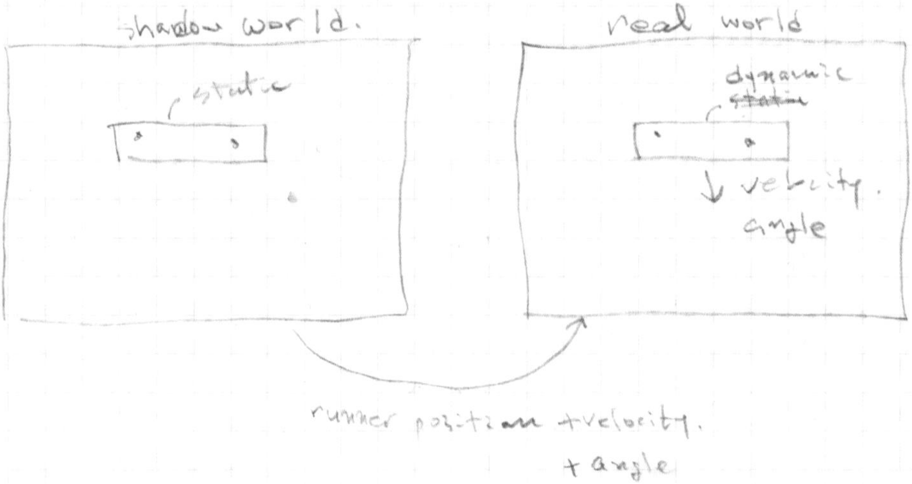

어 → 어 ↗ 어 ↓

shadow world.

real world

static

dynamic ~~static~~

↓ velocity.
angle

runner position + velocity.
+ angle

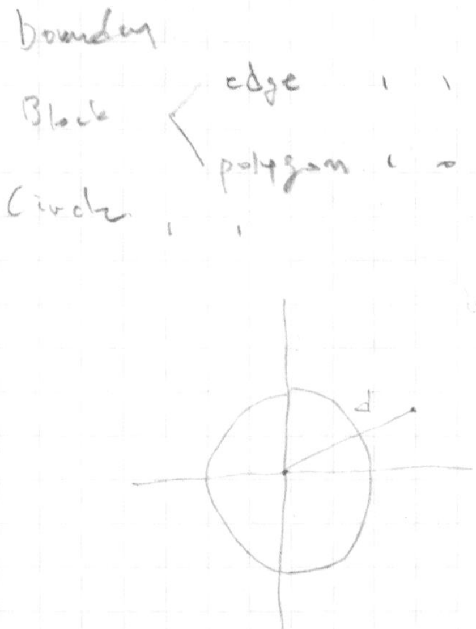

boundary

Block ⟨ edge
        polygon

Circle

-b , b+b/2   -b; b+b/2
-b, -b/2
0, -b/2
0, -b-b/2
go. b.   b, -b-b/2
                b. b/2
                0, b/2
                0. b+b/~

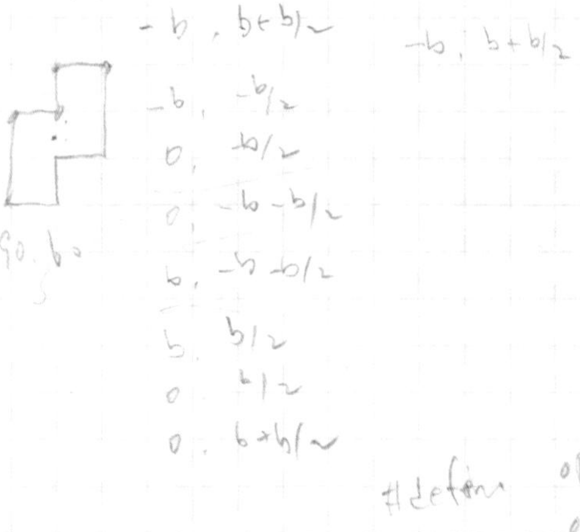

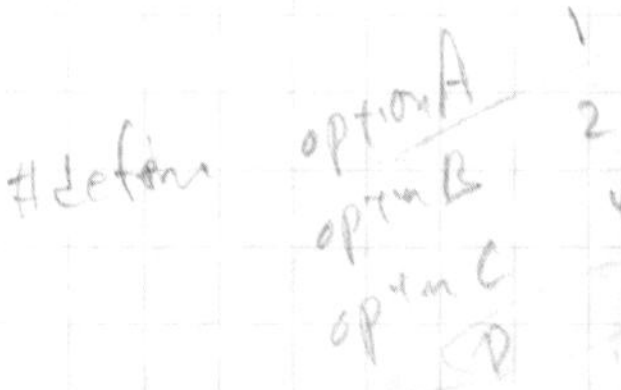

#define optionA
         optionB
         optionC
         D

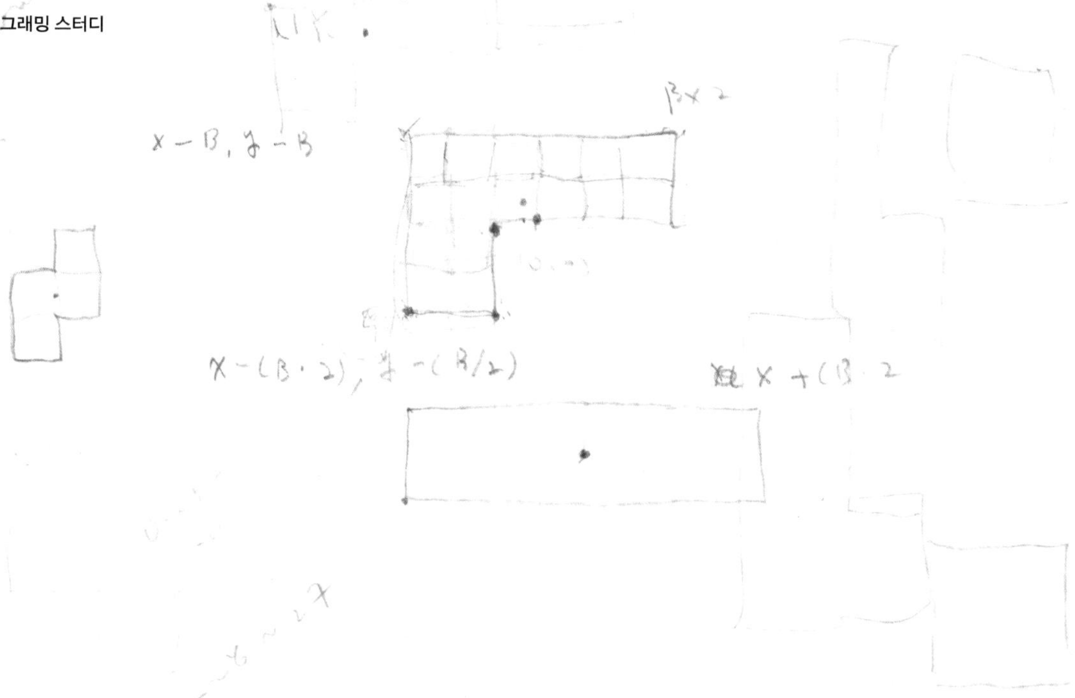

$x - B, y - B$

3×2

$x - (B \cdot 2), y - (B/2)$ $x + (B \cdot 2$

- Mic 2개
- Projector, Screen.
- PA

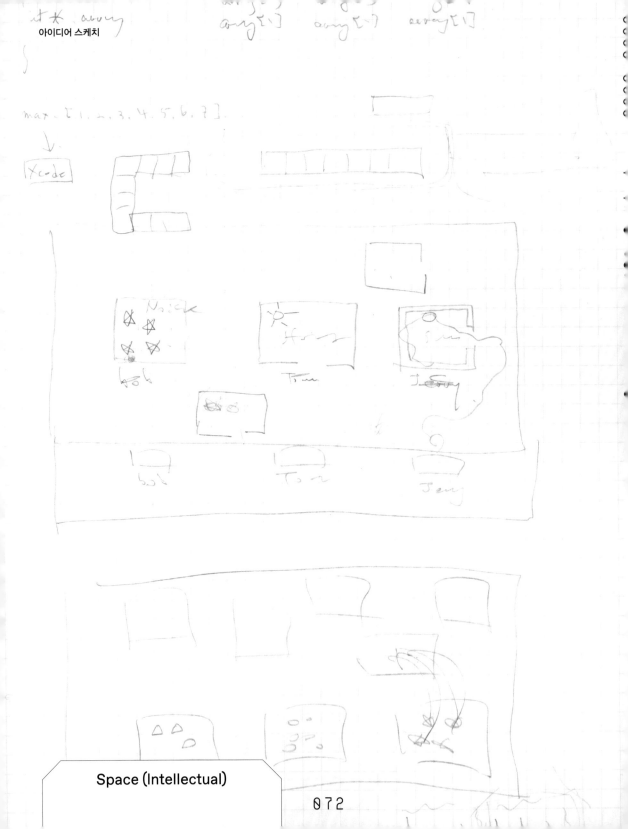

아이디어 스케치

Space (Intellectual)

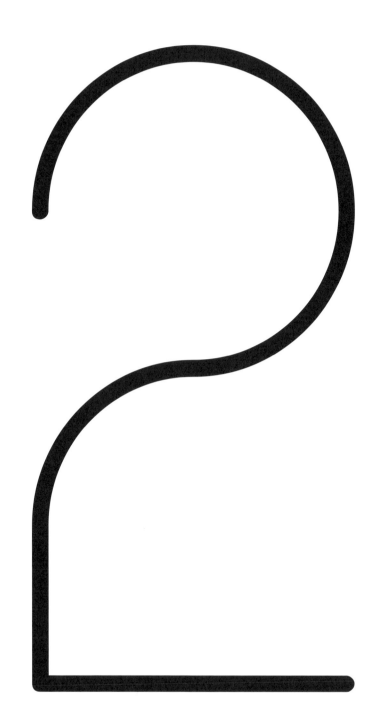

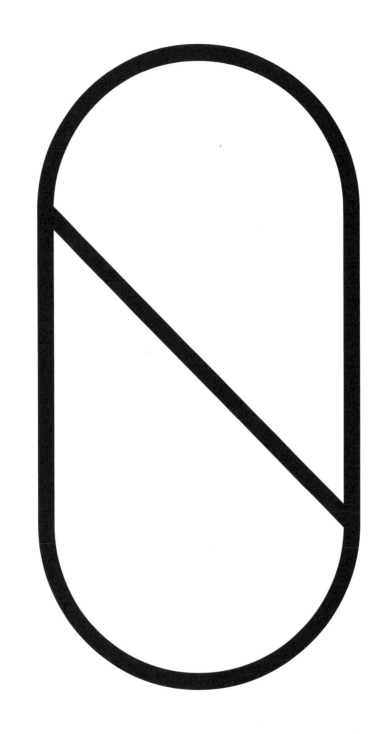

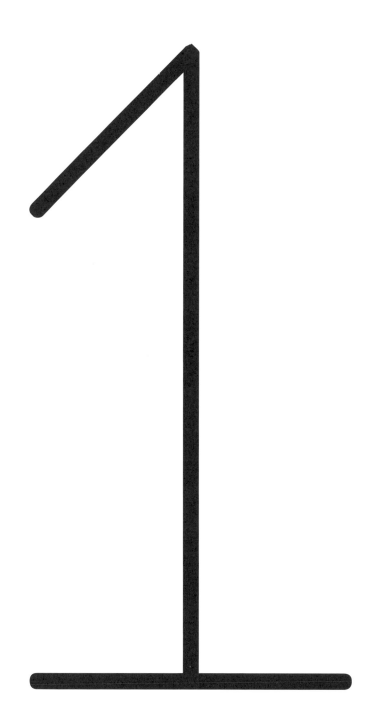

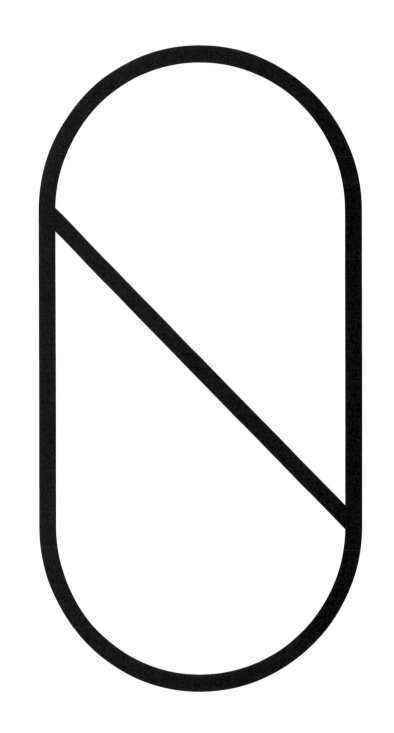

MEMORIAL EXHIBITION OF SEUNG-JO LEE

이승조 추모전에 초대되어
오프닝 공연과 더불어
‹op.sound› 작품을 전시했다.
‹op.sound› 시리즈의
첫 작품이었으며 16개의
스피커와 프로젝션 매핑을
이용한 작업이었다.

Tacit was invited to the
memorial exhibition
of Seung-jo Lee and
presented the opening
performance with
op.sound works. It was
the initial volume in
the *op.sound* series,
utilizing 16 speakers and
projection mapping.

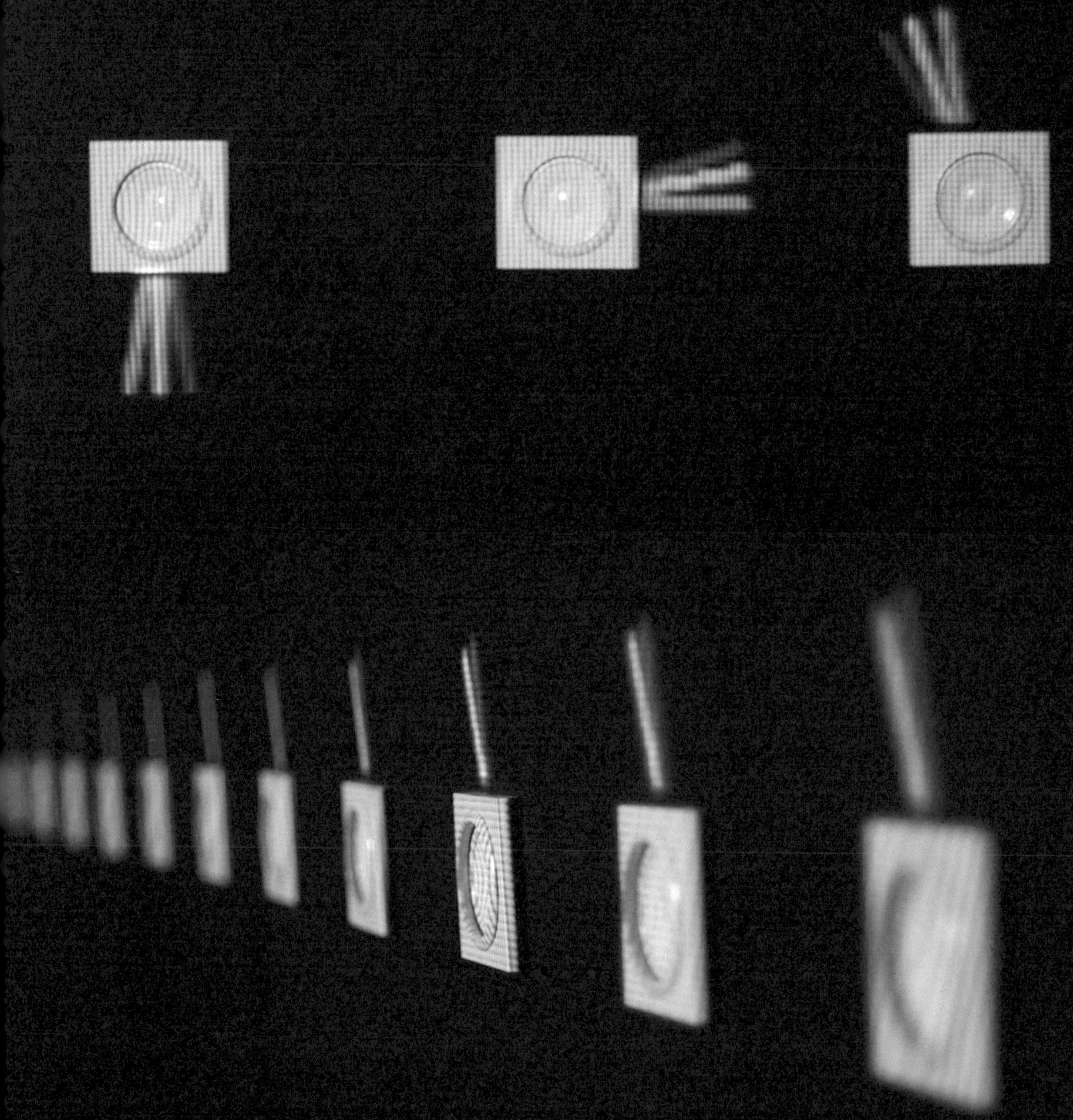

tacit.install[0]_
neighbors[i]

태싯그룹의 첫 전시회.
'이웃(neighbor)'라는 단어에
내포된 '경계'와 '밀착'의
의미에 주목해, 이웃의
변화에 따라 달라지는 양상을
알고리즘을 통해 풀어냈다.
POSTECH의 알고리듬
전문가 안희갑 교수가
기술자문으로 참여했다.

Tacit Group's first
exhibition. Paying special
attention to themes
of 'boundary' and
'closeness' implied in
the term 'neighbor', Tacit
Group addressed the
pattern that alternates
according to a change
of neighbors using an
algorithm. Ahn Hee-gap,
an algorithm expert at
POSTECH, served as a
technical advisor.

neighbors [i]

당신의 이웃은 안녕하십니까?
Algorithmic Audiovisual Exhibition

Tacit Group

한국과학창의재단   교육과학기술부   송원문화재단

PAMS CHOICE

tacit.perform[0] 공연이 팸스초이스에 선정됐다. 이는 태싯그룹의 활발한 해외 공연의 계기가 되었다.

The 2009 *tacit.perform[0]* performance was designated as a PAMS Choice. This served as an opportunity to expand upon Tacit Group's active overseas performances.

시작
1, 2, 3, 4, 5 차례대로

7번 만나기
남상원 제일 늦게 들어오기
이진원 먼저 9번으로 넘어갈 것

22번 만나기 (작게 시작 점점 커지기 -
그러나 너무 크지 않게!!!)
26번 다시 만나서
28번은 박재록 먼저 넘어갈 것

42번 만나기 (크게 만나서 점점 작아지기)
장재호 먼저 49로 넘어갈 것 (49번에서
넘어가지 말고 재록 기다려)
박재록 제일 늦게 넘어갈 것 (그 이전에
50번으로 가지 말 것!!!)

About Tacit Group

Tacit Group은 오디오 비주얼 퍼포먼스 그룹으로, 여러 장르를 크로스오버하는 총체적인 미디어 아트 공연을 만들면서 현대 예술이 나아갈 수 있는 좀 더 가까이 실험을 하고 있다. 헤어니 만 퍼포먼스 벨널조이트센터, 공간(Space), 두씨어센터 같은 공간 까지 디지털 미디어의 고유한 특성을 극대화한 공연이라 할 수 있다. 단순한 음으로 시작되었던 본 어디오 수록 공연자 사이에 나누는 대화, 그리고 관객과 나누는 시각의 대화를 만들어 간다. 재료들처럼 복잡한 음악으로 발전되는 과정들을 동시에 공연자들 사이의 처럼 그리고 공연자와 관객의과 내용을 이미지와 무대에 언어의 음이 으로 소통하는 개념을 강조하는 것이라. 관객과의 의사소통과 그리고 문학을 오키는 총체적 공연의의 새로운 도전을 보여줄 것이다.

Members

장재호 / Jaeho CHANG
이진원 / Jin Won LEE
남상원 / Sangwon NAM

Tacit Group is an audiovisual performance group established in early 2008 with vision of making new performance art while incorporating various disciplines like electro-acoustic music, contemporary visual art, literature. They are heavily influenced by digital technology and working on audiovisual performance, interactive installation, electro acoustic music, algorithmic composition, real-time projection mapping, computer graphics, and algorithmic art. The group aims to find a form of contemporary performance that communicates general public in broader sense.

Showcase Project Description

01 훈민정악 (Hun Min Jeong Ak)

〈훈민정악〉은 채팅이라는 한글 사용 환경이 음악으로 전환되는 작품입니다. 공연 초반부에 연주자가 한글이 작동되는 것을이 하면 이에 반응한 사운드가 발생합니다. 단순한 음으로 시작되었던 본 어디오 수록 공연자 사이에 나누는 대화, 그리고 관자가 나누는 시각의 대화를 만들어 간다. 재료들처럼 복잡한 음악으로 발전되는 과정들을 동시에 공연자들 사이의 처럼 그리고 공연자와 관객의과 내용을 이미지와 무대에 언어의 음이 으로 소통하는 개념을 강조하는 것이라. 관객과의 의사소통과 그리고 문학을 오키는 총체적 공연의의 새로운 도전을 보여줄 것이다.

Hun Min Jeong Ak employs the mechanism of computer chatting environment; its interactive usage of language. At the beginning of the performance, presented to the audience are the simple notes created in corresponding to the consonants of Korean alphabet. As the music proceeds, the music becomes more complicated since the players write from words, sentences and to dialogues between performers and their audience. In this sense this piece can be described as sonification of literary dialogue transmitted via sensory medium.

02 Puzzle 15

〈퍼즐이 음악이〉되는 〈Puzzle 15〉는 tacit group이 선보이는 작품입니다. 이 공연에서는 2인의 공연자가 15개의 이미지로 갈려진 퍼즐을 맞추어 가는 게임을 합니다. 서로가 화면 앞에 있는 2개의 퍼즐을 맞추어 나간 2개 이상의 퍼즐 조각들이 올지 어맞지 어있는 오늘의 조합의 음악으로 입고레이드 되는 시스템을 기반으로 하는 악작입니다. 이 시스템을 알리다로 자로으로 발성된 되는 작업이나고 이기고자 하는 속 경기자의 마이너이다이 곧 곡이 연주 과정이 되는 작업입니다. 이러한 방식의 자각 방법과 이를 통로 자각 방법과 이를 통로 자각 방법과 이를 통로가 음음자가 연주 방성이나 각각 방성이 실시간으로 보여집니다. 그림으로서 관객으로 음이 만들어지는 과정에 몰입하게 되고 어떤 그림이 완성될까 하는 기대감과 누가 이길까 이길까 기능을 즐기는 작품이 빠져니다.

Puzzle 15 is one of the TACIT's game series. In this performance, two players race to assemble 15 puzzle pieces to complete their faces projected behind them in real time. When the player aligns more than 2 pieces of puzzle correctly those linked images creates more complicate harmony. Depending on the dynamic of the two player's performance results of each game play differs one from another with different composition of harmony and codes. In this sense the game play becomes playing music and composition itself.

03 In C

이 곡은 미니멀 음악의 선구자 테리 라일리(Terry Riley)의 작품으로 연재도 어쿠스틱 악기 여러 대로 연주되도록 의도된 악곡입니다. 53개의 짧은 악구(phrase)를 이루어진 이 곡은 연주자들이 주어진 53개의 악구를 차례로 연주해야 하지만 차이마다 악구를 얼마나 바로 반복 연주를 하느냐 연주할 때마다 화성과 리듬이 조금에 다양한 변형이 일어나는 작업입니다. 그러나 합주곡에서 같은 변형이 일어나도 안나이 하는 동이 임보에 기반을 반영하는 지시를 따라야 하는 것입니다. 이 작품을 tacit group은 비트메핑을 활용하여 영상과 전자음악을 결합한 멀티미디어 퍼포먼스로 재탄생 시킵니다.

This music is work of Terry Riley who is pioneer of minimalist music that is basically intended to perform with many acoustic instruments. This music composing of 53 of short phrases should be played in order. however, each phrase can be repeatedly performed as they want so that various variations would occur to combination of harmony and rhythm in each performance. However, performers should follow some instructions of composer as written on the score such as meeting at the same phrase. Tacit Group is recreating this work into image and electronic music-mixed multimedia performance using digital technology and network.

04 Game Over

무대위에는 여섯 명의 연주자들이 서로를 상대로 테트리스 게임을 벌입니다. 하나씩 내려오는 테트리스 블록과 이 블록이 만드는 블록의 모양이 들어지는 결과물이 얼마나게 함께 자양하는 다른 연주자와 결과물에 각기 다른 연주곡이 만들어 집니다. 랜덤하게 주어진 블록들과 연주자들의 게임판정대 경기 시간이 조에 게임의 음악이 결과는 매우 자유롭게 남아주고 인자로의 속블록에다.

Shown on the back of the stage is the six columns of Tetris game being played by the performers. Slowly falling down Tetris blocks and certain combination that are forming the rows are in sync with the corresponding notes. Despite the fact that the blocks are given to the players at random, to a certain extend of the algorithm, each player has freedom to form the shape of the row in order to make desired harmony. The question remains for the player is that how well do you want to score or composition of harmonies made of such blocks.

tacit.perform[1]

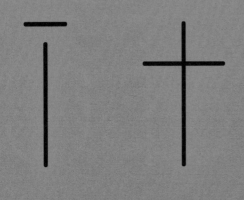

태싯그룹의 공연 시리즈인
tacit.perform의 두번째
공연. ‹훈민정악›과 ‹Game
Over›가 업그레이드된
버전으로 공연됐으며, 실험
무용 음악가 N2(남상원)이
합류해 다양성을 더했다. LIG
아트홀에서 개최됐다.

The second performance
of *tacit.perform*, part of
the group's performance
series. *Hunminjeongak*
and *Game Over*
were performed in
upgraded versions, with
experimental dance
musician N2 (Nam
Sangwon) joining to add
diversity. It was held at
the LIG Art Hall.

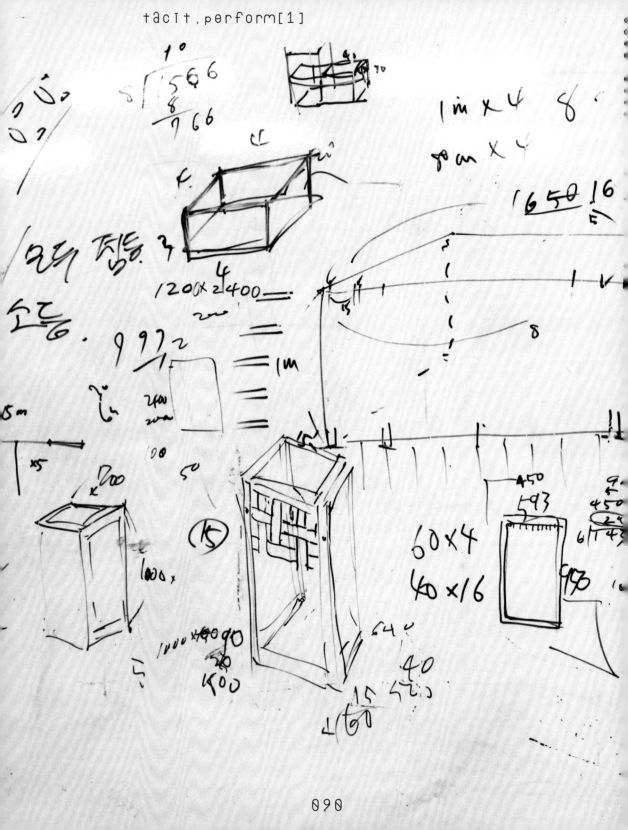

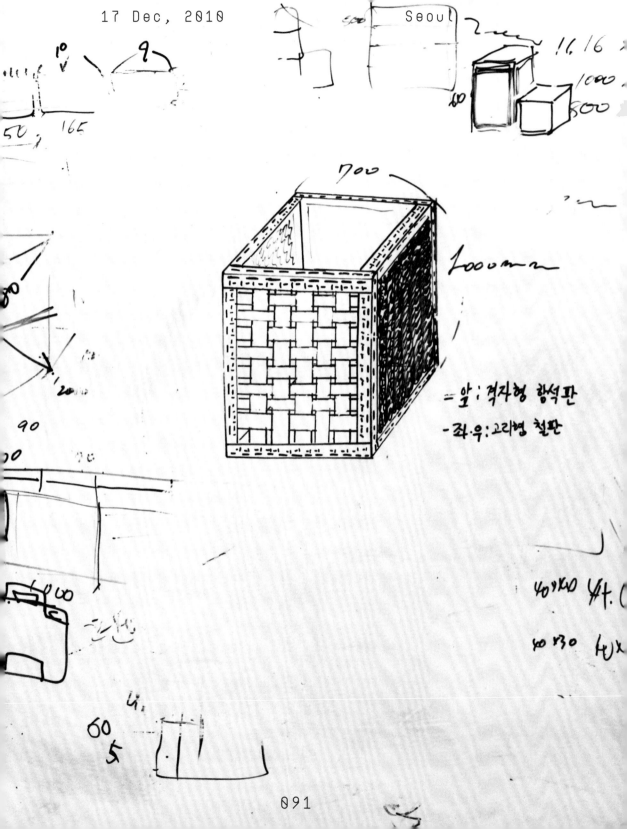

700

1000mm

=앞: 격자형 항석판
-좌·우: 고리형 철판

16.16

1000

800

50, 165

10

9

90

60
5

40×100 ¼.

40×30 40×

ga

david

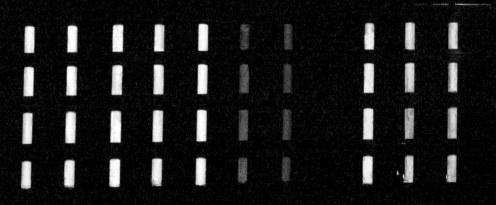

tacit.perform [1]

한글과 게임, 그리고 예술이 만난 미디어 아트 공연

@LIG ART HALL
2010.12.18[Sat] - 19[Sun] 4pm/7pm

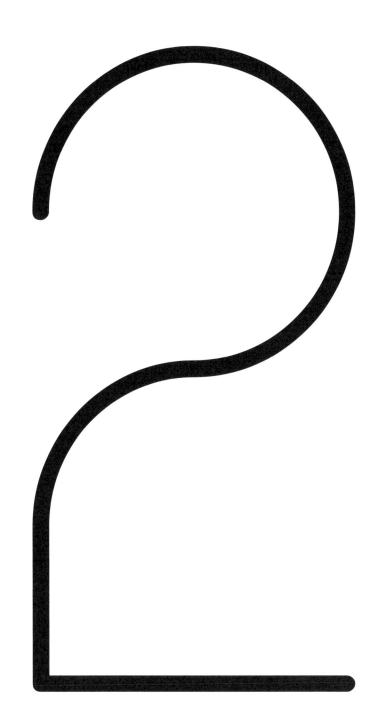

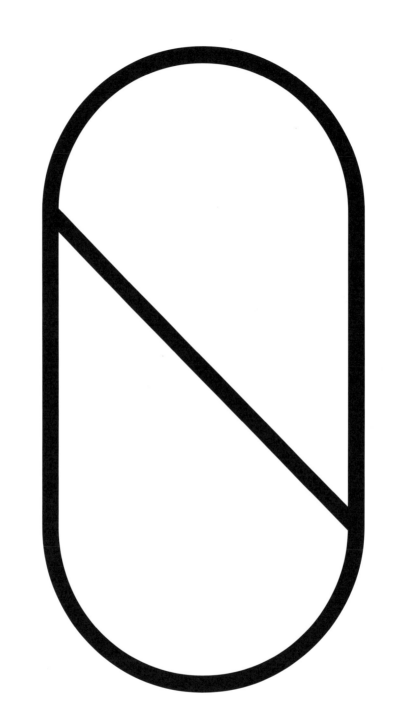

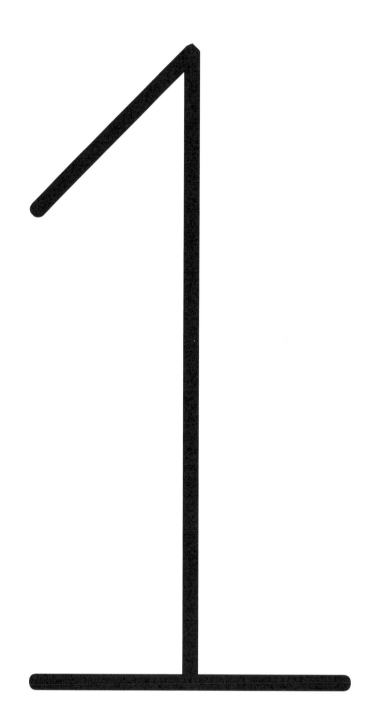

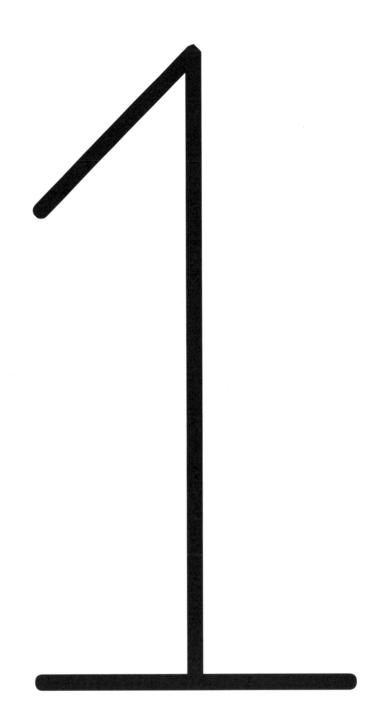

18 FEB, 2011

S.U.N.
SHOWCASE

프랑스 몽펠리에 Kawanga
스튜디오에서의 레지던시와
쇼케이스 공연. 프랑스를
중심으로 활동하는 안무가
남영호와 협업했으며,
이후 프랑스와 한국에서
공연되었다.

Residency and showcase
performance at the
Kawanga studio in
Montpellier, France.
Tacit Group collaborated
with Nam Young-ho, a
choreographer who is
primarily active in France.
This work was
subsequently performed
in France and Korea.

AARHUS FESTIVAL

45년 역사를 지닌 덴마크의 종합예술제인 오르후스 페스티벌의 초청 공연. 3회의 공연과 1회의 강연을 통해 태싯그룹의 작품 세계를 펼쳐보였다.

An invitational performance at the Oruchs Festival, a comprehensive art festival in Denmark with a 45 year history. Through three performances and one lecture, the sphere of Tacit Group's work unfolded.

금천예술공장에서
주최한 '다빈치 아이디어
공모전'에서의 전시.
태싯그룹의 ‹Puzzle 15›을
설치 작품으로 만든 ‹Face
Puzzle›을 전시하였다.

Exhibition at the Da Vinci
Idea Contest hosted by
Geumcheon Art Factory.
Face Puzzle, which is an
installation work of Tacit
Group's Puzzle 15 was
displayed.

작품 구성

주위에서 쉽게 접할 수 있는 퍼즐을 모티브로
한 인터랙티브 작품이다. 타일퍼즐의 논리를
알고리듬화하여 음악과 영상, 관객의 참여가
미디어아트로 승화되게 하였다. 관객은
실시간으로 비추어지는 자신의 얼굴을
4×4 퍼즐로 맞추면서 동시에 태싯그룹이
프로그래밍해 놓은 알고리듬을 이용해 작곡/
연주하는 독특한 경험을 하게 된다. 작품은 빔
프로젝터를 통해 영사되는 영상과 스피커를 통해
연주되는 음악 그리고 관객의 참여로 구성되어
있고 컴퓨터가 네트워킹을 통해 이 세가지 요소를
결합한다.

적용 기술

작품에 적용되고 있는 기술은 타일퍼즐
알고리듬과 작곡 알고리듬으로 모두 태싯그룹을
통해 직접 개발됐다. 타일퍼즐 알고리듬은 어린
시절 흔히 가지고 놀던 15 퍼즐의 기본 논리를
그대로 적용한 것이다. 총 16개의 섹션에 15개의
타일이 올려져 있다. 단 한 개 존재하는 빈칸의
전후좌우에 위치한 타일은 빈칸으로 이동할
수 있으며 각 타일이 원래의 위치로 돌아 가면
게임은 완료된다. 이 기본적인 논리를 C, C++,
Max/MSP 프로그램을 이용하여 알고리듬으로
구현한다. 또 다른 기술인 작곡 알고리듬에도
역시 C, C++, Max/MSP 프로그램이 이용된다.
타일들이 제대로 짝을 이루어 이웃하게 되면
그룹으로 지정되면서 태싯그룹이 프로그래밍한
작곡 알고리듬에 의해 음악으로 치환된다.
관객이 게임을 진행하는 방식에 따라 음악은
예측불가능하게 전개된다. 결국 최종 게임을
완성하여 모든 타일이 하나의 그룹으로 묶이면,
완성된 음악이 흘러 나오게 된다.

추진 체계

작품의 추진 방식은 크게 4단계로 분류될 수 있다.
1단계 타일퍼즐 알고리듬 설계
2단계 작곡 알고리듬제작
3단계 타일퍼즐의 알고리듬과 작곡 알고리듬의
접합 설계 4단계 최종적인 관객의 참여와 실시간
네트워킹을 통한 작품의 구현

기능

미디어아트는 대중들이 다소 난해하게 여기는
장르이다. 하지만 ‹Face Puzzle›은 어린 시절
누구나 가지고 놀았던 조그만 타일 퍼즐에서
아이디어를 착안하여 관객이 즐겁게 (FUN)
미디어 아트를 접할 수 있도록 고안되었다. 관객은
타일 퍼즐 게임에 참여함으로써 동시에 최첨단
미디어 아트 작품의 연주에도 참여하게 된다.
관객은 자신이 연주하고 있는 음악의 난해함에도
불구하고 직접적으로 미디어아트를 경험할 수
있고 동시에 즐길 우 있는 독특한 경험을 하게 될
것이다.

활용방안

‹Face Puzzle›은 모바일 어플리케이션으로
확장될 수 있다. 최근 확산되고 있는 스마트 폰은
페이스 퍼즐의 운영에 필요한 모든 기능 즉 자판,
스피커, 동영상 카메라를 장착하고 있다. 또한
와이파이나 3G를 통해 서로의 얼굴 혹은 영상을
배경으로 하여 실시간 퍼즐 배틀을 벌일 수 있다.
여기에 초현대 전자음악 뿐 아니라 대중음악,
전통음악 등 다양한 음악을 접목 시킨다면 교육
효과를 가진 독특한 게임으로 활용될 수 있을
것이다.

tac
perf
[2]

세번째 단독 공연. 신작 ‹Analytical›과 ‹Operational›, 그리고 ‹Space›를 리메이크한 ‹Intellectual›과 ‹Game Over›를 리메이크한 ‹Structural› 등이 공연되었다.

For the third solo performance, the subtitle 'Structural Sounds' was attached, which was taken from the title of the work *Structural*. *Structural* is the sequel to *Game Over*. *Hunminjeongak* and *SPACE* were also performed.

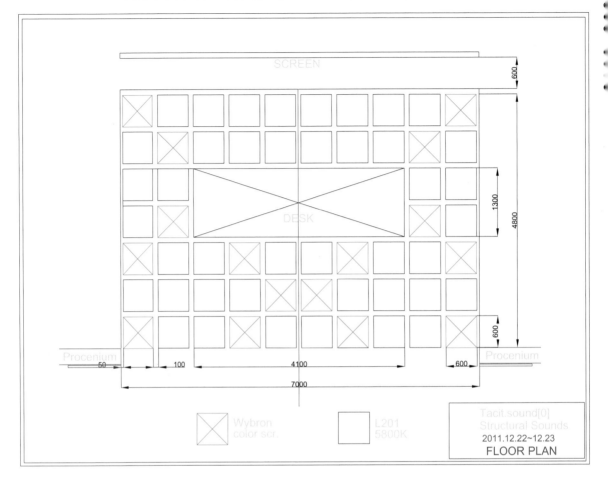

name (이름)
: 자신의 이름을 정함

sound (type freq amp)
: 사운드를 만듬 (type = 0~4)

select
: 사운드를 선택 (select를 타이핑한 후 리턴
키를 누르지 말고 화살표 키로 사운드를
선택)

deselect
: 사운드 선택 취소

zone (type)
: zone을 만듬 (type = 0~2)

select zone
: zone을 선택 (select를 타이핑한 후 리턴
키를 누르지 말고 화살표 키로 zone을 선택)

deselect zone
: zone 선택 취소

kill
: 선택된 사운드를 없앰

kill me
: 나의 모든 사운드를 없앰

kill zone
: 선택된 zone을 없앰

kill all zone(s)
: 모든 zone을 없앰

kill (이름)
: 다른 플레이어의 사운드를 공격하여 죽임

no kill
: 공격 명령 취소

scatter
: 흩어지게 함

114

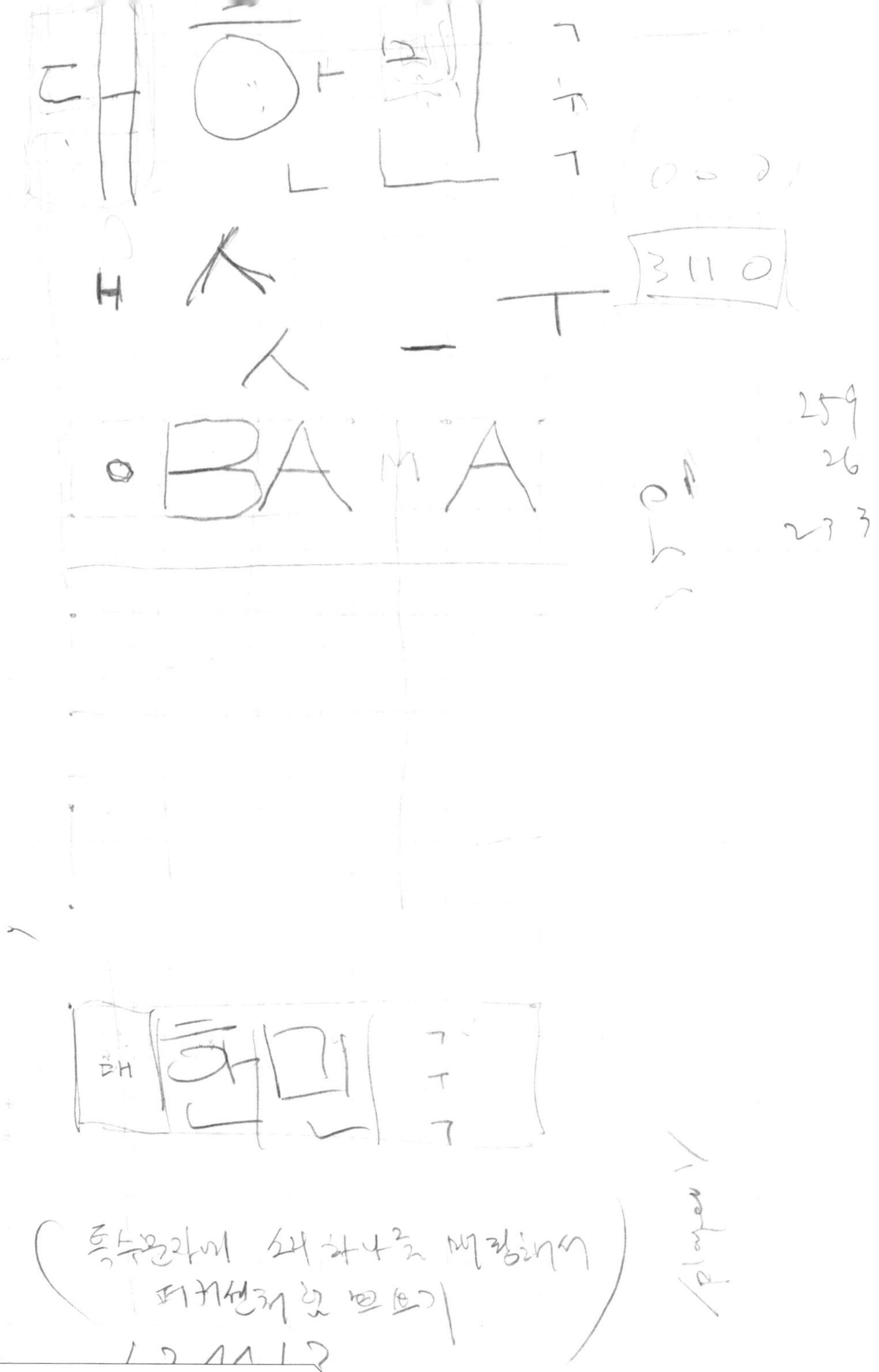

대 ㅎ 아 희 ㅜ

ㅇ ㄴ ㄴ

ㅐ ㅅ ㅡ ㅜ

ㅅ

° BAMA

259
26
233

매 화 민 ㄱ
ㅜ
ㄱ

(훈민정가에 쾨 화나를 배경하여)
피커선기 및 믜[ㅂ]기

Hunminjeongak

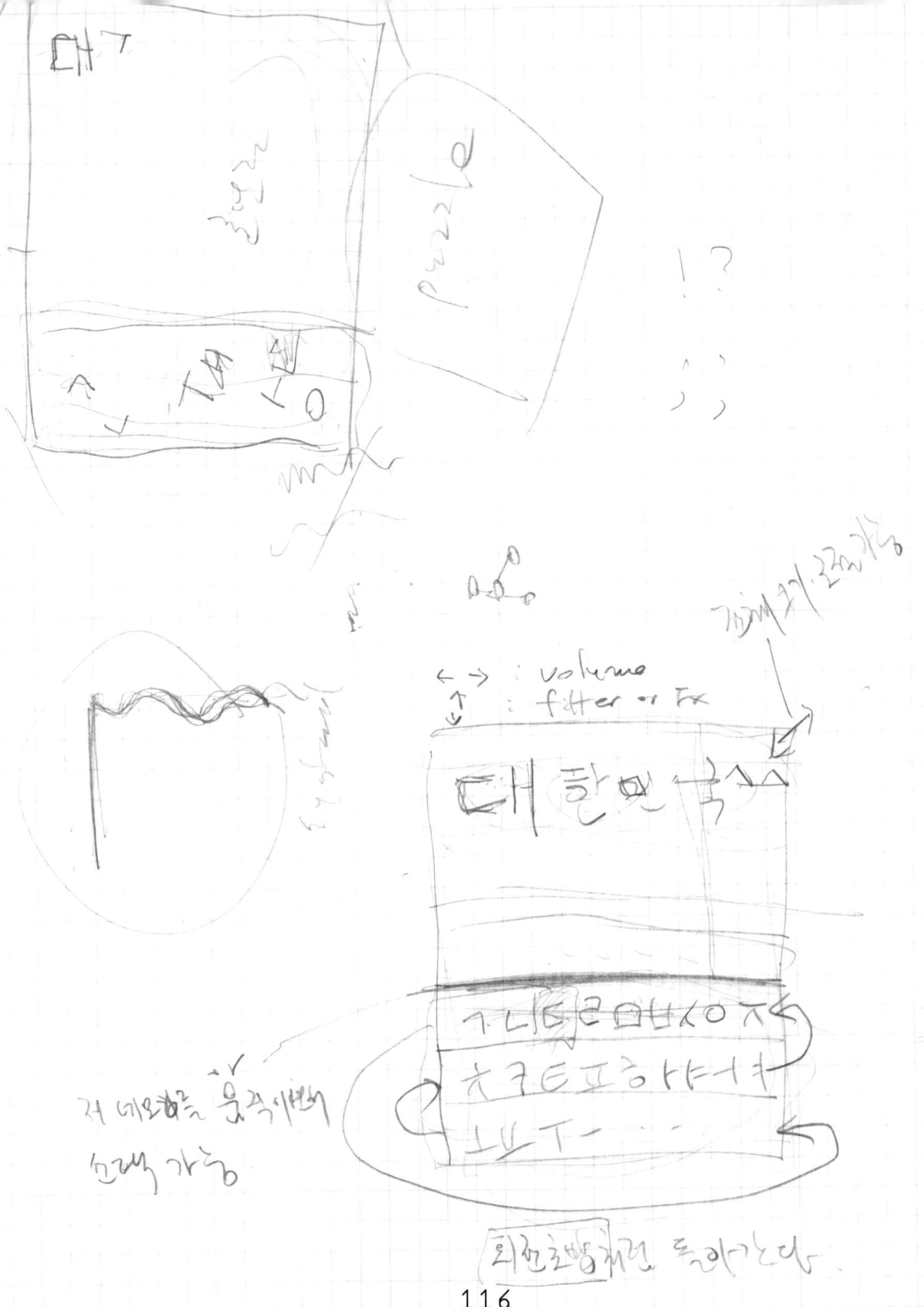

대기

puzzle

!?

volume
filter + fx

대한민국ㅅ△

ㄱㄴㄷㄹㅁㅂㅅㅇㅈㅊ
ㅊㅋㅌㅍㅎㅏㅑㅓㅕ
ㅗㅛㅜ ─ ─

회전초밥처럼 돌아간다

116

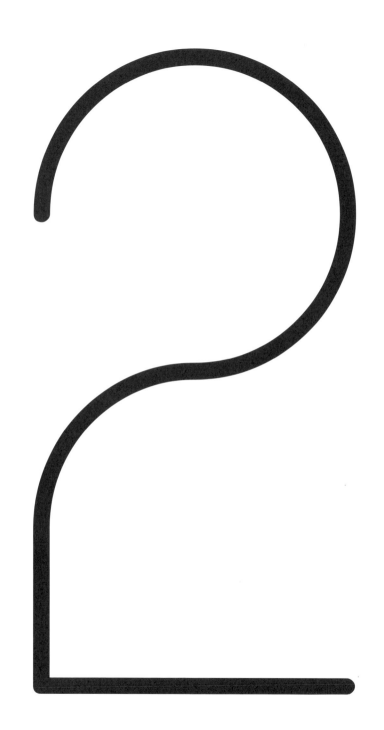

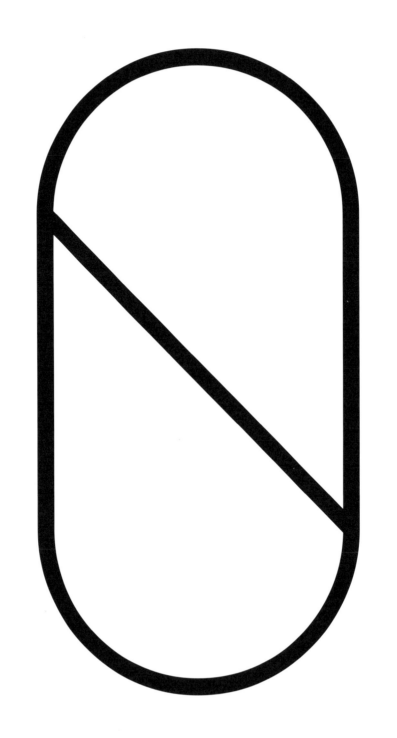

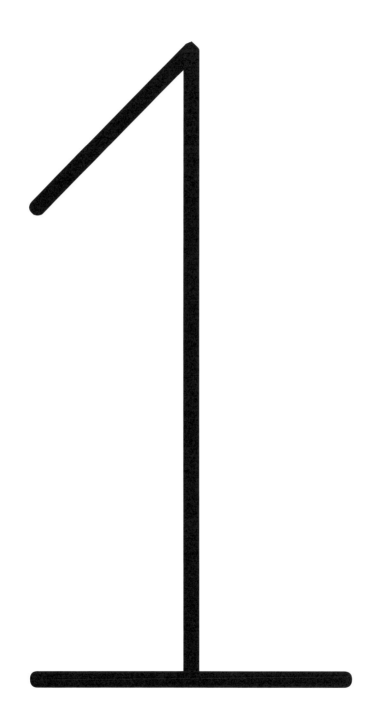

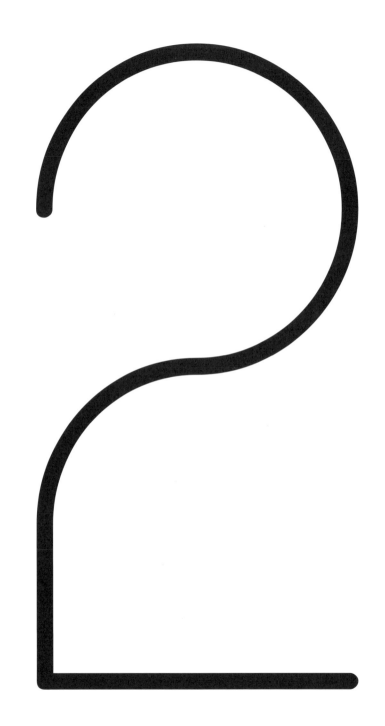

S.U.N. @ AGORA

안무가 남영호와 협업한
‹S.U.N.› 작품을 프랑스
몽펠리에의 Agora에서
공연했다.

SUN in collaboration
with choreographer Nam
Young-ho was performed
at Agora in Montpellier,
France.

1부

제일 처음 라이팅 들어오면서 신디 약하게 첨부터 나오기
호흡도 첨부터 호흡리버브샌드;0
마리 신디 0.1로 시작 0.25까지
카리나 왼쪽앞에 서고 셋이 돌고난 후 딜레이 넣어서 터지기

2부

카리나 솔로후 프랭크 선무도 솔로에서 호흡 넣기
프랭크 솔로에서 양발로 뛰고 돌아서서 스크린 보면서 팔 올릴때
　　　서서히 신디 들어가기

1부

제일 처음 라이팅 들어오면서 신디 약하게 첨부터 나오기
호흡도 첨부터 호흡리버브샌드;0
마리 신디 0.1로 시작 0.25까지
프랭크 소리 지를때까지 신디 들어가기
3명 호흡 계속 들어감

마지막의 연속된 호흡에 딜레이 넣어서 터지기

2부

제일 처음의 깔리나에게 빅 리버브(혹은 딜레이)
까리나와 프랭크 듀엣에는 호흡 없애기(프랭크는 아예 안나옴)
　　둘이서 붙을때 없애기
까리나와 프랭크 듀엣 시작하고 30초정도 뒤
　　백 조명으로 스크린 뒤에서 마리 혼자 할때 마리호흡켜기
마리 센 솔로때 마리 마이크 켜기(세명이 둥글게 모였다가 흩어질때)
　　한명씩 하 세번 한다음에 셋이 모였을때 시작
　　딜레이 센드 이용해 chaos처럼 만들기
　　천천히 움직이는 부분에서 볼륨 낮추기
　　프랭크 나오기 전까지 나오기
프랭크 선무도 솔로에서(중앙으로 돌아와 자세 잡은 후) 호흡 넣기
프랭크 솔로에서 양발로 뛰고 돌아서서 스크린 보면서 팔 올릴때
　　　서서히 들어가기

3부

호흡 다 들어가기
시작하면서 3명 신디 왕창 들어가기

나 ; U 장샘;+5dB master;+3db

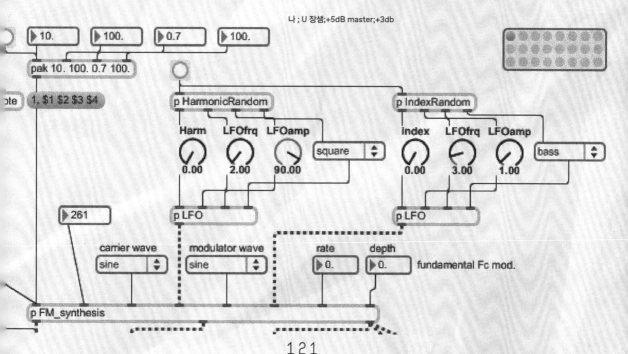

Puzzle 15

"Puzzle 15" is a work that involves a classic puzzle game. While two performers compete with each other solving the puzzle, the computer generates melody and rhythmic patterns according to the matched tiles of the puzzle. As a result, various combination of musical elements are made that are unexpected and accidental.

광주 아시아예술극장의 창작
레지던시 공모에 선정되어,
tacit.perform[3]을 위한
작품들의 프로토타입을
만들었다.

It was selected in a
creative residency
contest at the Gwangju
Asian Arts Theater and
created prototypes for
tacit.perform[3].

17 Sep, 2012   Gwangju

123

US TOUR

23 NOV–6 DEC, 2012

US TOUR –
Legion Arts (Cedar
Rapids), MCA
(Chicago), Lincoln
Center (New York)

태싯그룹의 첫 미국 투어.
뉴욕 링컨센터, 시카고
현대미술관 등에서 10여
일에 걸쳐 초청 공연을
펼쳤다. 테리 라일리의
작품을 태싯그룹이 재해석한
‹In C›에 감동을 받은
링컨센터 디렉터의 초청으로
이루어졌다. ‹훈민정악›
채팅의 경우 영어가 아닌
한글로 진행됐는데, 이는
‘한글의 건축적인 멋을
보여줘야 한다’는 디렉터의
요청에 의한 것이었다.

Tacit Group's first US tour.
Invitational performances
were held over 10 days
at Lincoln Center in New
York and the Museum
of Contemporary Art
in Chicago. Invitation
was extended by the
director of Lincoln Center,
who was impressed by
the reinterpretation
of Terry Riley's work
by Tacit Group. The
Hunminjeongak
symposium was
conducted in Korean, not
English, at the request
of the director: 'We must
show the architectural
beauty of Korean
alphabet'.

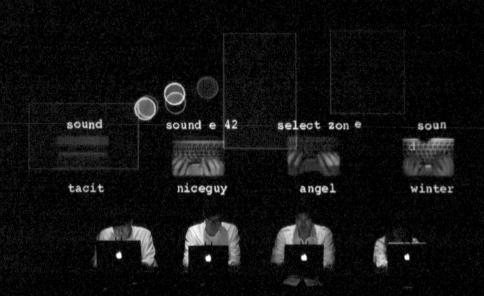

Legion Arts
presents the
North American debut of

TACIT GROUP

"Connecting the dots between sound waves in space and visual experience"

Aarhus, Denmark

Using laptops as musical instruments, South Korea's **Tacit Group** is revolutionizing live performance one megabyte at a time. The six-person group uses real-time projection mapping and computer graphics to create compelling soundscapes and stunning visuals. They represent a new breed of composer, one with a deep sense of play and a virtuosic command of algorithms. *Tour supported by the Korean Arts Management Service and the National Performance Network.*

Fri-Sat | Nov 23-24

CSPS HALL
Tickets $15 advance | $18 door | $5 student rush
CSPS | 1103 Third St SE | Cedar Rapids | 319.364.1580
Project of Legion Arts | www.legionarts.org

23 Nov–6 Dec, 2012 US

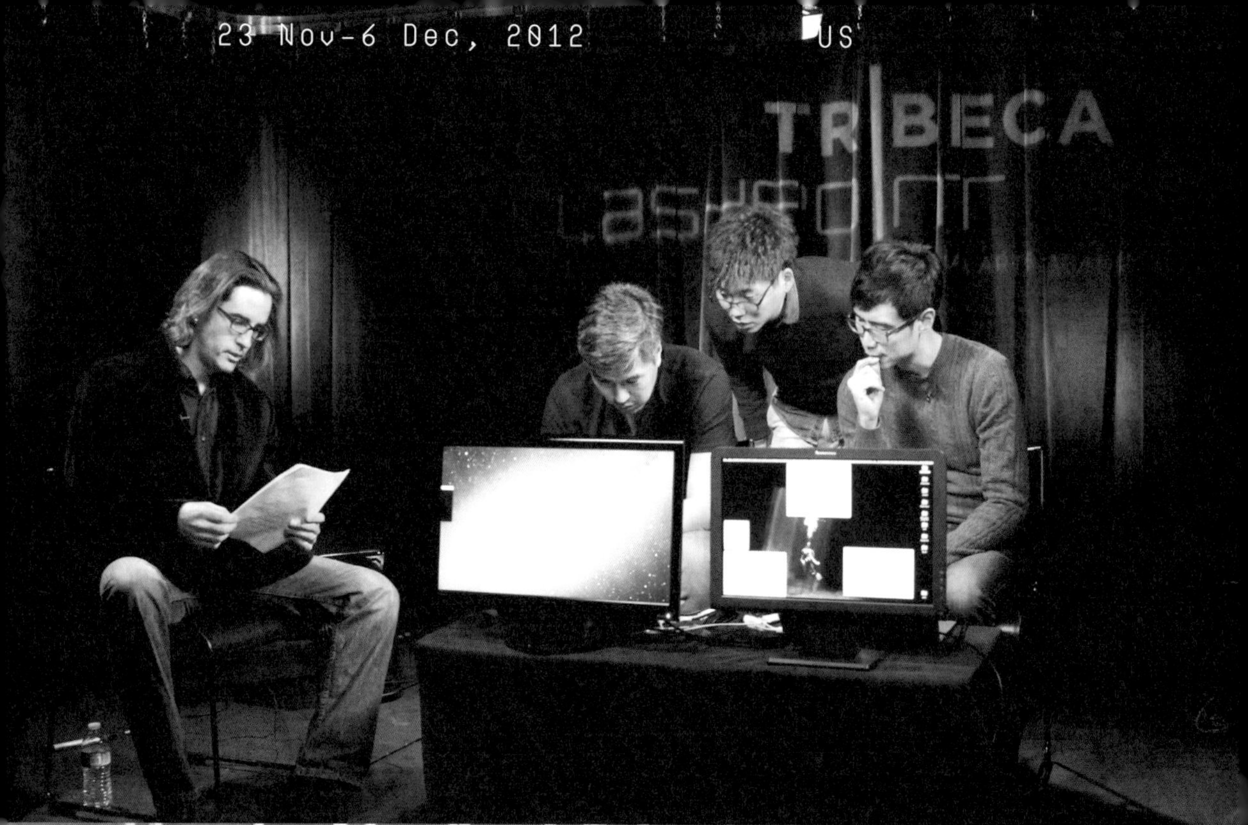

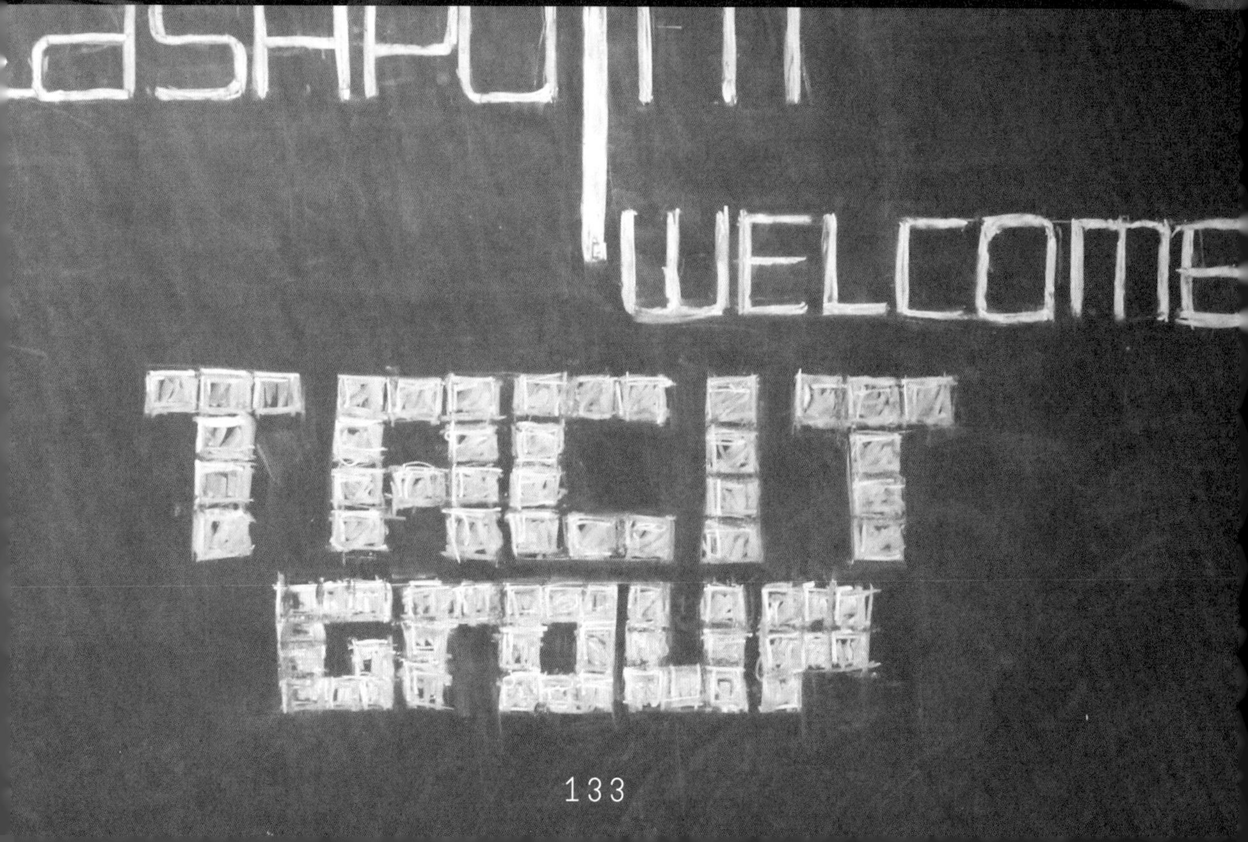

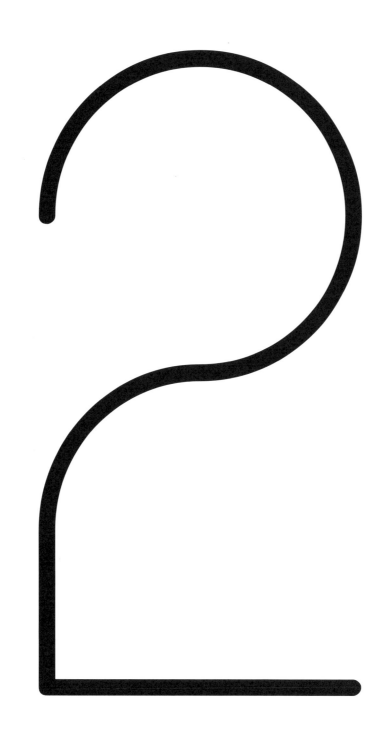

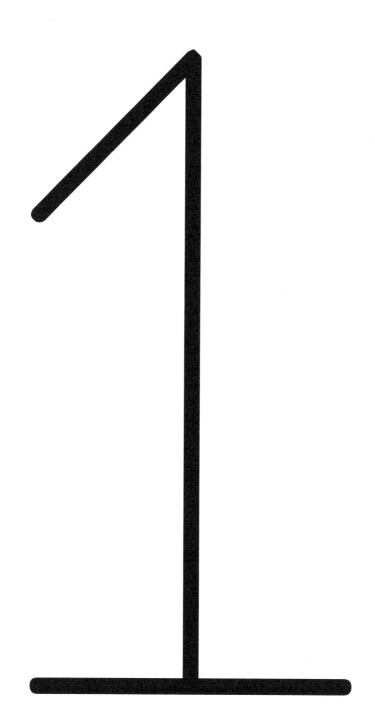

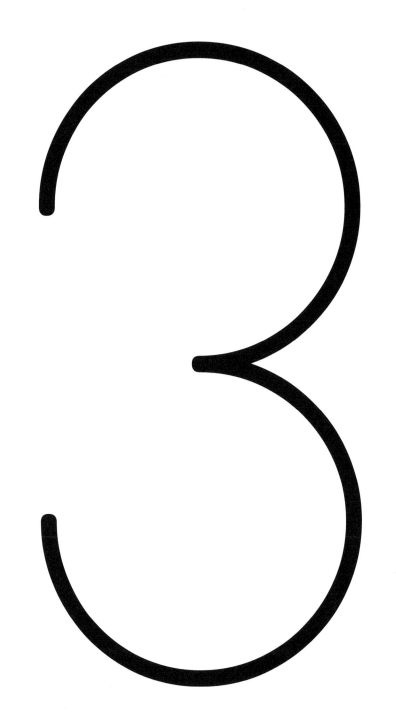

19 AUG, 2013

RESIDENCY @ GWANGJU ASIA ART CENTER

광주 국립아시아문화전당
아시아예술극장의 개관
준비 프로그램 ‹레지던시
쇼케이스›의 선정작 공연.
태싯그룹은 ‹LOSS›를 통해
사운드라는 소리 생명체가
탄생하고 진화하고 번식하는
모습을 선보였다.

Selected work
performance for
Residency Showcase, a
preparatory program for
the opening of the Asian
Arts Theater at the Asian
Cultural Center, Gwangju.
Through *LOSS*, Tacit
Group documented
the birth, evolution and
reproduction of a sound
creature called sound.

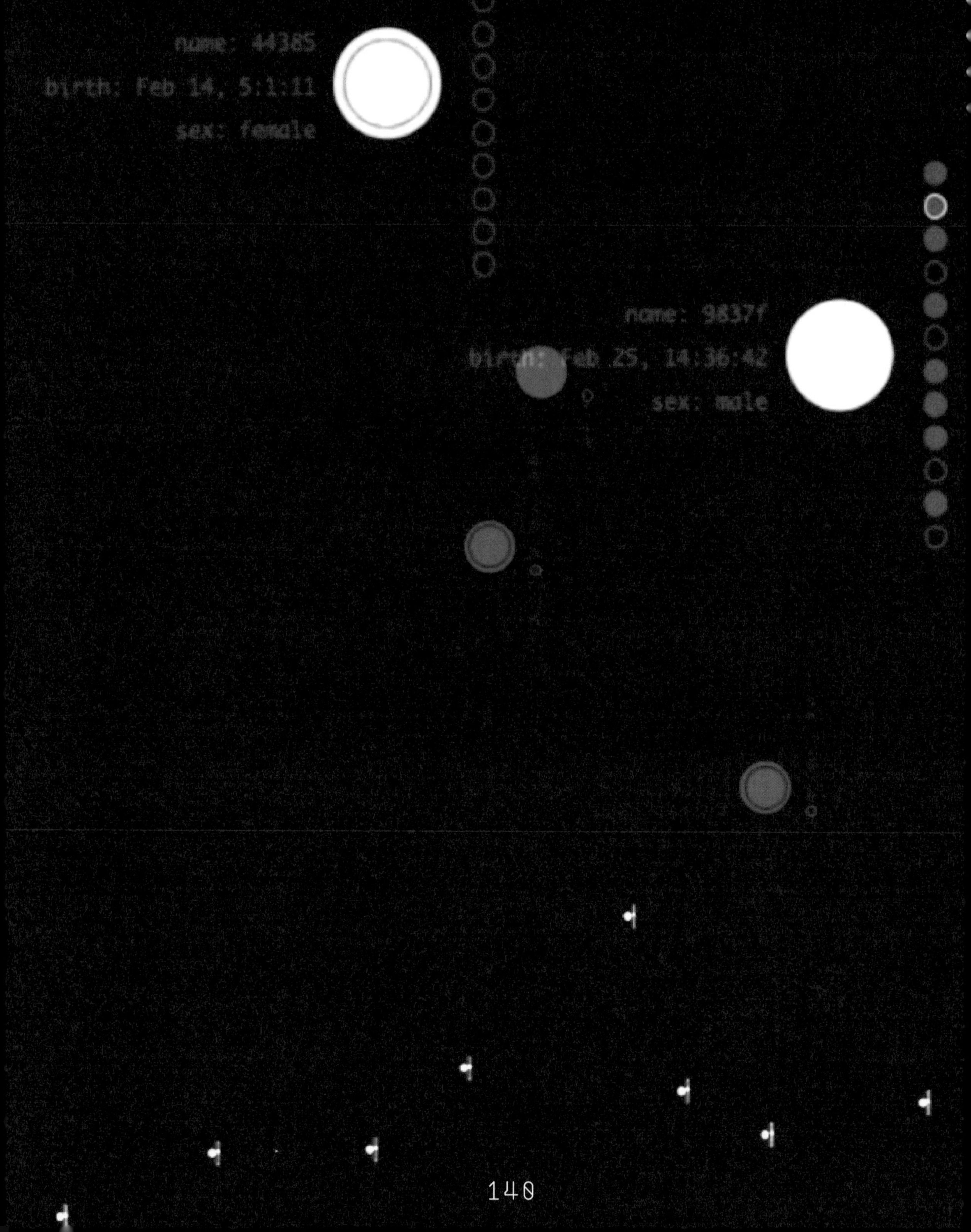

name: 4438S

birth: Feb 14, 5:1:11

sex: female

name: 9837f

birth: Feb 25, 14:36:42

sex: male

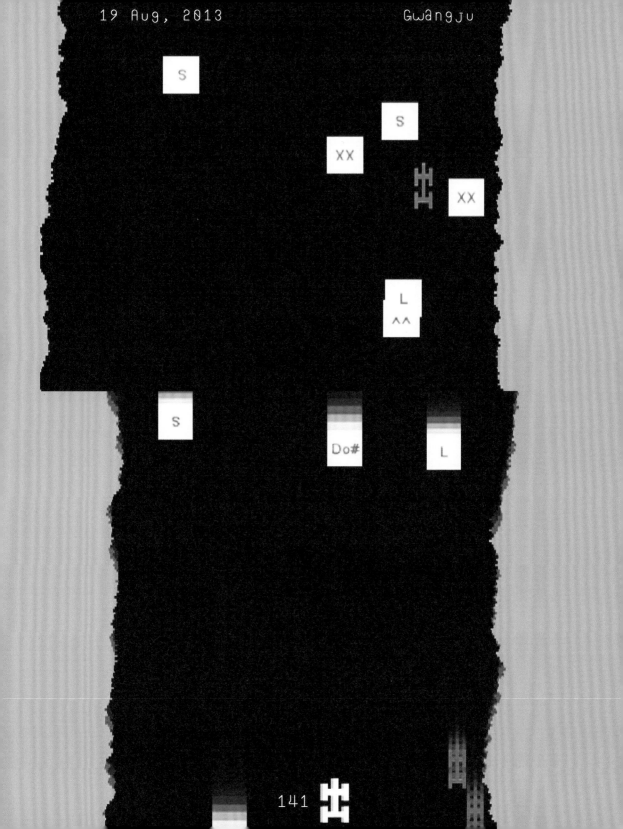

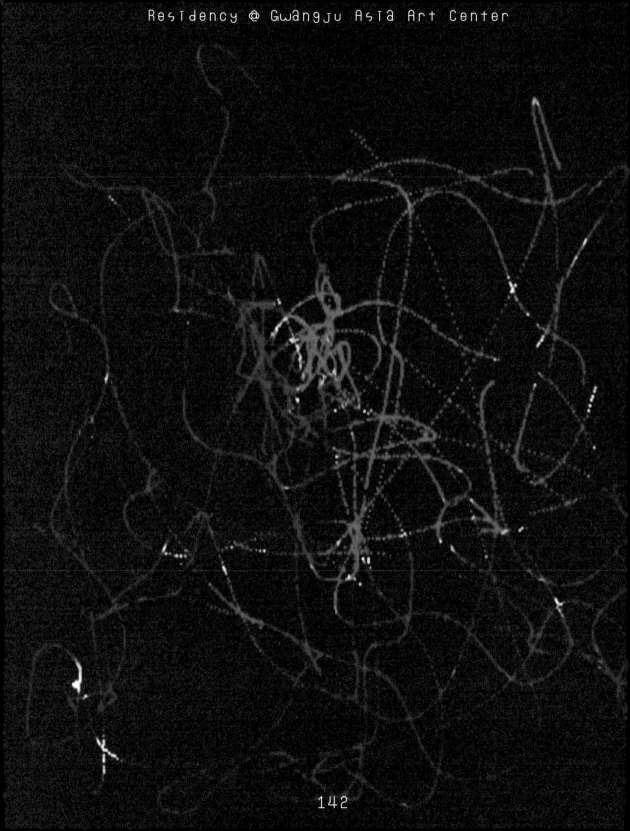

tacit.perform[3]

ㅜㅗ
ᅲ

ㅗrm

국립현대미술관 서울관
개관 기념 주제전 ‹알레프
프로젝트›의 연계 행사로 열린
태싯그룹의 네번째 단독공연.
‹LOSS›의 업그레이드 버전이
발표됐으며 '연주자가 없는
공연'으로 화제가 됐다.
아케이드 게임 팩맨과 스티브
라이히의 ‹Six Pianos›에
영감을 얻은 ‹Six Pacmen›이
처음으로 발표되기도 했다.
Graycode(조태복)가
객원으로 참여했다.

The fourth solo
performance of the Tacit
Group held in conjunction
with the thematic
exhibition *Aleph Project*
in commemoration of the
opening of the National
Museum of Modern and
Contemporary Art, Seoul.
An upgraded version of
LOSS was announced,
becoming a topic of much
discussion for being 'a
performance without a
performer.'

Six Pacmen, inspired by
the arcade game Pac-
Man and Steve Reich's
Six Pianos, was also
released for the first time.
Graycode (aka. Jo Tae-bok)
participated as a guest.

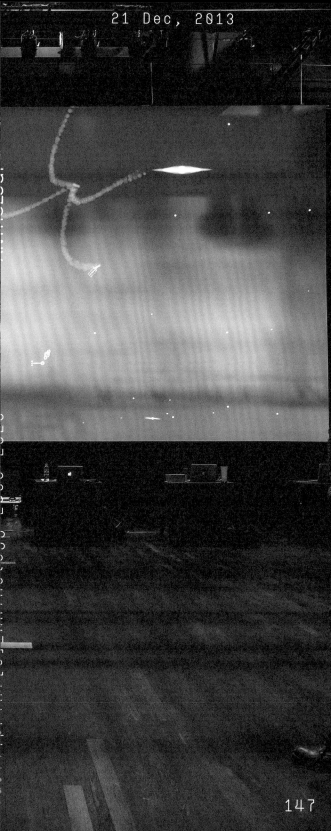

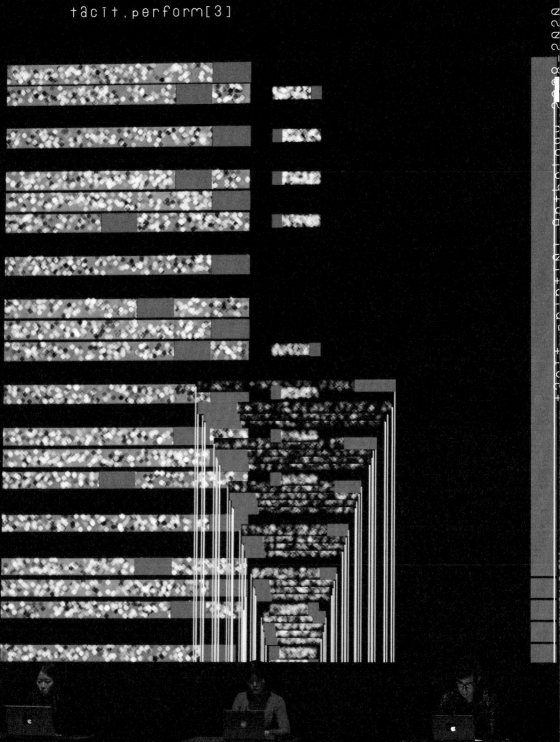

21 Dec, 2013
15
15

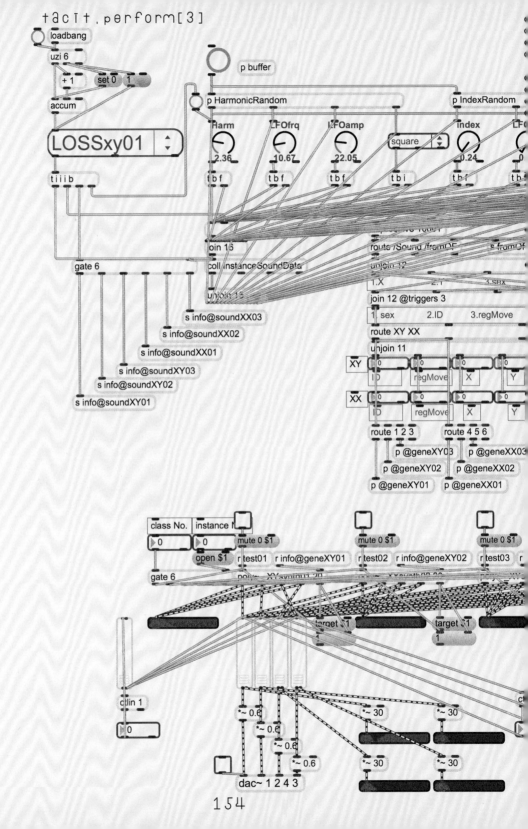

_LOSSsound_04g
2013.11.23

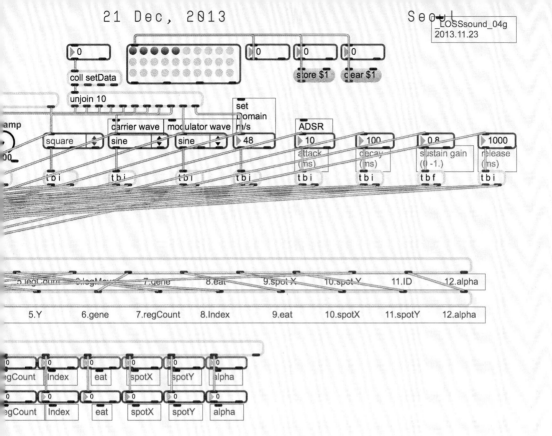

coll setData

unjoin 10

set Domain

amp

square | sine | carrier wave | modulator wave | m/s | 48

ADSR

10 | 100 | 0.8 | 1000

square | sine | sine | 48

attack (ms) | decay (ms) | sustain gain (0 -1.) | release (ms)

t b i | t b i | t b i | t b i | t b i | t b i | t b f | t b i

5.legCount | 6.legMax | 7.gene | 8.eat | 9.spotX | 10.spotY | 11.ID | 12.alpha

5.Y | 6.gene | 7.regCount | 8.Index | 9.eat | 10.spotX | 11.spotY | 12.alpha

regCount | Index | eat | spotX | spotY | alpha

regCount | Index | eat | spotX | spotY | alpha

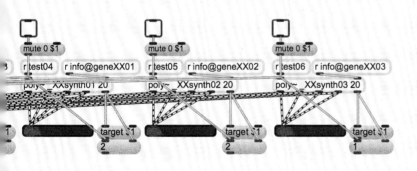

mute 0 $1 | mute 0 $1 | mute 0 $1

r test04 r info@geneXX01 | r test05 r info@geneXX02 | r test06 r info@geneXX03

poly~ _XXsynth01 20 | poly~ _XXsynth02 20 | poly~ _XXsynth03 20

target $1 | target $1 | target $1

2 | 2 | 1

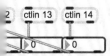

ctlin 13 | ctlin 14

0 | 0

155

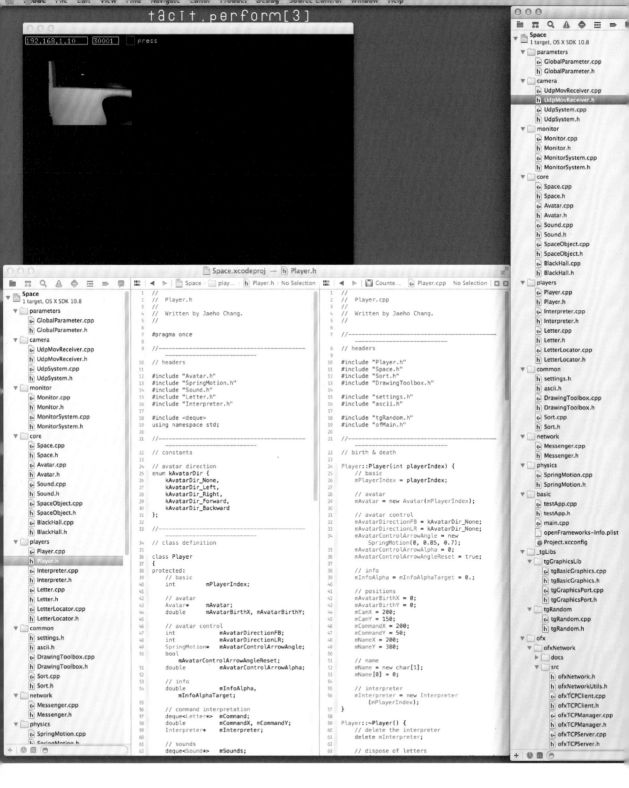

Space x tod proj — h Space.h

Space > core > h Space.h > No Selection

```
"Player.h"
"LetterLocator.h"
"Messenger.h"
"BlackHall.h"

"MonitorSystem.h"
"tgGraphicsPort.h"
"UdpSystem.h"

=deque>
espace std;


_____


kc port
pace::getGPort()
  returns tgGraphicsPort *

rs
he number of players
    Space::getPlayerCount()

he instance of a player
    Space::getPlayer(int playerIndex)
    - returns Player *

rs
he number of avatars = the number of players
    Space::getPlayerCount()

he instance of an avatar
    Space::getPlayer(index)->getAvatar()
    - returns Avatar *

objects
he collection that includes all the Avatar's and the Sound's

he number of SpaceObject
    Space::getSpaceObjectCount()

he instance of a SpaceObejct
    Space::getSpaceObject(int objIndex)
    - returns SpaceObject *

nger (osc)
pace::getMessenger()
  returns Messenger


_____


efinition


s a static class !


e {

phics port
 tgGraphicsPort*  mGPort;

ayers
 deque<Player*>  mPlayers;

ceObject instance collection
 deque<SpaceObject*> mSpaceObjects;

ck halls
 deque<BlackHall*>  mBlackHalls;

ter locator
 LetterLocator*  mLetterLocator;

work
 Messenger*     mMessenger;

 UDPSYSTEM*     mUdpSystem;

 MONITORSYSTEM*  mMonitor;

th & death
 void     setup(int playerCount);
 void     exit();

cess
 void     update();
 void     draw();

input
 void     keyPressed(int playerIndex, int asciiCode);
 void     keyReleased(int playerIndex, int asciiCode);

ceObject collection
 void     addSpaceObject(SpaceObject* obj);
 void     removeSpaceObject(SpaceObject* obj);

ect access
 tgGraphicsPort*  getGPort();
 int             getPlayerCount();
 Player*         getPlayer(int playerIndex);
 int             getSpaceObjectCount();
 SpaceObject*    getSpaceObject(int objIndex);
```

◀ ▶ | Counterparts Space.cpp No Selection

```cpp
//
// Space.cpp
//
// written by Jaeho Chang
//

//----------------------------------------------------------
// headers

#include "Space.h"
#include "settings.h"
#include "ascii.h"

#include "tgRandom.h"

#include "ofMain.h"

//----------------------------------------------------------
// init member variables

tgGraphicsPort*
Space::mGPort = 0;

deque<Player*>
Space::mPlayers;

deque<SpaceObject*>
Space::mSpaceObjects;

deque<BlackHall*>
Space::mBlackHalls;

LetterLocator*
Space::mLetterLocator = 0;

Messenger*
Space::mMessenger = 0;

UDPSYSTEM*
Space::mUdpSystem = 0;

MONITORSYSTEM*
Space::mMonitor = 0;

//----------------------------------------------------------
// birth & death

void
Space::setup(int playerCount) {
    // graphics port setup
    mGPort = new tgGraphicsPort(kDisplayWidth, kDisplayHeight, GL_RGB, kMSAA);

    double camX = 0;

    // create players
    for (int i = 0; i < playerCount; i++) {
        // create a player
        Player* newPlayer = new Player(i);

        // color setup
        newPlayer->setBaseColor(255 * (i == 0), 255 * (i == 1), 255 * (i == 2), 100, 200);

        // position settings setup
        double x = (ofGetWidth() / (playerCount + 1.)) * (i + 1.);

        if(i==0)camX = x;

        newPlayer->setAvatarBirthXY(x, 300);
        newPlayer->setCommandXY(x, 330);
        newPlayer->setNameXY(x, 500);
        newPlayer->setCamXY(x, 400);
        newPlayer->setCamSize(120, 90);

        // add to the list
        mPlayers.push_back(newPlayer);
    }

    // create black halls (TEST)
    mBlackHalls.push_back(new BlackHall(300, 50, 100, 40));
    mBlackHalls.push_back(new BlackHall(600, 70, 80, 40));

    // letter locator
    mLetterLocator = new LetterLocator();

    // network
    mMessenger = new Messenger();

    //x starting point, y is the same for 6 mov
    //arg : x offset, space, y axis
    mUdpSystem = new UDPSYSTEM(camX-(G_CAM_WIDTH/2), 96, 340);
//    mUdpSystem = new UDPSYSTEM(camX, -512, 350);

    mMonitor = new MONITORSYSTEM();
}

void
Space::exit() {
    // delete the messenger
    if (mMessenger) delete mMessenger;

    // delete the letter locator
    if (mLetterLocator) delete mLetterLocator;

    // delete the SpaceObjects
    mSpaceObjects.clear();
```

국립현대미술관 웹진 ART:MU 인터뷰
Tacit Group (태싯그룹)

태싯그룹에 대해 소개해 달라.

한국예술종합학교 음악테크놀로지과의 장재호
교수와 테크노 뮤지션 가재발 (본명 이진원) 두
사람으로 구성된 미디어 아트 팀입니다. 이번 2013년
공연(tacit.perform[3])부터는 Graycode라는
이름으로 활동해 온 미디어 아티스트 조태복이
객원으로 합류하였습니다. 처음에는 한국예술종합학교
음악테크놀로지과 대학원에서 선생님과 제자로 만났는데,
결국 같이 팀을 만들게 되었습니다. 최근 순수예술 쪽에
팀으로 창작 활동을 하는 아티스트들이 늘고 있긴 합니다만,
스승과 제자가 함께 하는 경우는 드물 것 같습니다. 조태복
역시 한국예술종합학교 음악테크놀로지과 출신입니다. 3대에
걸친 스승과 제자인 셈이죠.

장재호: 저는 클래식 전자음악이라는 매우 난해한 음악을
전공했습니다. 일반적인 대중이 접근하고 이해하기에는 다소
무리가 있는 분야입니다. 하지만, 아티스트로서 대중 혹은
관객에게 다가가고 싶고 그들과 호흡하고 싶다는 마음이
컸습니다. 클래식 전자음악의 진입장벽들을 게임이나,
한글 채팅과 같은 방식으로 좀 무너뜨려보자는 의도에서
태싯그룹을 시작하게 되었습니다.

가재발: 저는 테크노나 가요처럼 완전히 대중적인 작업을
해 왔습니다. 대중이 좋아해 주는가? 클러버들이 신나게
춤을 출 수 있는가? 하는 것이 이전 제 작업의 가장 중요한
기준이었습니다. 그러다 보니 대중의 눈높이를 의식하지 않고
내가 하고 싶은 음악을 하고 싶다는 생각을 하게 되었습니다.
그 즈음에 장재호 교수님을 만나게 되었고, 서로의 중간
지점에서 태싯그룹을 시작하게 된 것 같습니다.

그룹명 태싯그룹은 무슨 의미를 담고 있는가?

태싯그룹(Tacit Group)의 '태싯'은 침묵이라는 뜻입니다.
라틴어 'Tacet'에서 유래된 이 단어는, 앙상블이나 교향곡
등에서 한 악장 전체를 쉴 때 악보에 적는 용어로
쓰입니다. 존 케이지(John Cage)의 '4분33초'라는 작품의
악보에도 사용되었는데, 연주자가 4분 33초 동안 아무것도
연주하지 않는다는 의미였습니다. '4분33초'는 20세기
음악사에서 매우 중요한 한 획을 그었다고 평가 받는데, 당시

예술의 개념을 완전히 무너뜨린 혹은 무한대로 확장시켜
주었기 때문입니다. 여기서 침묵은 다른 소리들을 듣게
하고 그것의 의미를 새롭게 발견시키는 역할을 합니다. 즉,
침묵은 'nothing'이 아니라 'something else'인 것입니다.
태싯그룹의 '태싯'은 이러한 침묵의 의미를 21세기에
적용하여 디지털 테크놀로지로부터 기존 음악과는 전적으로
다른 새로움을 발견하려는 의지를 담고 있습니다.

태싯그룹의 작품은 영상과 사운드가 긴밀하게 연결되어 있는 것 같은 느낌을 받는다. 어떤 식으로 작업이 이루어지는가?

태싯그룹의 작품들은 모두 '알고리듬' 아트'의 맥을 갖고
있습니다. 알고리듬 아트는 결과보다는 과정과 방식에 초점을
맞추는 특징을 갖고 있습니다. 종종 풍경(windchimes)에
비유되는데, 창작자의 역할은 풍경이라는 하나의 시스템을
만드는 데서 끝나고, 소리의 조합 즉, 결과는 바람이 만드는
식이죠.
대부분 예술 작품은 창작자가 그 완성품을 먼저 상상함으로
작업을 시작합니다. 그러나 태싯그룹의 창작은 결과 보다는
'방법'을 먼저 생각하는 것부터 시작합니다. 이 '방법'은 수학
공식, 물리학의 개념, 유전학, 게임 등에서 영감을 받습니다.
영상과 사운드는 창작의 '방법'을 다양한 방식으로 표현하는
가운데 만들어집니다. 즉, 영상과 사운드는 태싯그룹 작품의
근본인 '방법' 혹은 '알고리듬'으로부터 나온 것이고, 따라서
유기적인 관계성을 가질 수 밖에 없게 됩니다.

해외에서 활발한 활동을 펼치고 있다.

팀을 결성한 직후인 2009년 8월, 두산아트센터에서 개최된
첫 단독 공연인 tacit.perform[0]이 꽤 큰 반향을 불러
일으켜서, 유럽, 미국, 남미 등 세계 각지로부터 초청을
받았습니다. 테트리스를 모티브로 한 <Game Over>와 테리
라일리의 <In C>를 재해석한 곡 들이 매우 유머러스하고
글로벌하게 비쳤졌던 모양입니다. 덴마크 오르후스
페스티벌에 헤드라이너로 초청되어 첫 유럽 데뷔를 가졌는데,
해외 언론으로부터 충격적인 (sensational) 데뷔라는 평을
받았습니다. 이후에 미국으로 건너가서 시카고 현대 미술관,
링컨 센터에서도 단독공연을 가졌습니다. 특히 링컨 센터
공연은 뉴욕 타임즈에 소개될 정도로 반응이 좋았습니다.
저희의 초기 대표작 중 하나인 <훈민정악>은 한글의
독창성과 채팅의 쌍방향성이 작품의 초점이긴 한데,
해외에서는 영어버전으로
채팅이라는 포인트만 살려서 공연하고 있습니다. 한글의 세계화라는 측면에서 언젠가

오리지널 작품 그대로 해외에서도 공연해 봤으면 하는 꿈이 있습니다.

태싯그룹이 추구하는 예술관은 무엇인가?

결성 이래 저희가 지속적으로 추구하는 것은 경계와 접점에 대해 질문입니다.. 예술과 기술 익스페리멘탈과 커머셜, 우연과 필연, 결과와 과정처럼 서로 공존하기 어려워 보이는 양극단의 요소들을 중간지점에서 만나게 하고 그 접점을 보여 주는 것이라고 할 수 있습니다. 경계 위를 걷는 것이 위험한 것처럼, 우리의 시도 역시 어느 쪽에서도 환영 받지 못할 리스크를 언제나 가지고 있다는 점을 잘 알고 있습니다. 예술의 입장에서 보면 너무 기술을 많이 사용하고 있고 기술 쪽에서 보자면 그 기술의 수준이 유치하다는 거죠. 실험예술에서 보면 게임과 같은 요소는 너무 친숙하고, 대중이 이해하기에 우리가 이야기 하고자 하는 것은 다소 어렵다는 겁니다. 하지만, 그래서 재미있지 않나 하고 생각합니다. 저희는 비난과 논쟁이 그렇게 싫거나 무섭다고 생각하지 않습니다. 오히려 환영한다고 할까요? 그래서 이 경계를 한 없이 날카롭게 만들어서 스스로를 더욱 위험하게 만들고자 노력하는 것이 저희의 할 일이라고 생각합니다.

이번 공연에서는 무엇을 보여주고자 하는가?

Space를 제외하고는 전부 신작입니다. 2011년에 처음 발표했던 Space조차도 이번 공연을 위해 완전히 업그레이드되어서 거의 신작이나 다름없습니다. 하지만, 가장 심혈을 기울인 작품은 역시 최신작 LOSS(Life of Sounds)입니다. LOSS는 경계에 대한 우리의 시도에 있어서 끝판왕이라 할 수 있는 작품입니다. 연주자가 없는 연주. 컴퓨터가 스스로 창조해 내는 연주가 기본적인 컨셉입니다. 연주자들은 작품이 시작되면, 몇 가지 유전적 명령어만 지정해 SOUND라는 소리를 내는 생명체를 만들어 내고는 바로 무대를 내려오게 됩니다. 나머지는 미리 작업된 알고리듬에 의하여 SOUND들이 진화하고 번식하는 과정이 저절로 연주되는 거죠.
알고리듬들은 우리가 창조해 낸 세계의 법칙 즉 필연이라고 할 수 있고, 연주자들이 지정하는 명령어는 우연이라고 할 수 있습니다. 이 필연과 우연이 얽혀있는 LOSS의 세계에서 SOUND 들은 서로 결합하여 새로운 생명체를 만들어 내고 그들의 유전자를 전달합니다. 작품을 만든 저희조차도 그들이 어떤 세상을 만들어 낼 지 예측할 수 없다는 것이 재미있는

거죠. Six Pacmen은, 이름이 재미있죠? 얼핏, 식스팩을 가진 남자들이란 뜻처럼 들리는데 사실 16비트 게임의 원조격이라 할 수 있는 팩맨이 6마리 등장한다는 의미입니다.
현대 음악 작곡가 스티브 라이히의 Six Pianos란 곡을 프로그래밍적으로 재해석한 곡입니다.
Drumming 역시 스티브 라이히의 작품을 재해석한 곡입니다. 드럼의 피치와 박자는 원곡이 정한 바를 그대로 따르고 있지만, 그 외의 모든 사운드적 요소는 철저히 연주자의 몫으로 돌렸습니다. 6명의 연주자들은 사운드의 장단, 크기, 음색, 질감, 노이즈 등을 컨트롤하면서 연주합니다. 사운드의 이러한 요소들이 그대로 맵핑 된 사각형의 BAR는 길이, 두께, 색깔, 선명도 등의 변화를 스크린을 통해 시각적으로 관객에게 전달하는 작품입니다.

미술관에서의 공연에 어떤 의의를 두는가?

정형화된 장르들이 그 전통적 경계를 벗어나는 일은 최근 그리 어렵지 않게 볼 수 있습니다. 그러나 태싯그룹의 공연이 미술관에서 이루어지는 것의 의미는 단순한 탈 장르, 혹은 크로스 장르와는 다르다고 봅니다. 태싯그룹은 지난 5년간 지속적으로 경계와 접점에 대해 질문을 던져왔는데, 여기에는 공연과 전시의 경계도 포함됩니다.
앞서 설명한 LOSS는 태싯그룹에 의해 창조된 소리들의 세계인데, 이 작품을 보여주는 방식은 공연이기도 하고 동시에 전시이기도 합니다. 연주자들 조차도 이 작품에서는 연주자이기도 하고 동시에 관객 혹은 관람객이 되기도합니다. 태싯그룹의 작품들은 그 자체가 이미 음악과 미술의 경계를 모호하게 넘나듭니다. 그래서 태싯그룹의 작품들은 콘서트 홀에도 어울리지 않고 일반적인 미술 갤러리에도 어울리지 않지만, 동시에 어느 곳에도 어울린다고 말할 수 있습니다. 이번 국립현대미술관에서의 공연은 단순히 미술관에서 음악 공연을 하는 것이 아닌, 지금 우리가 살고 있는 시대에 예술의 경계를 다시 세우려는 노력이라고 할 수 있습니다. 우리는 국립현대미술관에서의 이번 공연을 통해 음악과 미술에 대해 대부분 사람들이 갖고 있는 보편적인 경계에 물음을 던지고자 합니다.

tion 0x977c5355 __CFRunLoopDoTimer + 709
tion 0x977aa162 __CFRunLoopRun + 1730
tion 0x977a963a CFRunLoopRunSpecific + 378
tion 0x977a94ab CFRunLoopRunInMode + 123
0x9a2aa15a RunCurrentEventLoopInMode + 242
0x9a2a9ec9 ReceiveNextEventCommon + 374
0x9a2a9d44 BlockUntilNextEventMatchingListI
0x944d0a3a _DPSNextEvent + 724
0x944d026c -[NSApplication nextEventMatchin
0x944c66cc -[NSApplication run] + 855
0x014e5940 std::out_of_range::~out_of_range
0x014dda20 std::out_of_range::~out_of_range
0x00002842 0x1000 + 6210
0x00002769 0x1000 + 5993
e: com.apple.libdispatch-manager
ib 0x934969ae kevent + 10
0x9252dc71 _dispatch_mgr_invoke + 993
ib semaphore_wait

LOS   LOSS 2020

LOSS   LOSS 2020

LOSS e0e0

LOSS

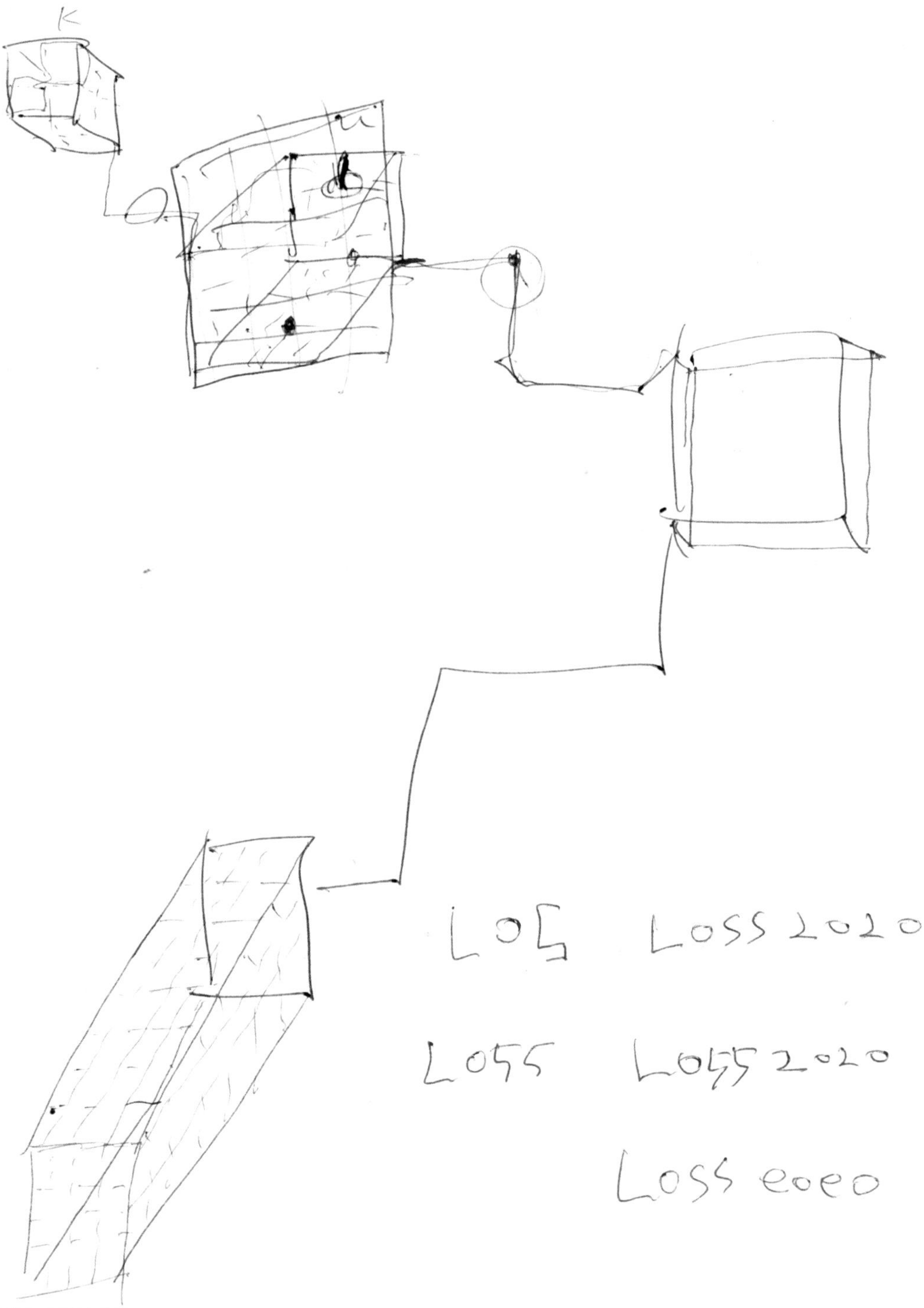

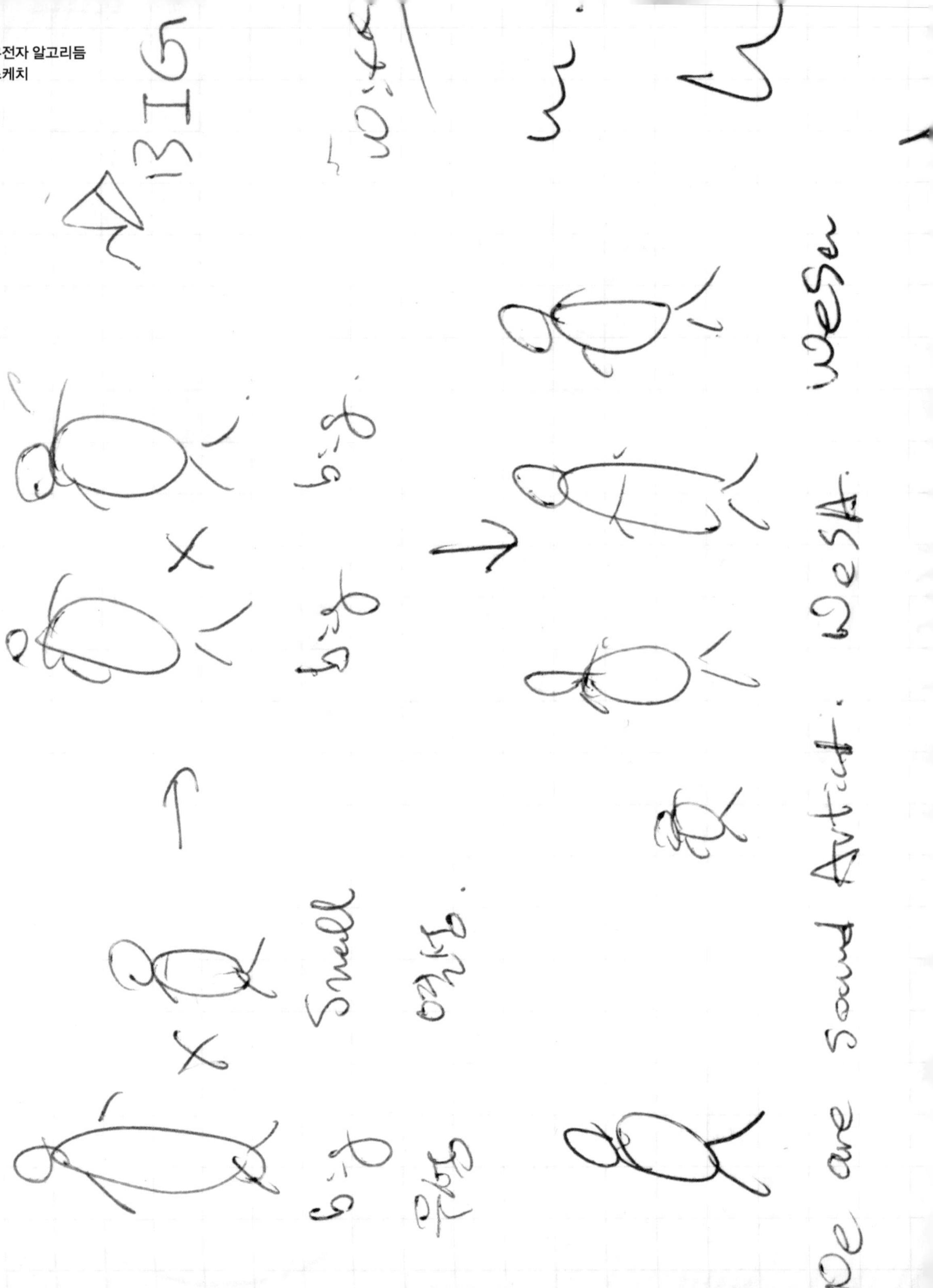

BIG

voice

WeSer

big big

big

Small

연결.

big

유전자

We are Sound Artist. WeSA.

WeSA.

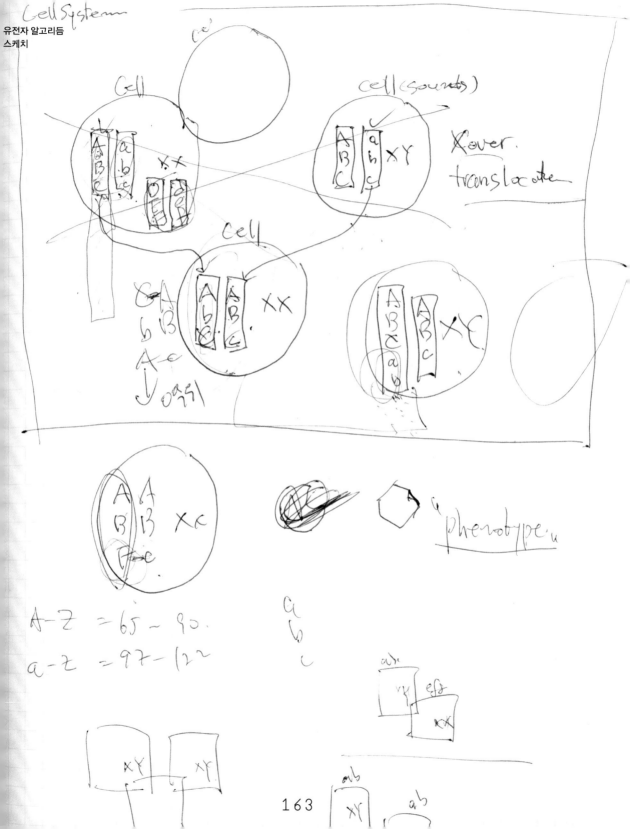

Cell System

유전자 알고리듬
스케치

163

pd pd⁺ p⁺d p⁺d⁺

pd

Pp⁺dd⁺   pp⁺d

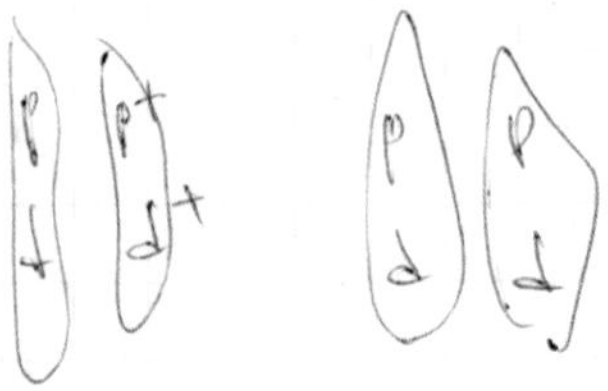

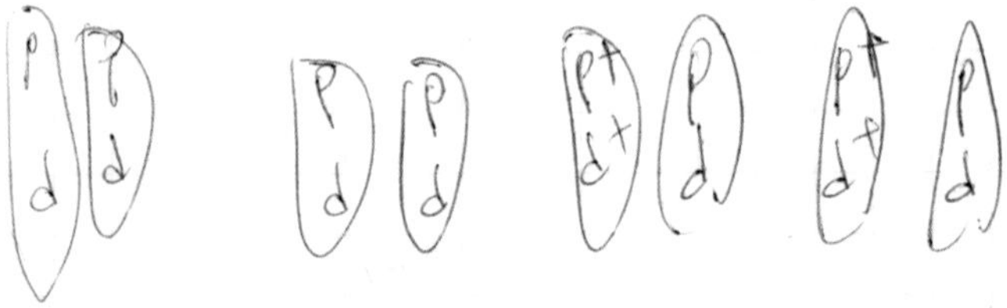

ppdd   ppdd   pp⁺dd⁺   pp⁺dd⁺

50%

pp⁺dd⁺
48%

cell   chromosome   cell

gene

cell - 세포

164

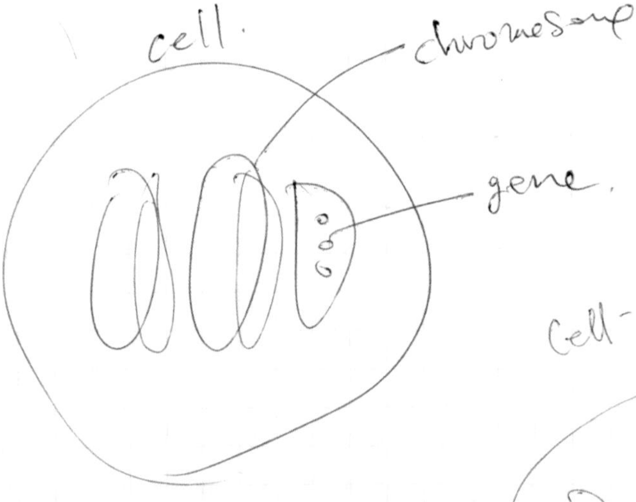

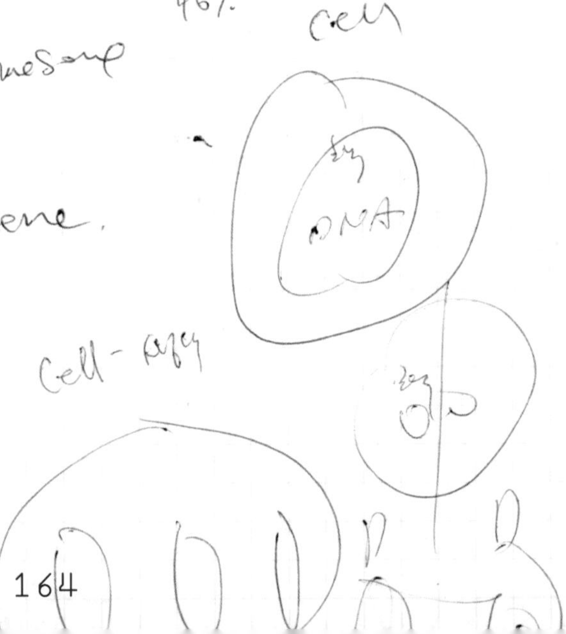

0 1 2 3 4 5 6 7   0 2 4 6   8 8 5 0

8 9 10 11 12 13 14 15   16 18 20 22

16 17 18 19 20 21 22 23   Brandt Krauer Trick

24 25 26 27 28 29 30 31   0 ~ 15

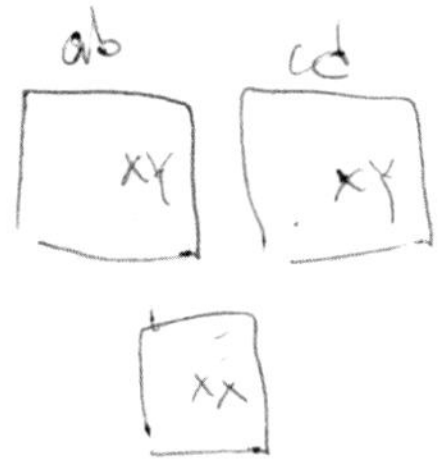

A a — 127   275

B b

C c

A A
A a) 255. 0. 0
a A
a a — 127. 0. 0

A B   B A — 255. 127. 0
A b   B a
a B   b A
a b   b a

B a.   255

A.

1 1
1 0
0 1
0 0

B A A B B A — 255. 127. 0
B a A b b A — 255. 64. 0
A   a B B a — 200. 127. 0
b a ~ b b a — 127. 64. 0

A a.   255 0 0   B a.
a a.   127 0 0   127   127

A C C A   255. 0. 127
A c c A   255. 0. 64
a C C a   200. 0. 127
a c c a   200. 0. 64

B B   B a.)
b B   a B.) 127. 127. 0
B b   B B.
~ b b

c A B C C B 200. 127. 127
c a B c c B
c A b C C b
c a b c c b. 200. 64. 64

255.

R G B,

A 1,6,5 C

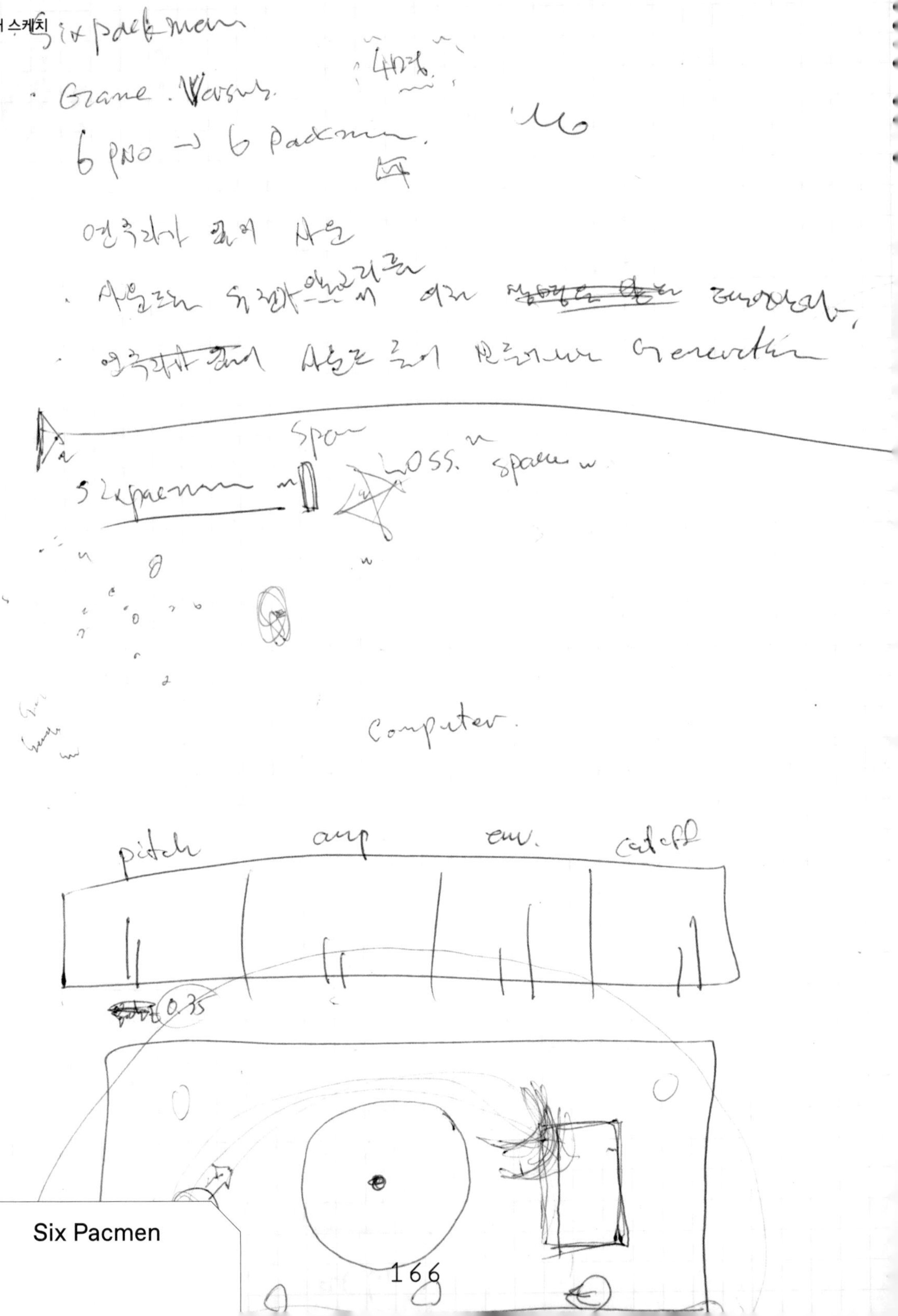

Six packman

· Game . Versus . 4가지

6 PNO → 6 Packmen 合

엉크리가 곡의 사운

· 사운드가 위켓 앞선거리를 악기 발생한다 얼마 재생하다,

· 악곡자가 곡의 사운드의 만큼으로 Generation

3 2 packman → Span LOSS. space

Computer.

pitch   amp   env.   cutoff

0.35

Six Pacmen

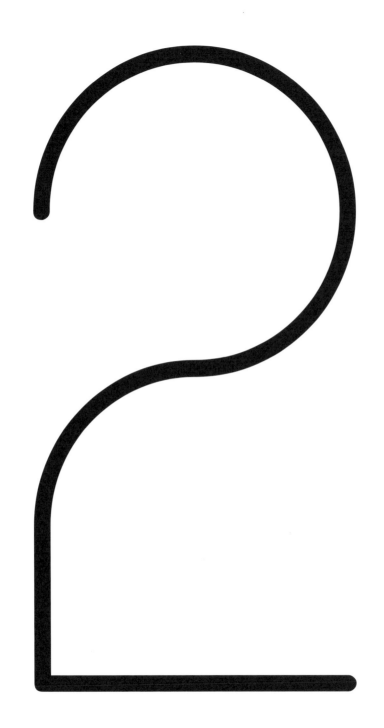

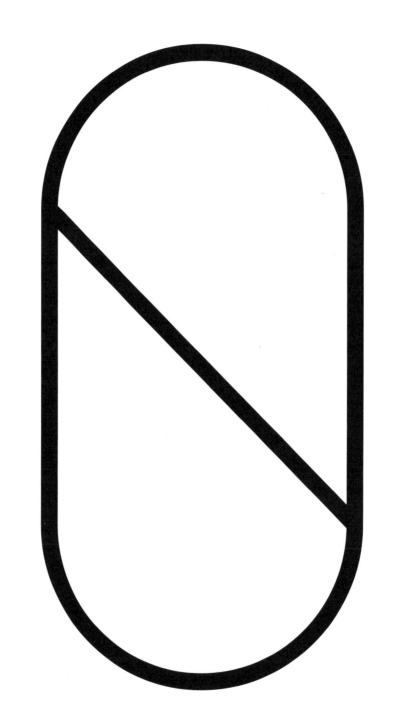

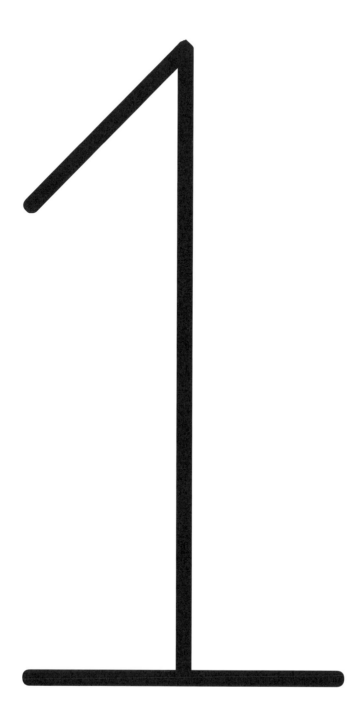

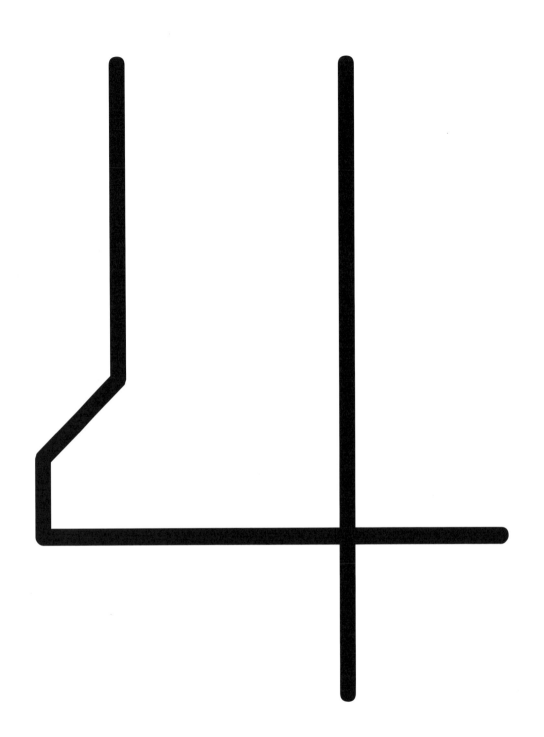

8 FEB, 2014

DISTORTION
FIELD 14

이화여대 ECC에서 '왜곡'을
주제로 열린 컨퍼런스로 주로
작가와 관객 간에 발생하는
왜곡장에 대해 다루었다.
태싯그룹은 공연분야에
초청받았다.

This conference was held
with the theme being
'distortion' which mainly
dealt with the distortion
field that occurs between
the artist and audience.
Tacit Group was invited to
perform. The conference
was held at Ewha
Womans University ECC.

171

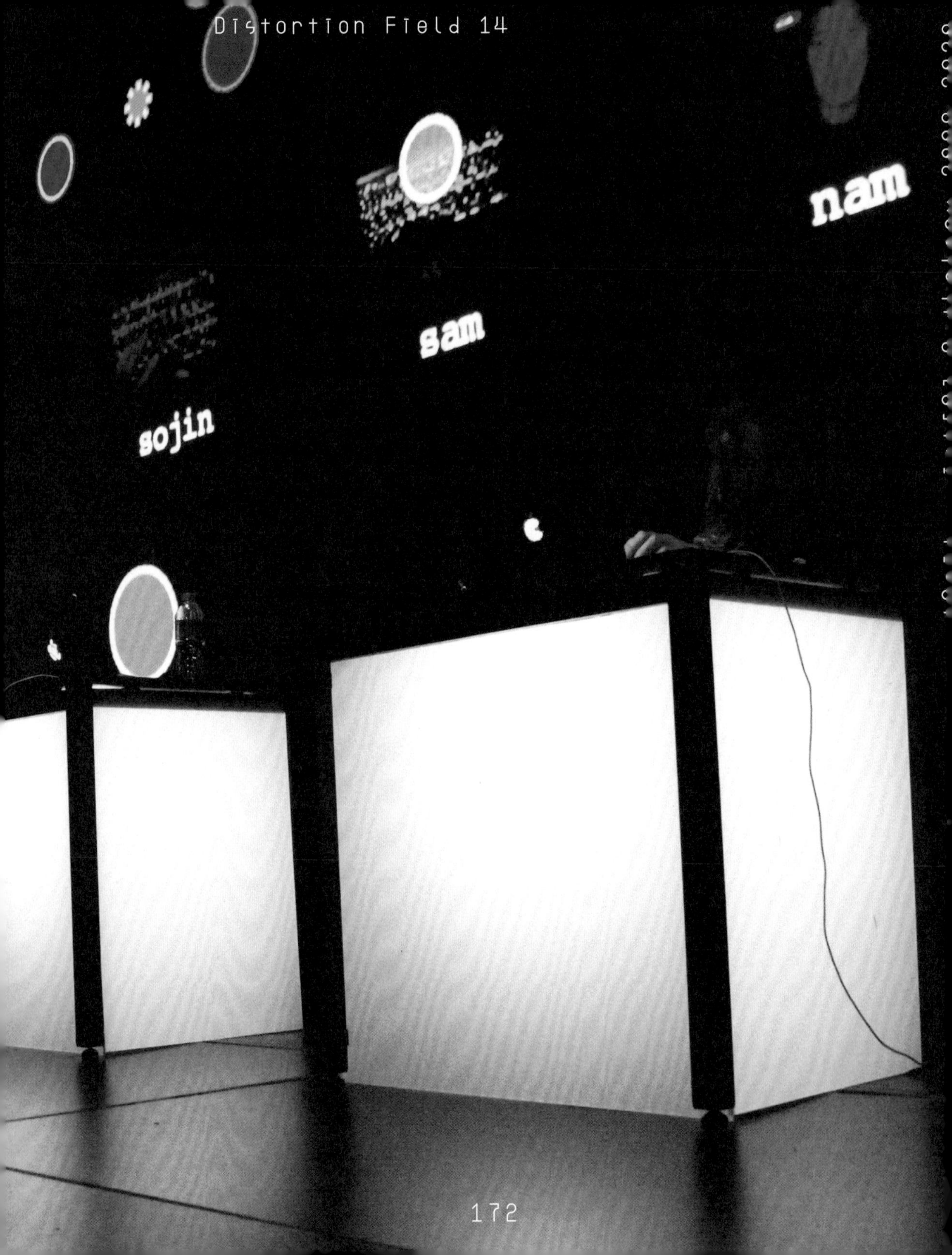
nam
sam
sojin

FESTIVAL
MORPH

태싯그룹의 유일한 클럽
퍼포먼스. 한국과 일본의 여러
EDM 뮤지션 및 DJ와 함께
했다.

Tacit Group's only
club performance. We
performed with several
EDM musicians and DJs
from both Korea and
Japan.

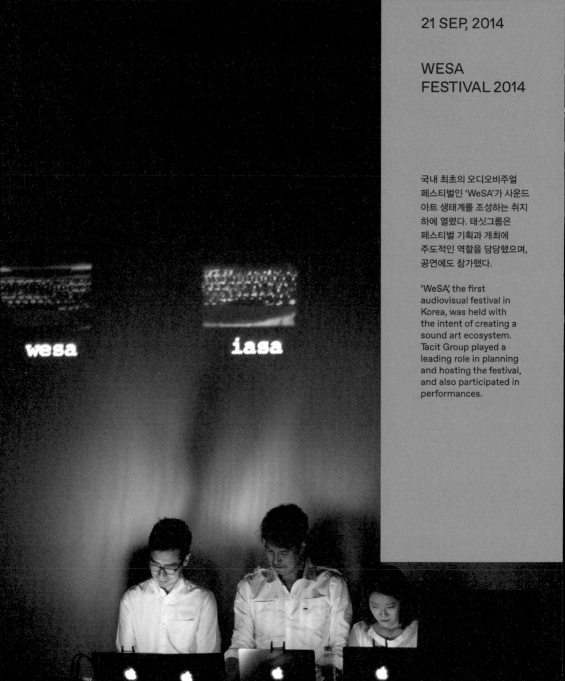

21 SEP, 2014

WESA
FESTIVAL 2014

국내 최초의 오디오비주얼
페스티벌인 'WeSA'가 사운드
아트 생태계를 조성하는 취지
하에 열렸다. 태싯그룹은
페스티벌 기획과 개최에
주도적인 역할을 담당했으며,
공연에도 참가했다.

'WeSA', the first
audiovisual festival in
Korea, was held with
the intent of creating a
sound art ecosystem.
Tacit Group played a
leading role in planning
and hosting the festival,
and also participated in
performances.

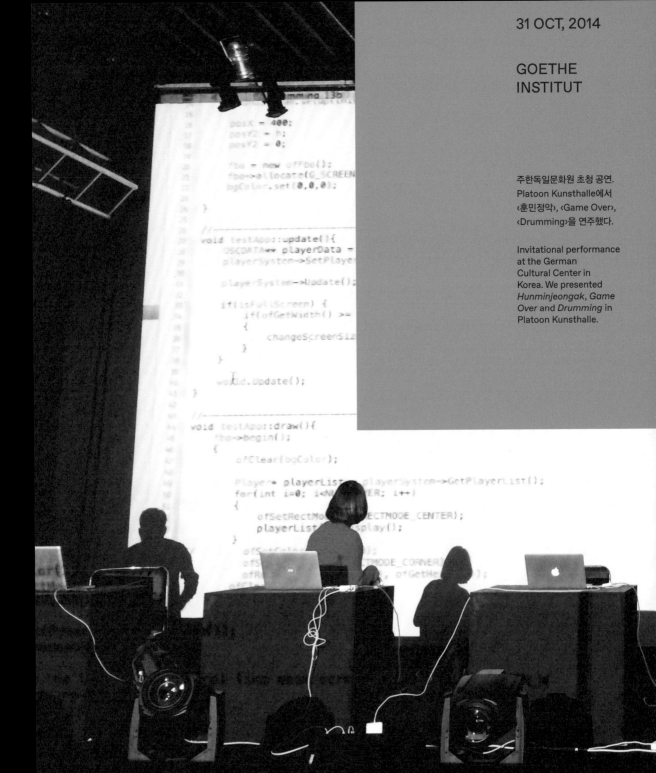

31 OCT, 2014

GOETHE
INSTITUT

주한독일문화원 초청 공연.
Platoon Kunsthalle에서
‹훈민정악›, ‹Game Over›,
‹Drumming›을 연주했다.

Invitational performance
at the German
Cultural Center in
Korea. We presented
Hunminjeongak, *Game
Over* and *Drumming* in
Platoon Kunsthalle.

```
                         h_testApp.h   No Selection
#pragma once

#include "oscManager.h"
#include "playerSystem.h"
#include "world.h"
#include "MonitorSystem.h"
#include "GlobalParameter.h"

//pitch : position of dot in the bar
//amp : height of the bar
//decay : length of the bar
//filter cutoff : color of the bar not the pitch dot
//pitch : falling speed of the bar

using namespace std;

class testApp : public ofBaseApp{
public:
    void setup();
    void update();
    void draw();

    void audioRequested(float *, int , int );
    void keyPressed(int);
    void changeScreenSize();

    int              w, h;
    ofxReceiver      oscReceiver;
    bool             isFullScreen;

    playerSystem*    playerSystem;

    world            world;

    ofSoundStream    soundStream;

    float            posX, posY1, posY2;
    int              counter;

    ofFbo            fbo;
    ofColor          bgColor;
    ofPixels         pixels;

    MONITOR          monitor;
```

태싯그룹은 다섯번째 단독
공연을 통해 청각과 시각의
경계를 집중 탐구했다. 데뷔
초부터 지속적으로 탐구해온
주제인 '사운드의 시각화'에
본격 도전한 것이다.
‹System1› ‹System2›
‹Organ› 등 영상이 귀로
들리는 작품을 선보였다.

Tacit Group focused on
exploring the boundary
between hearing and
sight through their fifth
solo performance. It is
a full-fledged challenge
to the 'visualization
of sound', a topic that
has been continuously
explored since the
beginning of the team's
debut. Tacit Group
presented works that can
be experienced through
the ears, such as *System1*,
System2 and *Organ*.

리듬감이 있는 소리들의 경우 (멜로디는 많고!

Pulse 파의

width와   Height 에   따라서

↓

* 소리가 날지 안날지

음색(?)

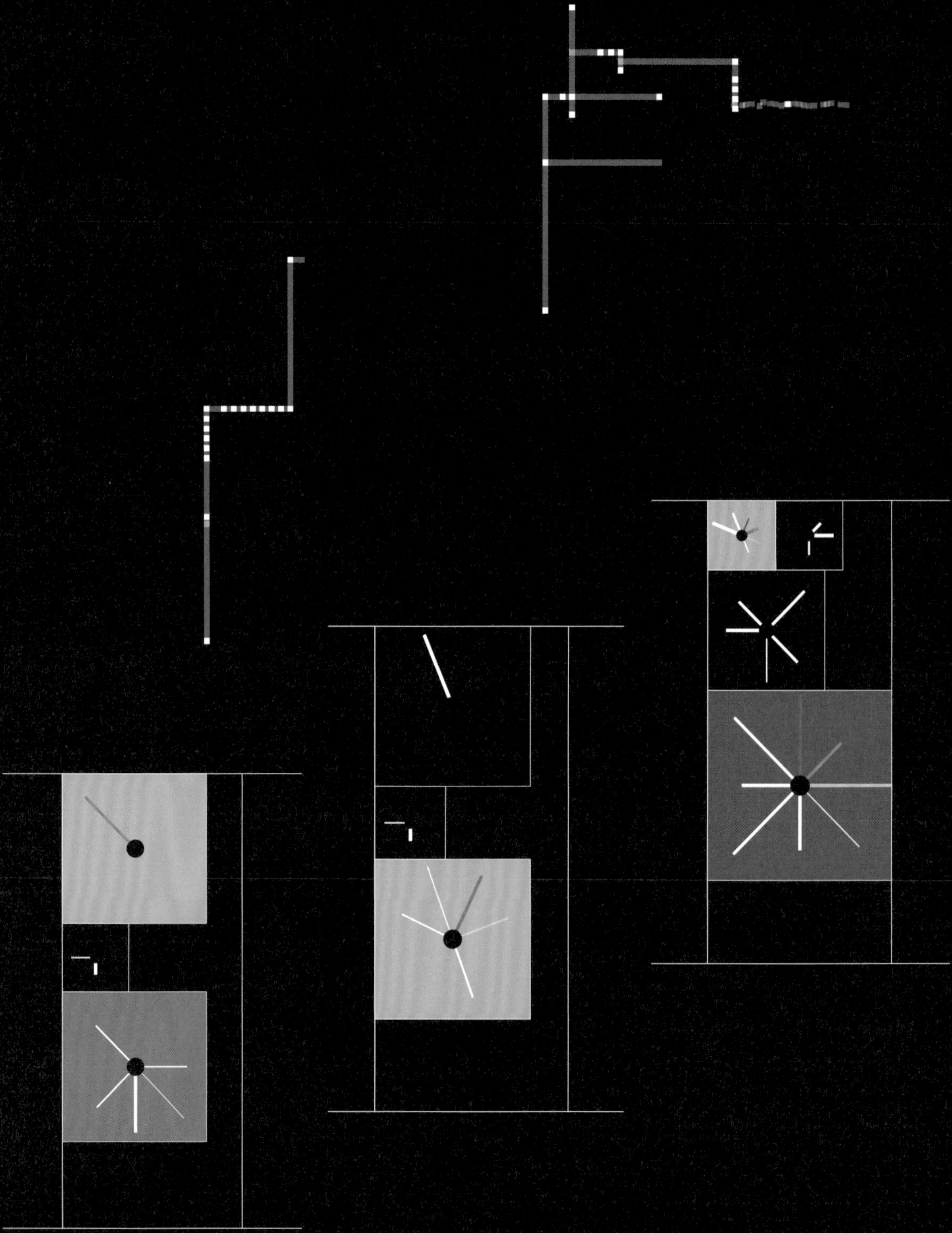

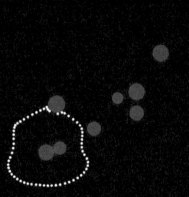

t a c i t . p e r f o r m [4]

1 2 . 2 7 . s a t . 8 p m
2 8 . s u n . 5 p m
p l a t o o n k u n s t h a l l e

tacit.perform@gmail.com
http://facebook.com/tacit.group

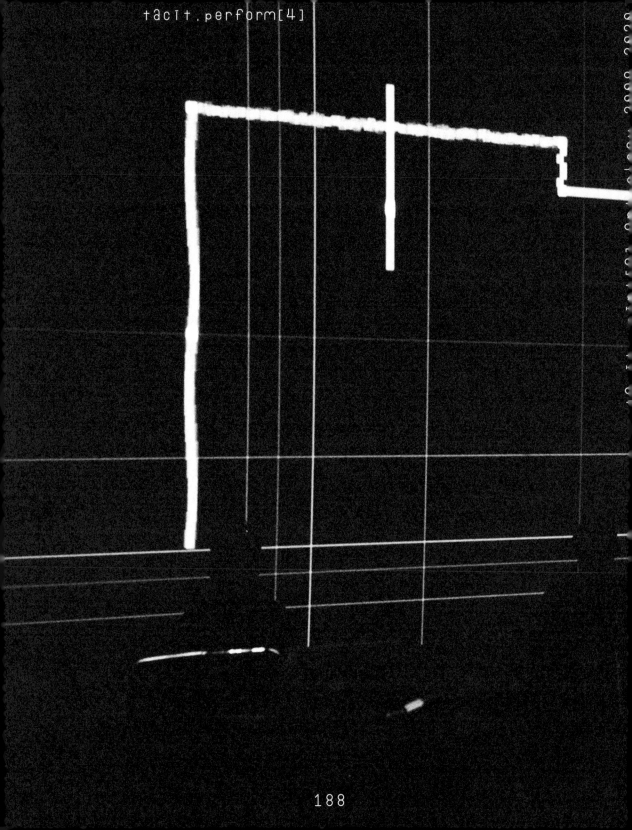

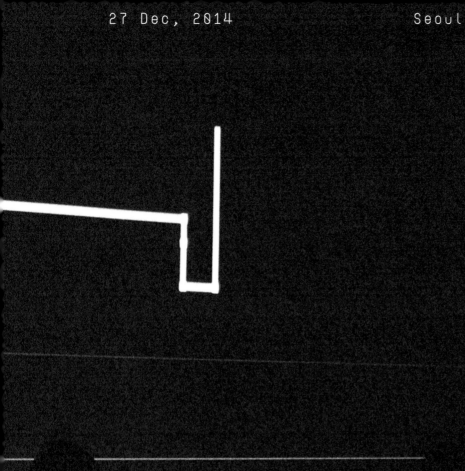

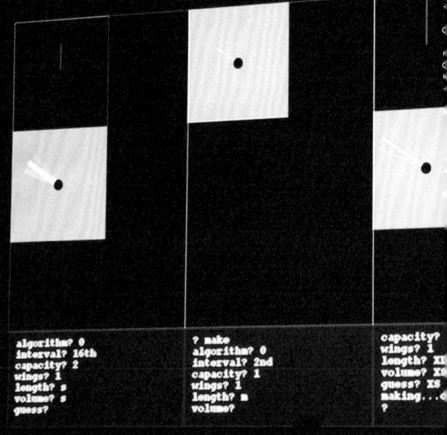

```
algorithm? 0          ? make                capacity?
interval? 16th        algorithm? 0          wings? 1
capacity? 2           interval? 2nd         length? X
wings? 1              capacity? 1           volume? XS
length? s             wings? 1              guess? XS
volume? s             length? m             making...
guess?                volume?               ?
```

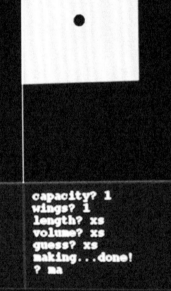

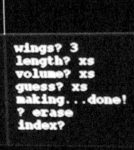

```
capacity? 1
wings? 1
length? xs
volume? xs
guess? xs
making...done!
? ma
```

```
wings? 3
length? xs
volume? xs
guess? xs
making...done!
? erase
index?
```

```
capacity
wings? 1
length?
volume?
guess? x
making..
?
```

tacit.perform[4]

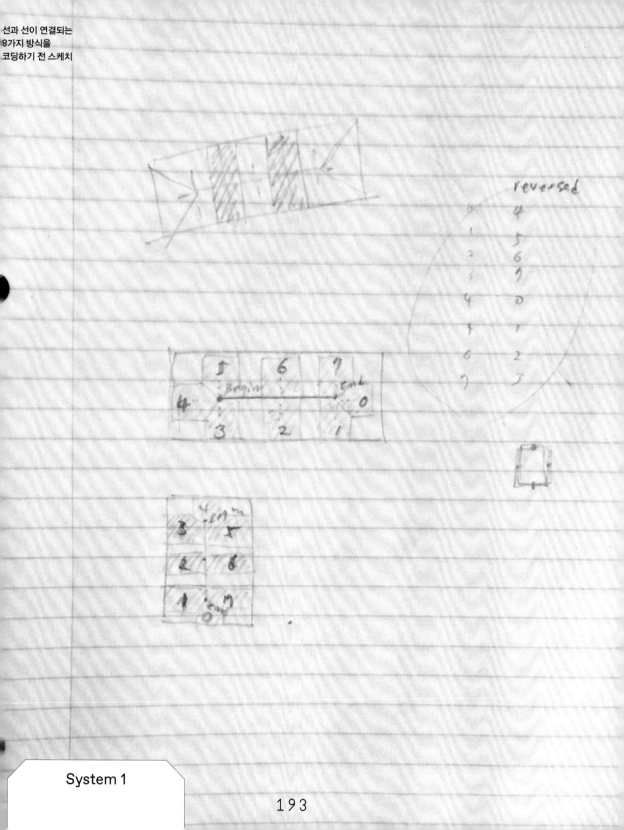

System 1

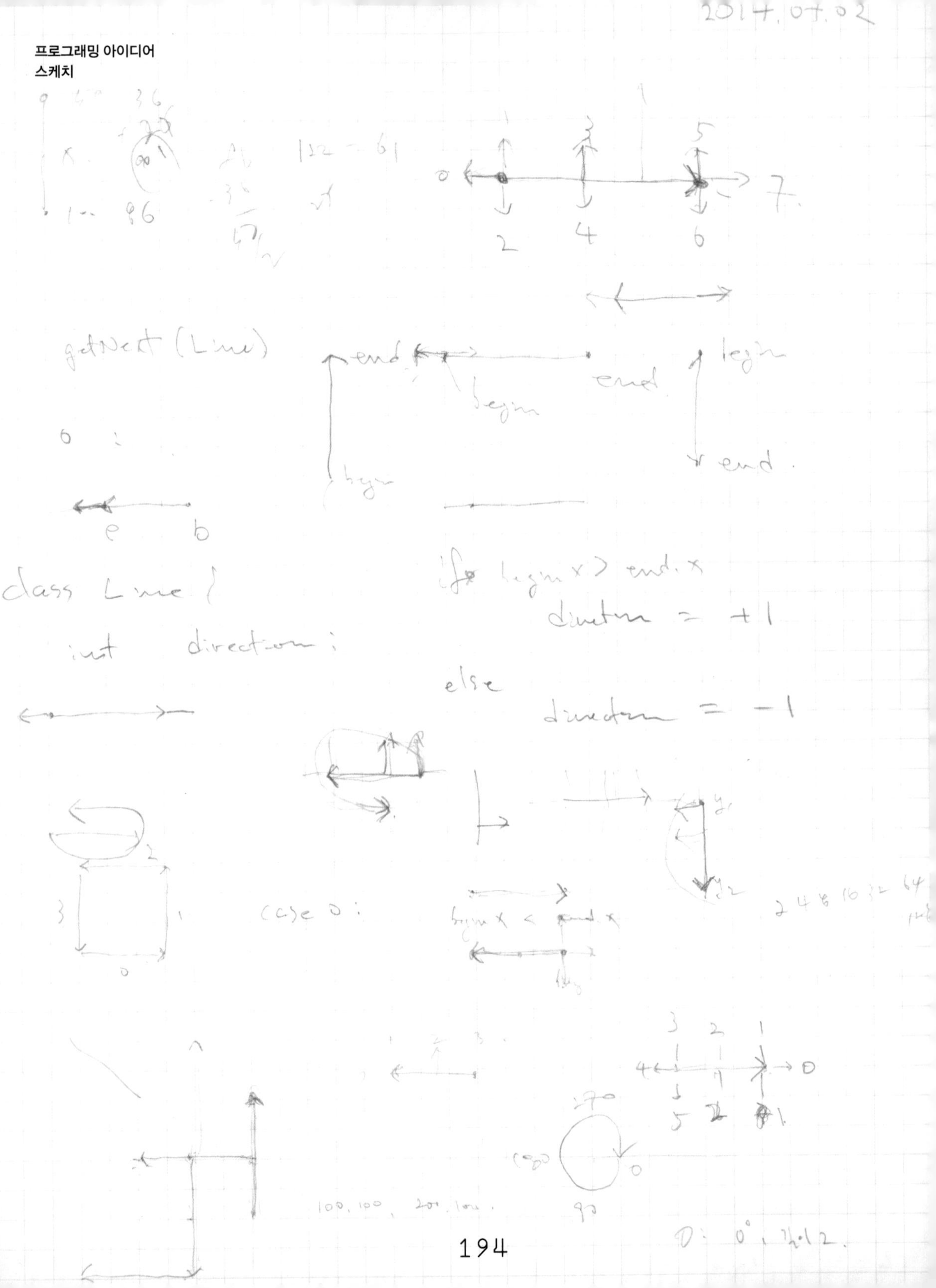

getNext (Line)

0 :

class Line {

int direction;

if begin.x > end.x
  direction = +1

else
  direction = -1

case 0:

begin.x < end.x

100, 100, 201, 100.

90

D: 0 : 2 : 1.2.

194

(300,200)

1. 스케일로 점이 말려 간다

2. 선이 그려간다 ——→

3. 선의 rotating

2014 07 04

BLADE

"2014. 07. 07"

PLAN? YOUR PLAN!
TIMM

1. 높이 최장음에 따라 리듬이 만들어짐.
   선의 높이에 따라 리듬의 길이가 결정됨

2. 점선. 남선 의 Rythm을 만들기

3.

P1   P2

P3

Play-r!
○ 리더시 ...

195

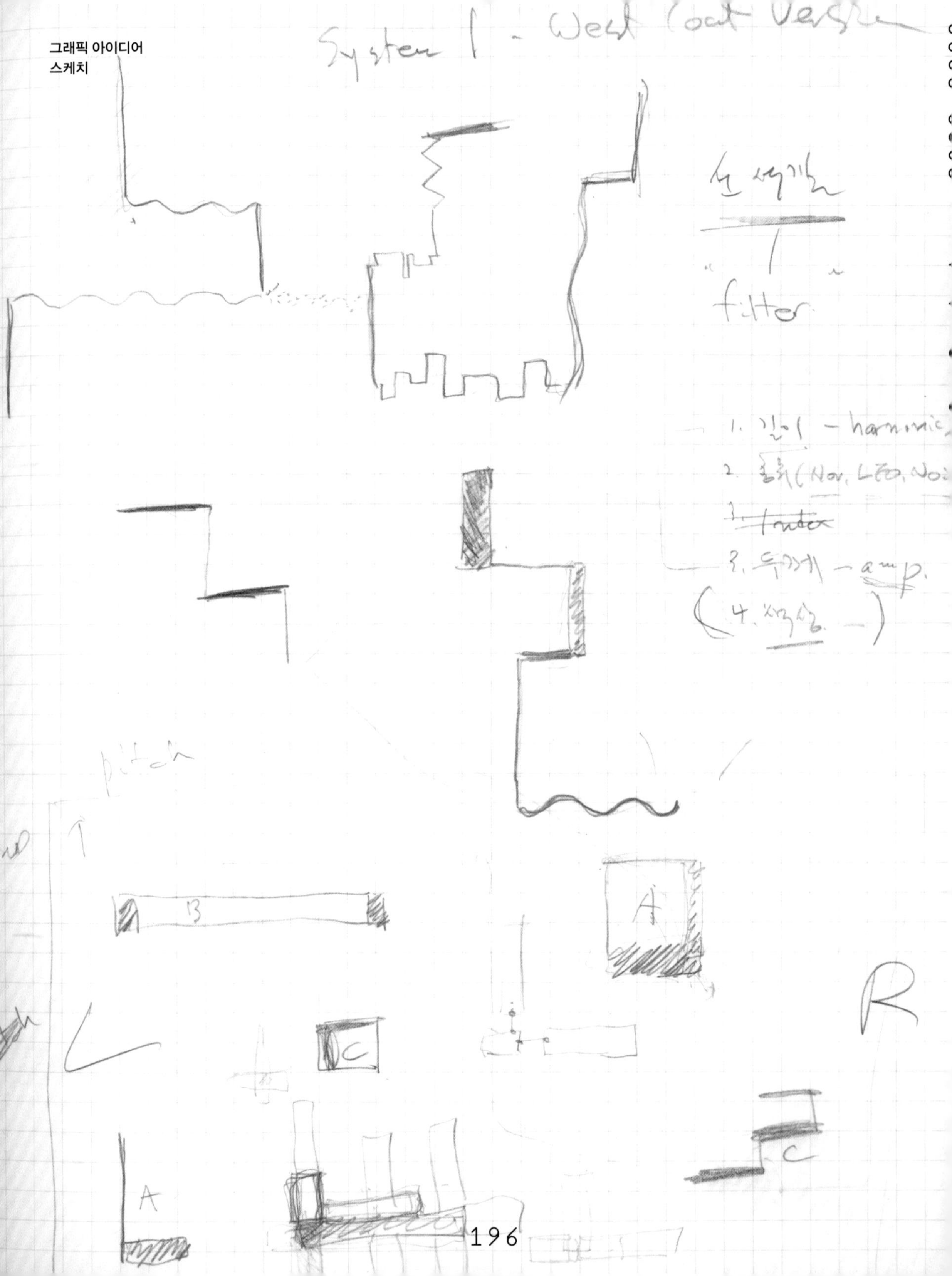

System 1 - West Coast Version

노 생기온

"filter"

1. 갈이 - harmonic
2. 줄위 (Nov, LFO, Noi
3. ~~Index~~
3. 누게 - amp.
(4. 성상. -)

pitch

B

A

C

A

R

C

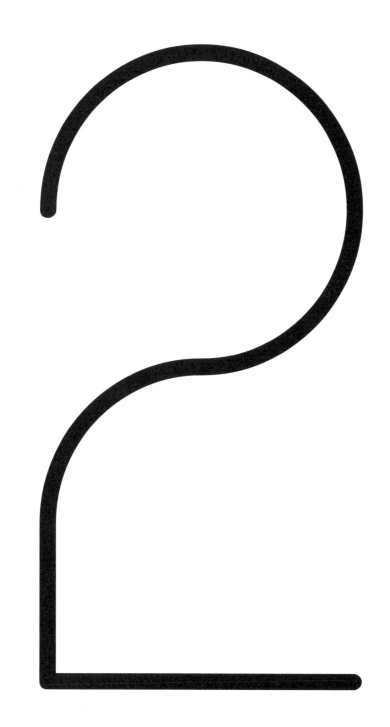

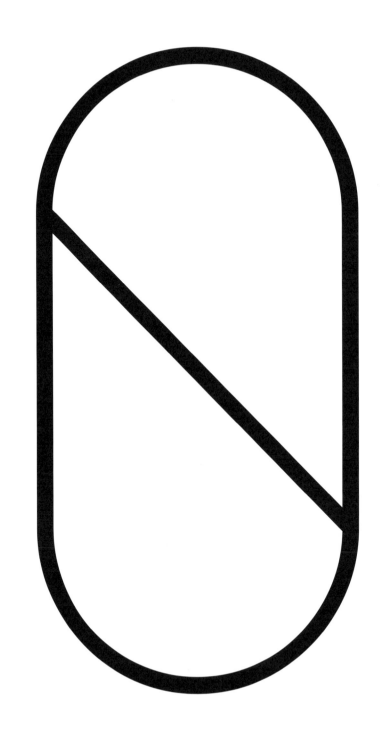

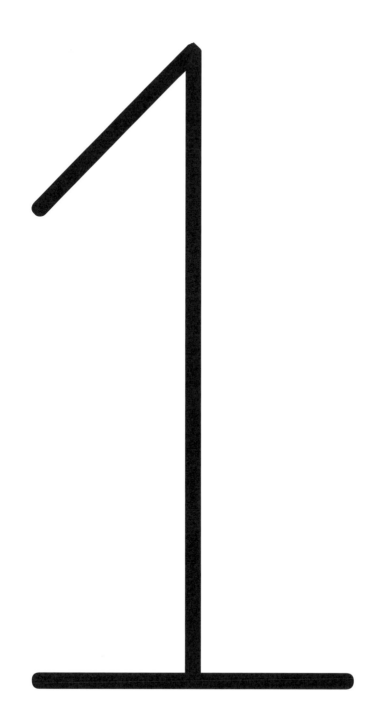

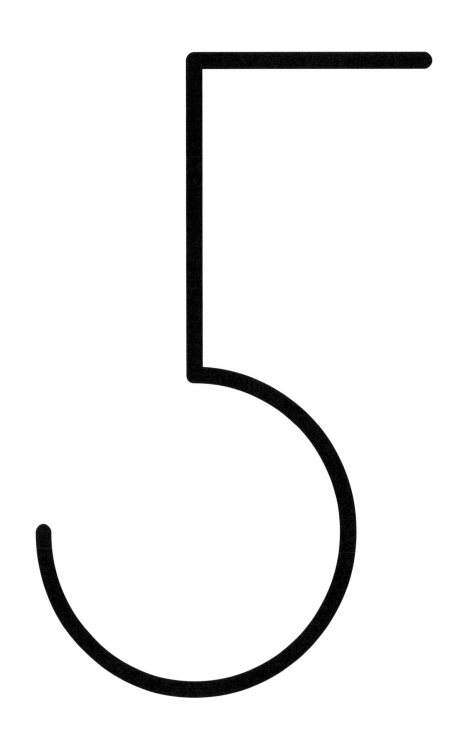

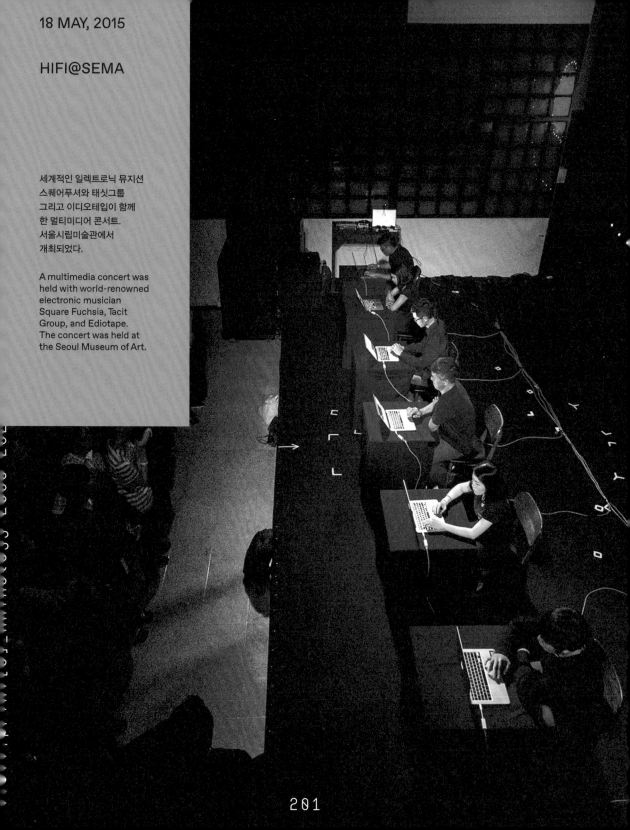

18 MAY, 2015

HIFI@SEMA

세계적인 일렉트로닉 뮤지션
스퀘어푸셔와 태싯그룹
그리고 이디오테입이 함께
한 멀티미디어 콘서트.
서울시립미술관에서
개최되었다.

A multimedia concert was
held with world-renowned
electronic musician
Square Fuchsia, Tacit
Group, and Ediotape.
The concert was held at
the Seoul Museum of Art.

LECTURE PER-FORMANCE, BRUSSELS

벨기에 한국문화원의 초청 공연.

Invitational performance at the Korean Cultural Center in Belgium.

훈민정악(Hun-min-jeong-ak)

"훈민정악"은 연주자가 타이핑하는 자음과 모음들의 조합이 음악을 만들어 가는 작품으로, 한글의 창제 원리에 바탕을 둔다. 한글의 창제 원리에는 크게 두 가지가 있는데, 하나는 글자가 그 요소들의 수평적, 수직적 조합에 의해 만들어지는 것이고, 또 다른 하나는 글자의 요소들이 언어의 실제 소리를 바탕으로 만들어진 것이다. 이 두 가지 원리는 컴퓨터 프로그램 안에 구현되어 연주자가 타이핑하면 글자를 이루는 각 요소들이 그에 상응하는 소리로 바뀌게 된다. 연주자들은 자음과 모음을 조합하여 추상적 모양을 만들거나, 의미있는 글자를 통하여 연주자들 혹은 관객과 대화를 해 나가는 즉흥적인 퍼포먼스를 펼친다.

Morse ㅋung ㅋung

모르스 코드(Morse Code)는 짧은 소리와 긴 소리, 이 두가지 소리의 조합으로 만들어진다. 이는 0과 1로 구성된 디지털 세계와 매우 흡사하고, 그 리듬은 매우 음악적이다. 태싯그룹은 이러한 모르스 코드에서 영감을 얻어 자신들만의 음악적 코드를 만들었다. 한글의 자음과 모음은 태싯그룹이 임의로 정한 '코드'를 갖고 있고, 연주자는 자음이나 모음을 골라 음악적으로 코드를 조합시킨다. 연주자가 코드를 고르는 행위는 음악을 만드는 동시에 글자를 만드는 것으로, 음악의 의미와 글자의 의미가 묘하게 혼합된 결과를 만들어낸다. 관객은 음악을 듣는 동시에, LED의 On과 Off로 구성되어 있는 글자 판을 통해 이 과정을 지켜볼 수 있다.

Game Over

연주자들은 서로를 상대로 테트리스 게임을 벌인다. 내려오는 테트리스 블록이 밑에 쌓이면 그 블록의 높낮이에 따라 들려지는 소리가 달라지고, 함께 경기하는 다른 연주자의 결과물과 함께 하나의 앙상블을 이룬다. 랜덤하게 주어진 블럭들과 연주자들의 게임 과정, 그리고 그 경기 시간에 따라 음악의 결과는 매우 즉흥적이고 우연적으로 흘러간다.

Tacit Group has performed in diverse places around the planet, including the Lincoln Center and the Audio Engineering Society in New York, the Chicago Museum of Contemporary Art, the Nam June Paik Art Center in Korea, and the Aarhus Festival in Denmark.

Group Members

Jaeho Chang

Jaeho Chang is a composer and media artist. His main interest is developing computer algorithms to compose music. His work also includes electro-acoustic music for dance or film, and sound installations. He also has been developing interactive music systems for media arts, and recently experimented with algorithmic image synthesis systems.

Jinwon Lee (aka Gazaebal)

Jinwon Lee is a well-known techno composer since the early 90s, who later evolved to a more experimental approach. With his electronic music and media art, he participated in both music performances as exhibitions in Korea and abroad.

More information
Official website: www.tacit.kr
Videos: https://vimeo.com/tacit

Concert Pogram

1. Lecture
Before starting their performance, the group members introduce their musical approach and tonight's performance. The lecture will be simultaneously translated in English.

2. Hun-min-Jeong-ak
Hun-min-jeong-ak is a compound of two Korean words: the name of a very old book on the principles of Hangeul, the Korean alphabet (Hun-min), and the name of a Korean traditional music genre (jeong-ak). While the performers type improvised letters and words, computers transform them into corresponding sounds.

3. Morse Kung Kung
Morse code consists of the alteration of short and long signals, making it very similar to the binary logic of computers, based on the alteration of 0 and 1. In Morse Kung Kung, a Morse code sequence is created, based on the alteration of vowels and consonants in Hangeul, the Korean alphabet, which are then converted in onto music.

4. Game Over
Game Over involves the classic computer game Tetris. The computer generates a melody according to the shape and configuration of the Tetris blocks that come down while the performers are playing.

4. Q&A
Feel free to ask your questions to the performers.

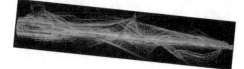

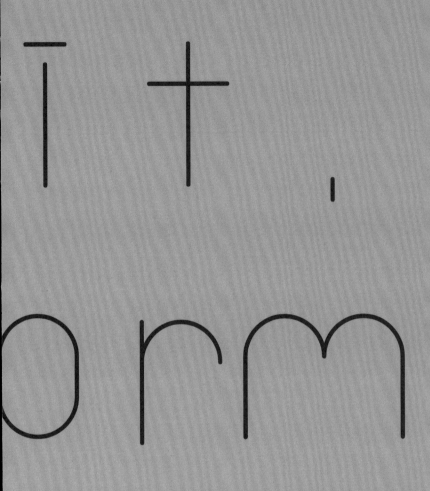

예술의 전당에서 여섯 번째
단독 공연을 펼쳤다. 사운드가
연주자의 손끝에서 발생하는
수동적인 존재가 아니라는
태싯그룹의 인식이 반영된
공연으로 ‹Morse ㅋung
ㅋung›과 ‹Gesture &
Texture›가 발표되기도 했다.

Tacit Group performed
the sixth solo
performance at the
Seoul Arts Center *Morse
ㅋung ㅋung* and *Gesture
& Texture* were also
released as performances
reflecting the ethos of
Tacit Group that the
sound is not a passive
entity simply bourne
from the fingertips of the
performer.

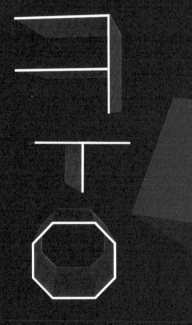

tacit.perform[5]

2015.10.31 Sat PM 7:30   후원 서울문화재단
2015.11.01 Sun PM 5:00   티켓 http://www.sacticket.co.kr
예술의전당 자유소극장   Tacit.kr

11–12 NOV, 2015

ABU DHABI

아부다비 뉴욕대학교 아트
센터 개관 초청 공연.

Invitational performance
at the Art Center at New
York University's Abu
Dhabi campus.

06

music

Wednesday, November 11, 2015 www.thenational.ae

Tacit Group's compositions use algorithms, complex computer equations that allow the group to improvise and seamlessly integrate a wealth of digital media into their performances. *Courtesy Tacit Group*

Tacit Group decoded

outh Korean music programmers will bring a multimedia feast to Abu Dhabi with an Arabic twist, writes Si Hawkins

9 the game-changing e *The Matrix* bewil- nces with its reve- our world is really rate computer pro- r fantasy, of course, ap are now apply- ystem to music - refer a less sinis-

y right, *The Ma-* , and we make he Korean col- nder Jin Won lassic way to ve do is wind e hang wind ut who makes wind makes s whatever it ay we explain s in music." y-pushing ake their t the NYU re tonight promise a xperience.

Each Tacit Group show is different, and almost as surprising for the players as for the audience. As Lee suggests, their compositions use algorithms: complex computer equations allowing the group to improvise and seamlessly integrate a wealth of digital media into their performances – there are electronic sonic effects, spectacular interactive visuals, and in a particularly novel twist, live onstage game-playing.

"Algorithmic arts usually have problems communicating with the public," admits fellow founder Jaeho Chang. "The reason we incorporated video games into our works was this, at the beginning."

Far from being boring or baffling, Tacit Group shows often look like a retro gaming contest – with a better soundtrack. Lee, Chang and their colleagues combine arcade classics with their music by actually rewrit-

ing each game's code, adjusting the rules to fit their performances. Their production Six Pacmen, for example, reinterprets Steve Reich's acclaimed composition *Six Pianos* to accompany a giant onstage game of Pac-Man, while *Game Over* customises another oldie.

"One day I was playing Tetris, and all of a sudden it looked like [musical] scores to me," Lee recalls of the enduringly popular falling-shapes game. A bad Tetris move by one of the six onstage performers "leads to the same note playing over and over", he explains. "Or no sounds at all."

That mix of media is a particular favourite of Chang's. "Not only do people like the piece," he says, "but also it clearly shows the main characteristics of our work". Lee concurs: "Kids are very excited by the computer game-based works, especially Game Over. They sometimes

scream if a player does some wrong block-matching."

Younger spectators even "sing along", says Lee, who has significant experience of audience interaction away from Tacit Group. From the late 1990s onwards he was a globally renowned techno artist, under the pseudonym Gazaebal, but eventually tired of creating beats for dance floor. Having enrolled on a university course back home in South Korea, he met Chang – his professor.

"I was mostly teaching algorithmic composition and Jin became interested in it while he was studying with me," Chang recalls. "In 2008 Jin and I started Tacit Group with other students in the Music Technology programme. We had a few chances of performing to the public in that first year. It was quite successful."

Seven years on, Tacit Group have performed across several

continents, which is a sizeable logistical task. "In Abu Dhabi there will be six players onstage and one on the side of the stage: we call him 'server'," Lee says. "He operates all the server computers, so he has the most difficult job, because he has to take care of the most detailed stuff: open this programme, close this programme, control the projector."

The collective will also perform a specially reworked piece at these shows. Their audiovisual interpretation of *In C*, a 1964 composition by the minimalist musician Terry Riley, has undergone several transformations already. "When we made In C originally, the visual part involved simple shapes such as circles," Lee states. "But when we made the second version, we put Korean letters that show the names of notes we play. This was a fascinating change for us because the audience liked it way more than

we expected." The new ver "involves Arabic letters inst which is technically simple culturally interesting, I th says the former DJ, who is " ing forward to seeing how p in Abu Dhabi feel". Indee may well receive repeat vis especially with the two sho ing free feature different p each night.

Lee says the group will p much material into this v possible. "We have fun or because we're not playing what a score says. It's me jazz: you have the rules, b we play is our own dec he says. "As long as you the simple few rules, yo whatever you want."

● Tacit Group perform at N Arts Center tonight and tor 8pm. Free entry upon rese on www.nyuad.edu

artslife@thenational.a

28 NOV, 2015

ACT FESTIVAL

광주 국립아시아문화전당의
개관 기념 초청 공연.

Invitational performance
to commemorate the
opening of Gwangju
National Asia Culture
Center.

KTONICS

ACT FESTIVAL
애트 페스티벌
2015-11-25/28 광주
GWANGJU

cont -r index

center (200, 200)

radius

ncenter.

4:59 5:40

광원씨 공간연결이 너무 길게 붙여진
오디오와 영상 페어로 초초 더 먹히기
잘돌롤 사이가 좋깄다.

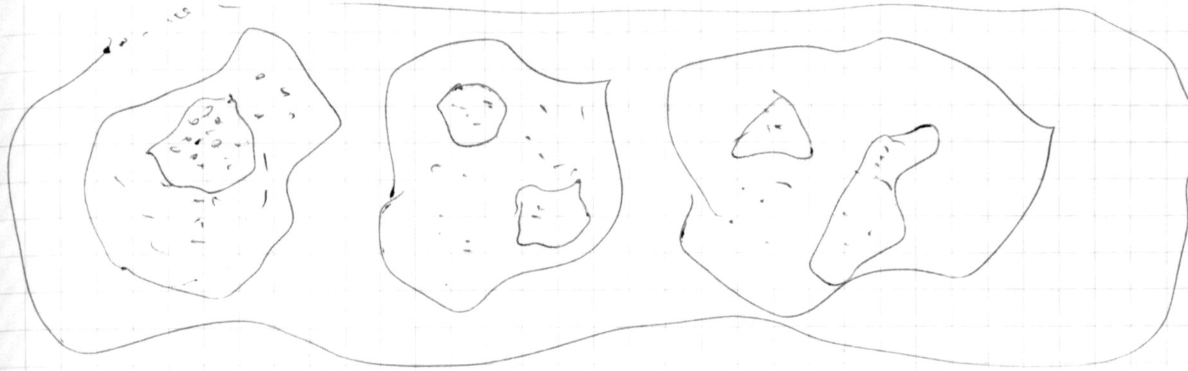

요간 ORGAN   OOSS

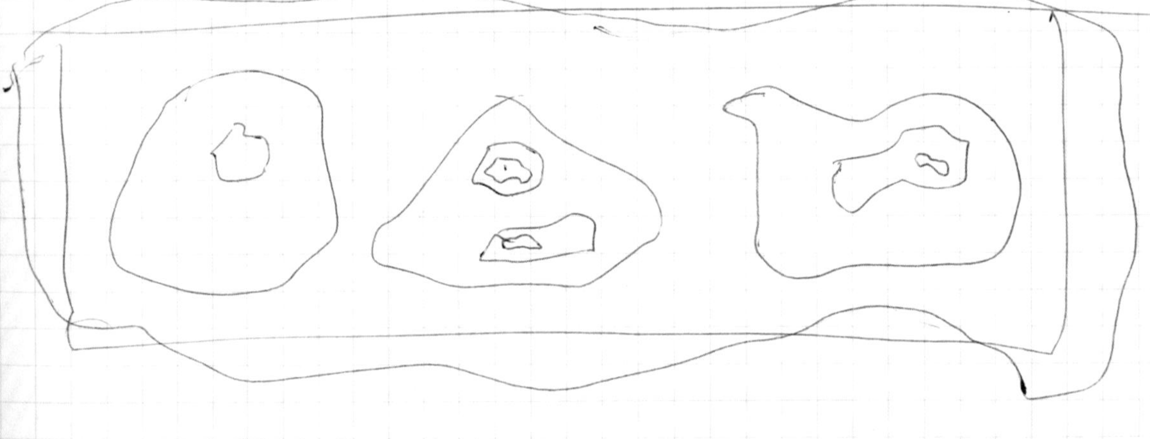

rate = 25ms.

	1.00	125	64 2° 20
	25 ×		12 ㅂ 60
1ms↓	125		16 ㄷ 80
62.5	62.5	62.5 60.25	

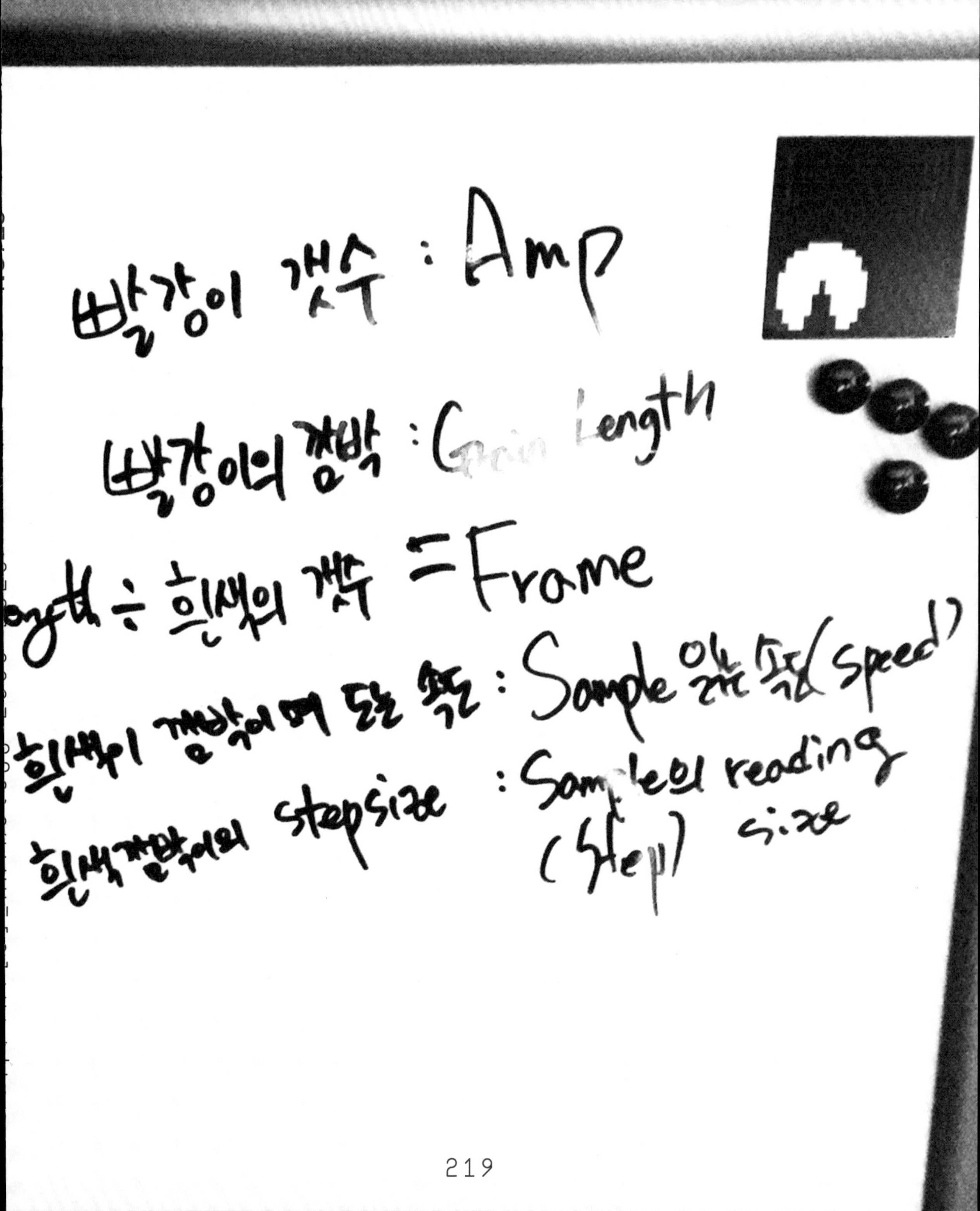

빨강이 갯수 : Amp

빨강이의 깜박 : Grain Length

양색 ÷ 흰색의 갯수 = Frame

흰색이 깜박이며 도는 쪽 : Sample 앞뒤 속도(speed)

흰색깜박의 stepsize : Sample의 reading
(step) size

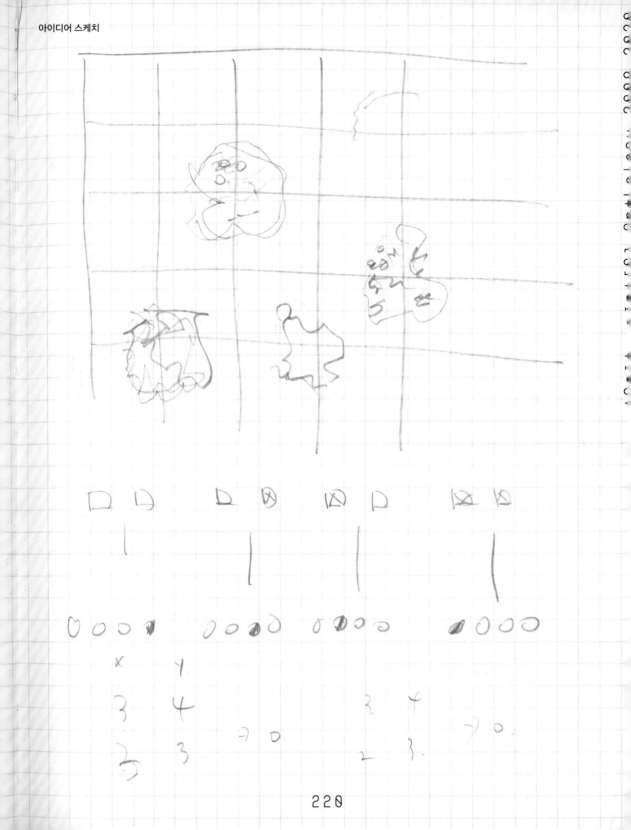

System 8   System _ Sine   Sine System

- · Sine 되면 이동.
  설 과 음~의 기본인
- · 소리의 가장 기본 사인파로 이동. 그리고 그의 회전을 이용만
  해서 곡을 만듦.
- · 규칙적으로 회전 - 음고 파악 가능.
  불규칙 - Noise.
- · 限 limited choice (사계의 방향)
- · 모든 소리로 정리되의 항으로 나타낼수 있다 - 푸리에

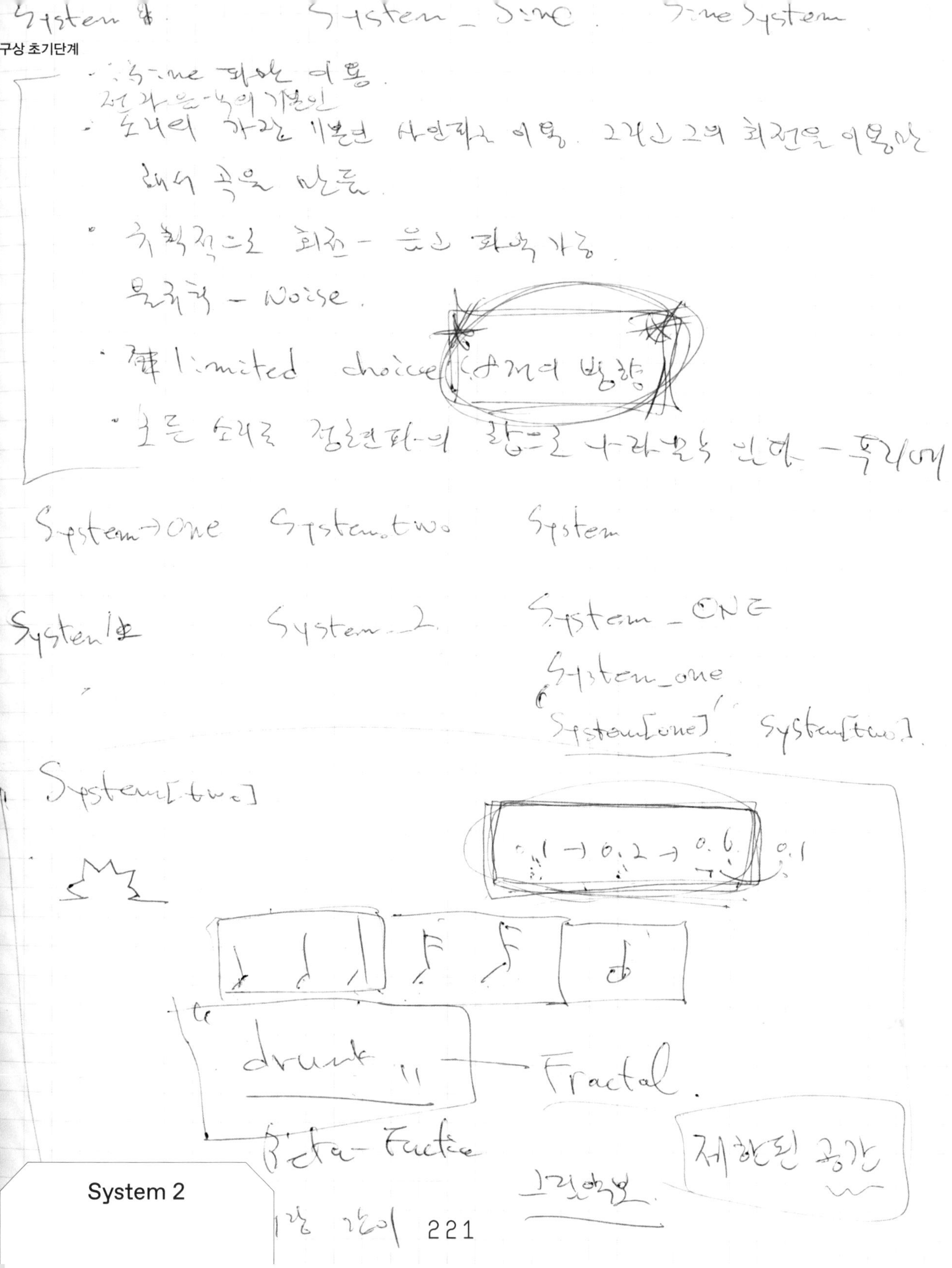

System → one   System two   System

System 1호   System_2   System _ ONE
                          System_one
                          System[one]   System[two]

System[two]

$0.1 \rightarrow 0.2 \rightarrow 0.6 \quad 0.1$

drunk " — Fractal.

Beta-Factor   그림악보

1권 2권이 221

Player System ~~System~~

Line Group Box

Line Group. - - - - -

~~Playground.~~
Player Ground. Group

Player Ground.

Line Group Box

Line Group.

Terminal

Player Interface

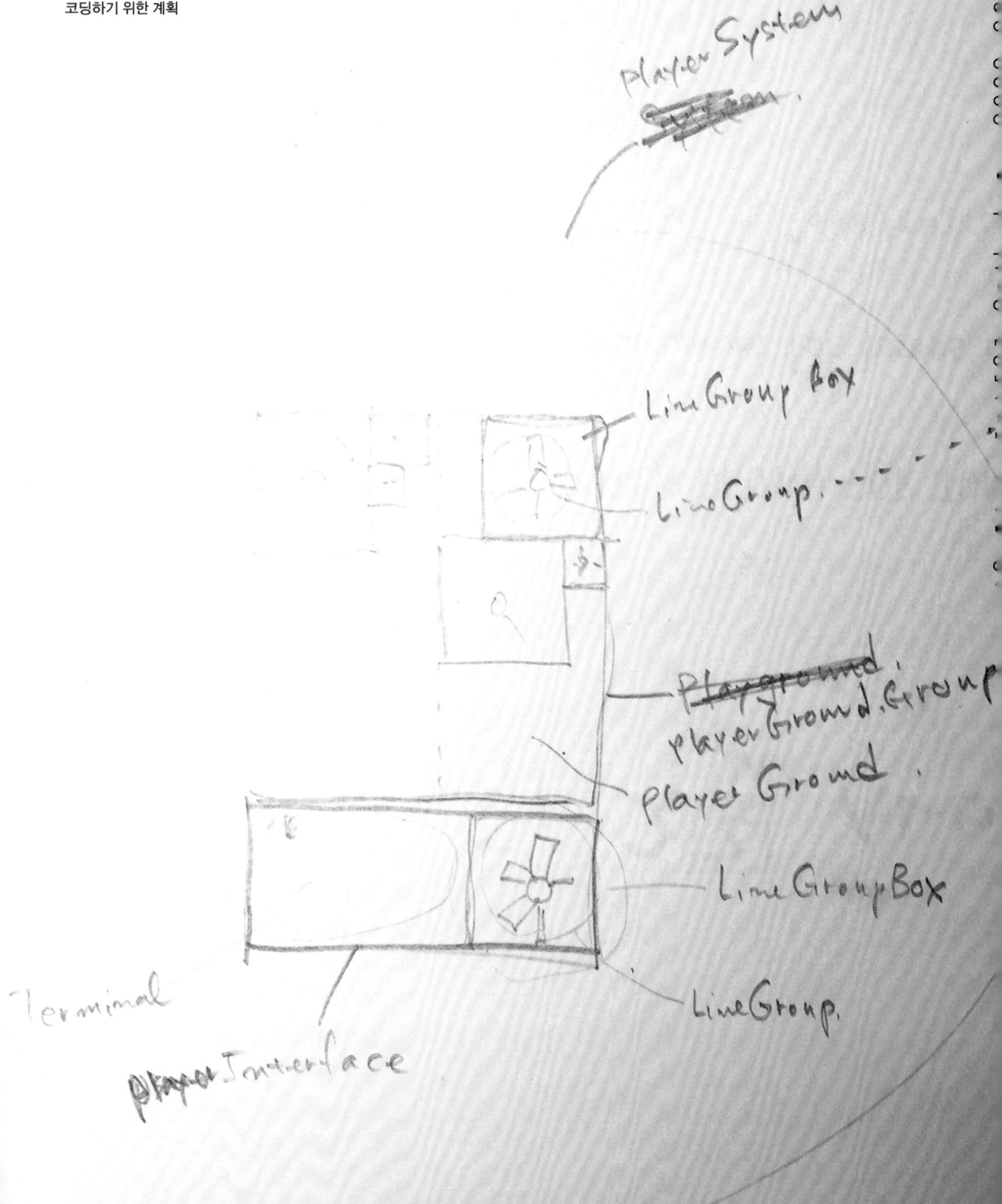

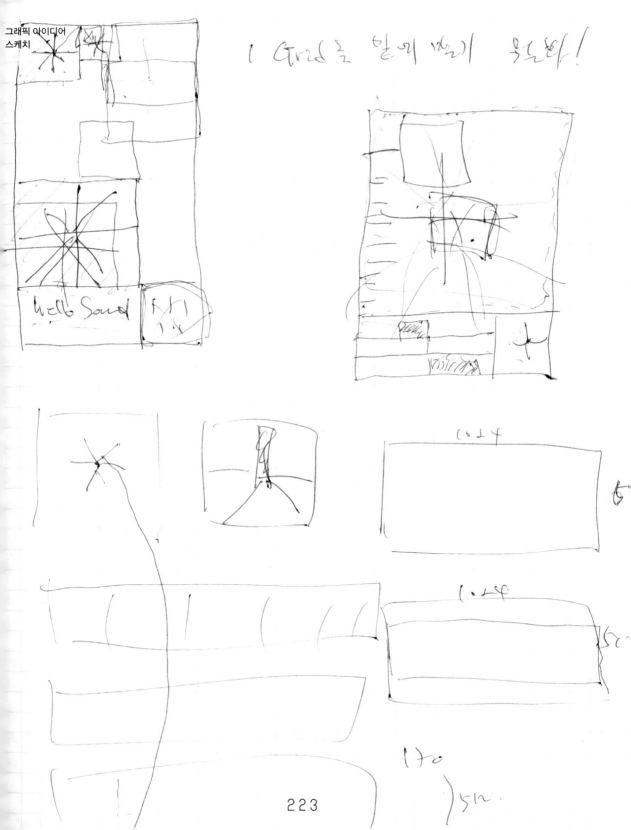

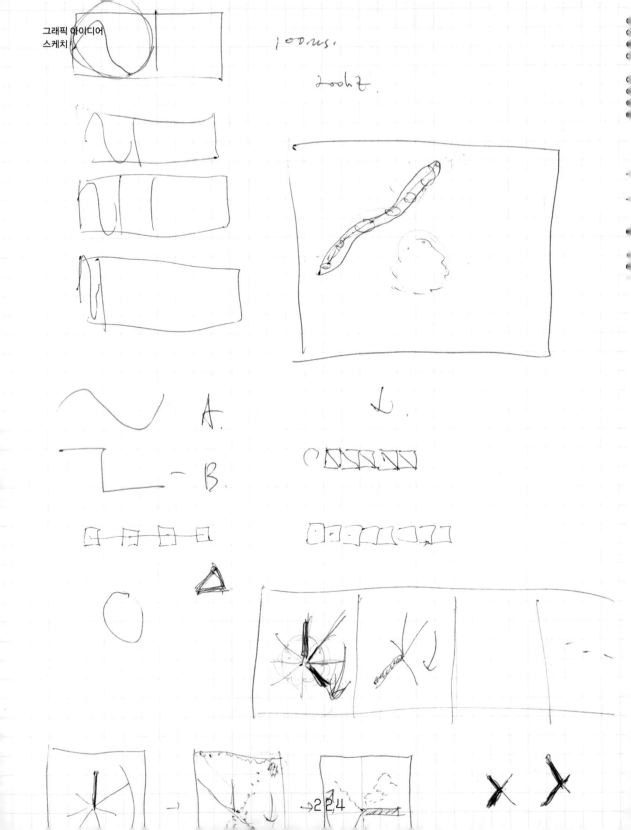

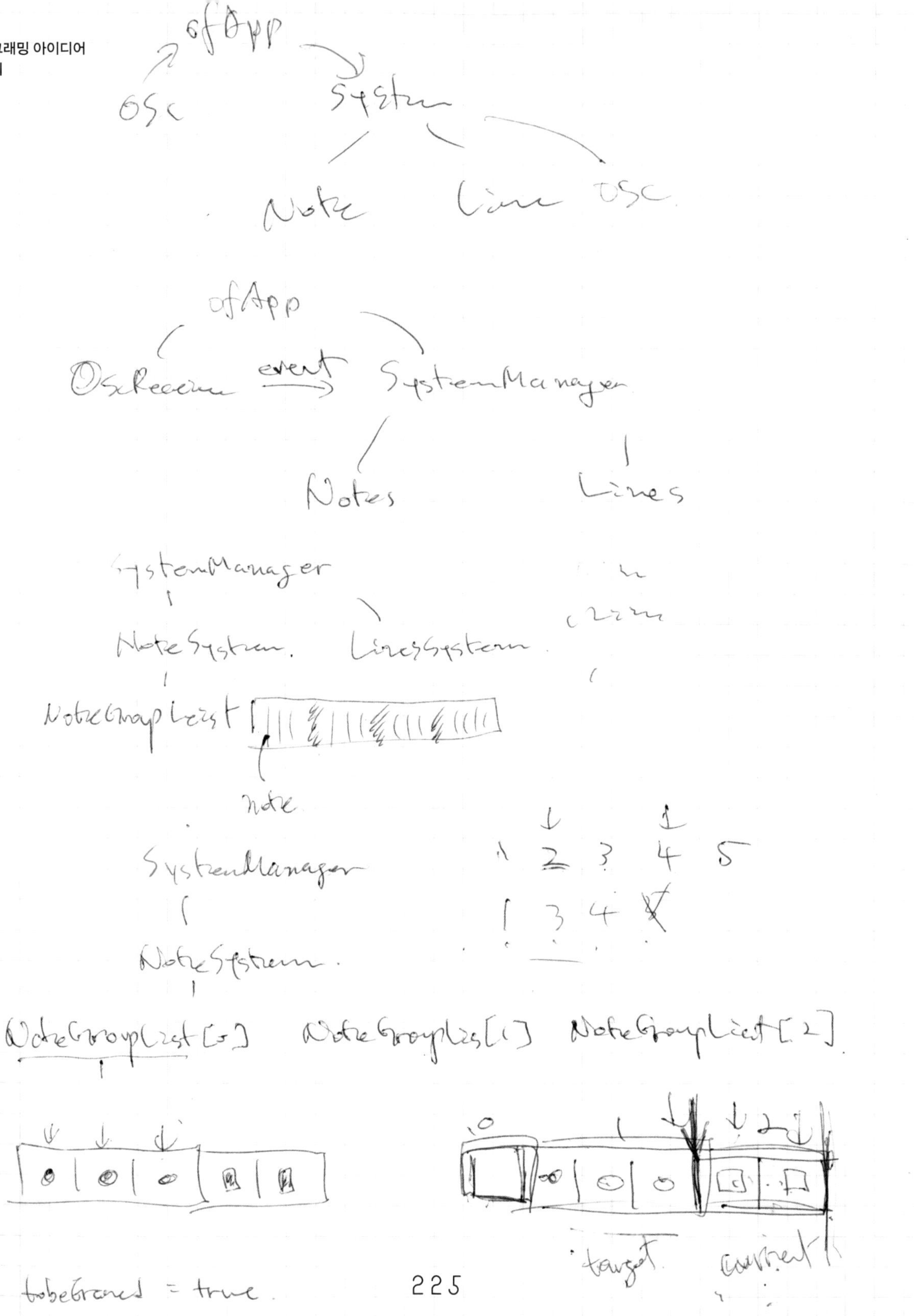

ofApp

OSC   System

Note   Line OSC

ofApp

OscReceiver → event SystemManager

Notes   Lines

SystemManager

NoteSystem.   LinesSystem.

NoteGroupList [|||§§|||§§|||§||§|||]

note

SystemManager   1 2 3 4 5

NoteSystem.   1 3 4 ⊀

NoteGroupList [ ]   NoteGroupList [1]   NoteGroupList [2]

target   current

tobeErased = true.

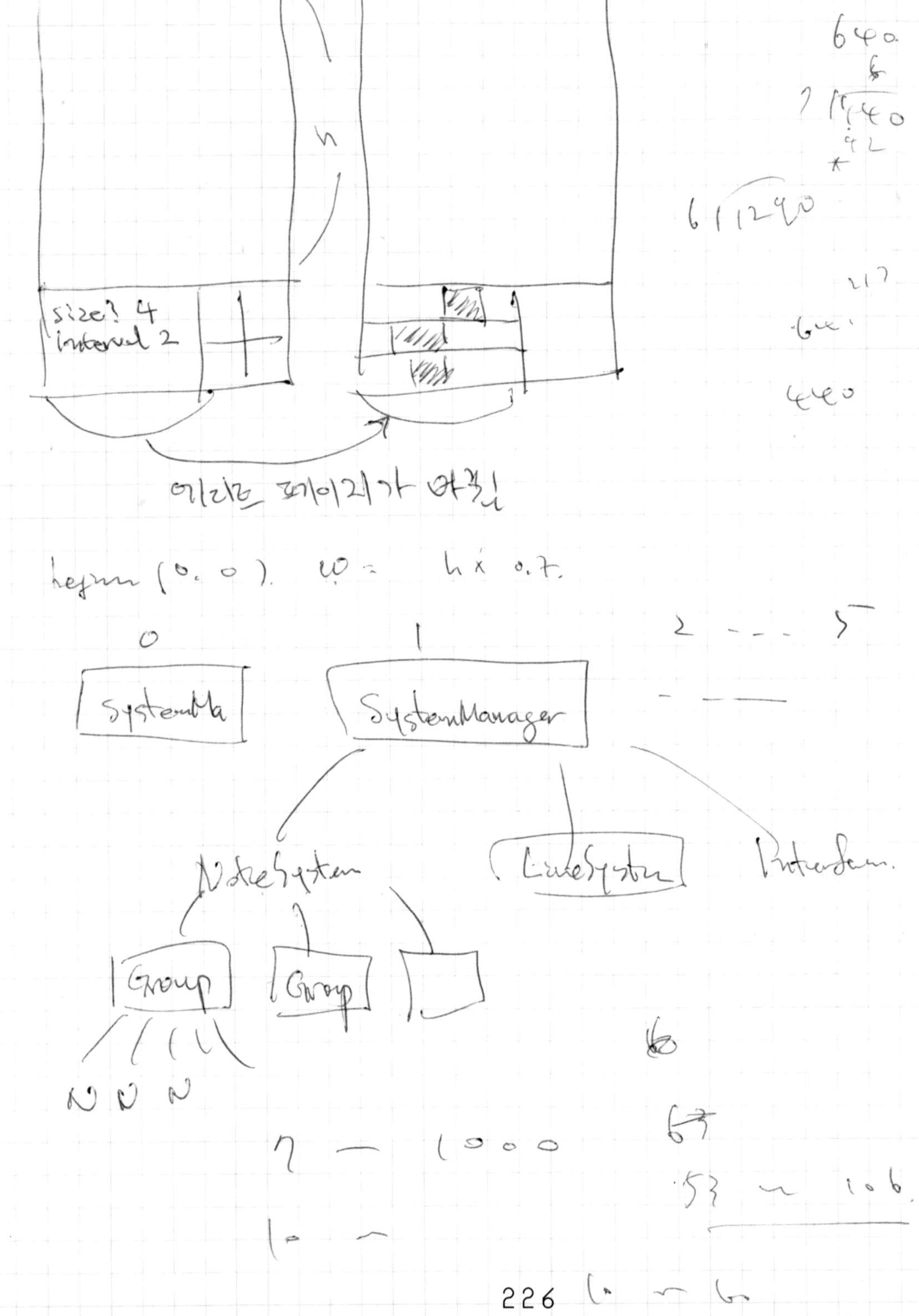

begin ~ w

1280

640

1440
42

61290

217
64

440

size? 4
interval 2

여기로 페이지가 바뀜

begin (0, 0). w = h x 0.7.

0   1   2 --- 5

| SystemMa | SystemManager | -- -- |

NodeSystem

LineSystem   Interface.

| Group | | Group | | |

N N N

? — 1000

5? ~ 106.

l= ~

226 l ~ b

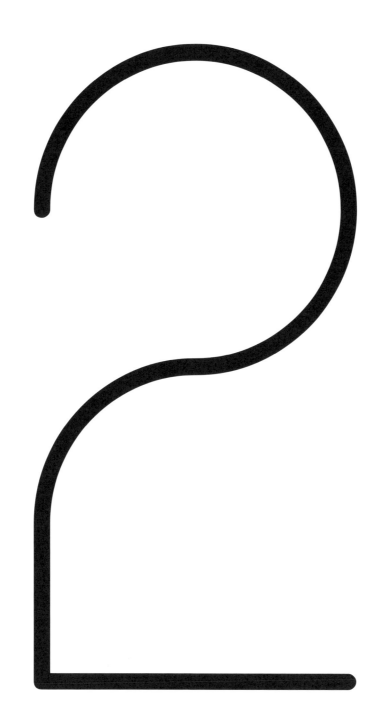

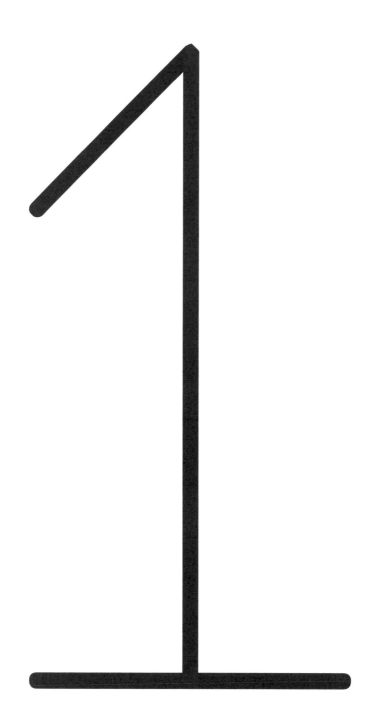

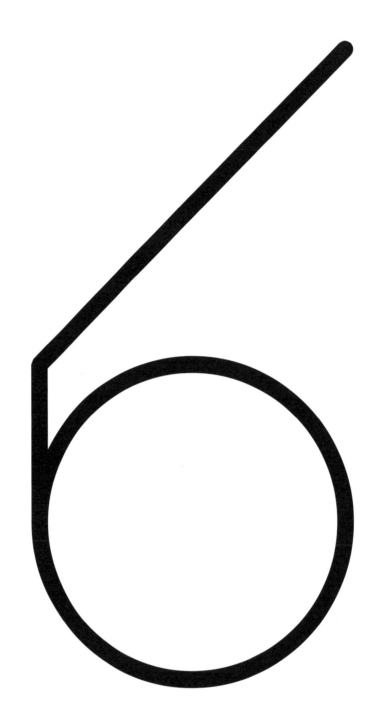

22 OCT, 2016

KT MASHUP
GIGA

슈게이징 락밴드
이디오테잎과의 콜라보
공연으로, 태싯그룹의
‹Drumming›과
이디오테잎의 ‹Even
Floor›를 새롭게 구성해
무대에서 함께 연주했다.
KT의 MASHUP GiGA
Festival의 일환으로
개최됐다.

As a collaborative
performance with
shoegaze rock band
Idiotape, Tacit Group's
Drumming and Idiotape's
Even Floor were
spontaneously fused and
performed on stage.
It was held as part of KT's
MASHUP GiGA Festival.

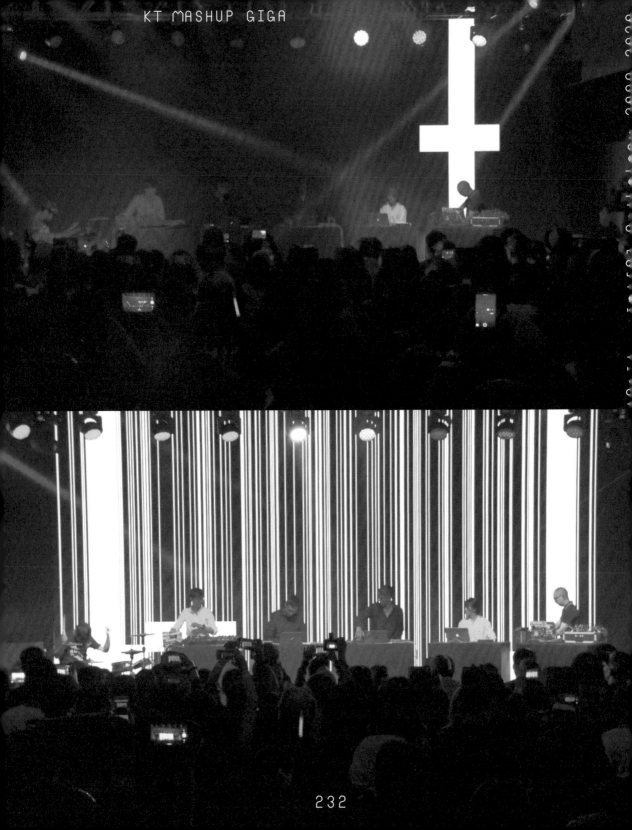

26 NOV, 2016

WESA
FESTIVAL 2016
IN DAEGU

대구예술발전소에서 열린
WeSA 비정기 페스티벌에서
렉처 퍼포먼스를 펼쳤다.
공연과 세미나가 결합된
형태인 렉처 퍼포먼스는
'이것도 음악인가요?'라는
테마로 ‹훈민정악› ‹Game
Over› 등을 공연하며
작품 설명과 코멘터리를
덧붙였다.

Lecture performance
was held at the WeSA
occasional festival held at
the Daegu Art Factory.
A lecture performance,
which is a combination
of performances and
seminars, included
Hunminjeongak and
Game Over using
the theme of 'Is this
also music?', with an
added explanation and
commentary on the work.

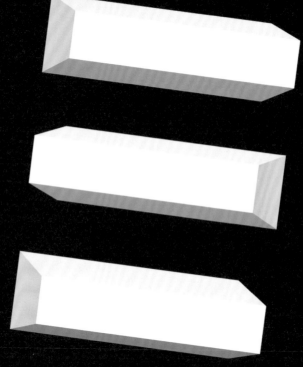

1 2 3 4 5 6 7 8 9 0

♩ = 15 frame.

♪ = 16 frame.

32 16 8 4 2 1

16 frame

1 2 3 4 5 6 7 8 9 10

2 4 8 16 32 64

3 6 12 24

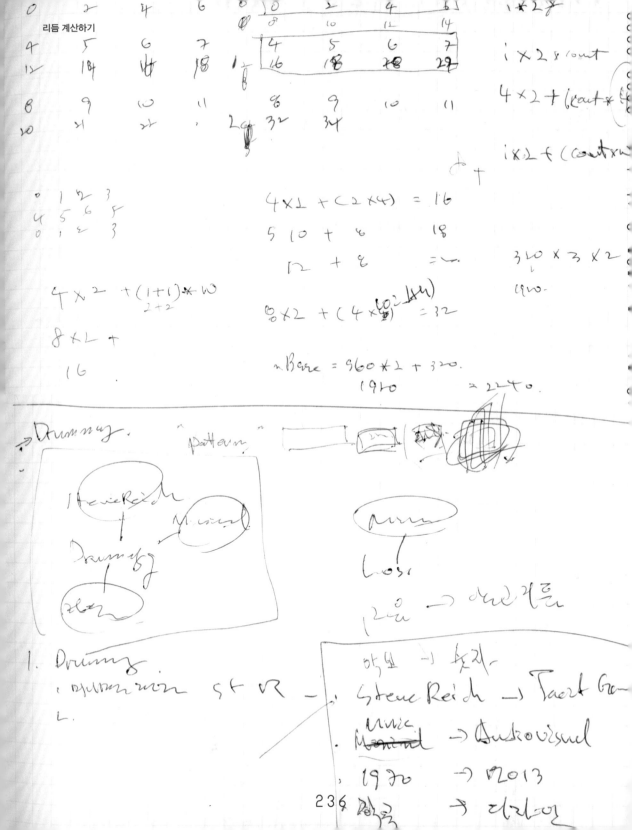

리듬 계산하기

0	0	1	1	2	2	3	3	4
24		29		34	57	39		44
5	4	6	5	7	6	8	7	9
25	49	30	58	35		40	53	45
	60						61	
10	8	11	9	12	10	13	11	14
26	59	31	50	36	54	41	62	46
15	12	16	13	17	14	18	15	19
27		32	55	37	51	42		47
20	16	21	17	22	18	23	19	24
28	63	56	33	38		43	52	64	48
25		26	21	27	22	28	23	29

OR ← AND

OR
X.OR.

238

922

Music metri

239

1. 에디멀모.

2. 누방.

3. Custom order.

4. X mas tree ⟶

기5 ~ 제12.

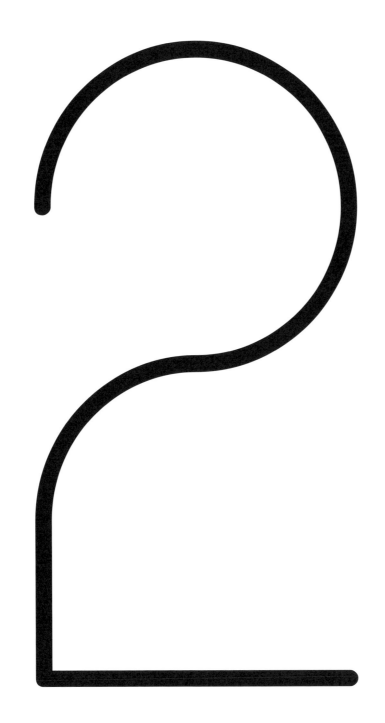

241

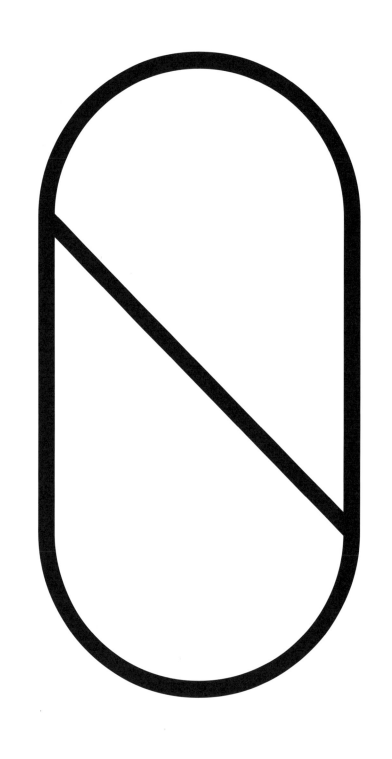

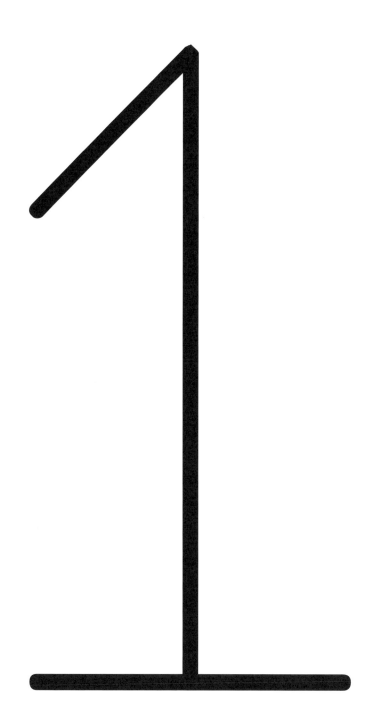

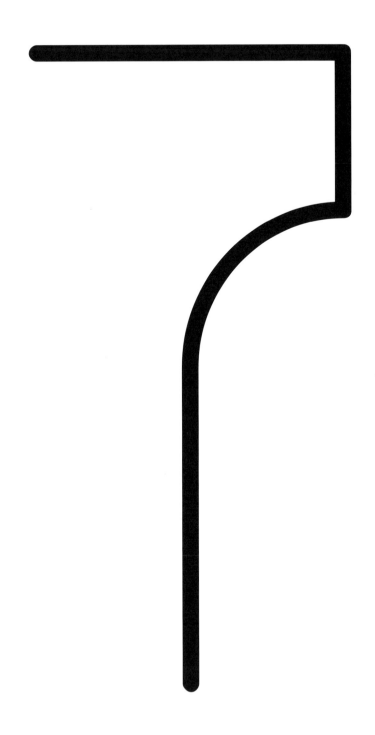

30 SEP, 2017

ARTIENCE
DAEJEON

예술(art)과 과학(science)의
합성어인 '아티언스'는
예술가와 과학자가 협력해
창작 활동을 벌이는 행사.
태싯그룹은 폐막식에 참여해
공연을 펼쳤다.

ARTIENCE, a
portmanteau of art and
science, is an event
in which artists and
scientists collaborate
to produce creative
activities. Tacit Group
participated in the
closing ceremony with a
performance.

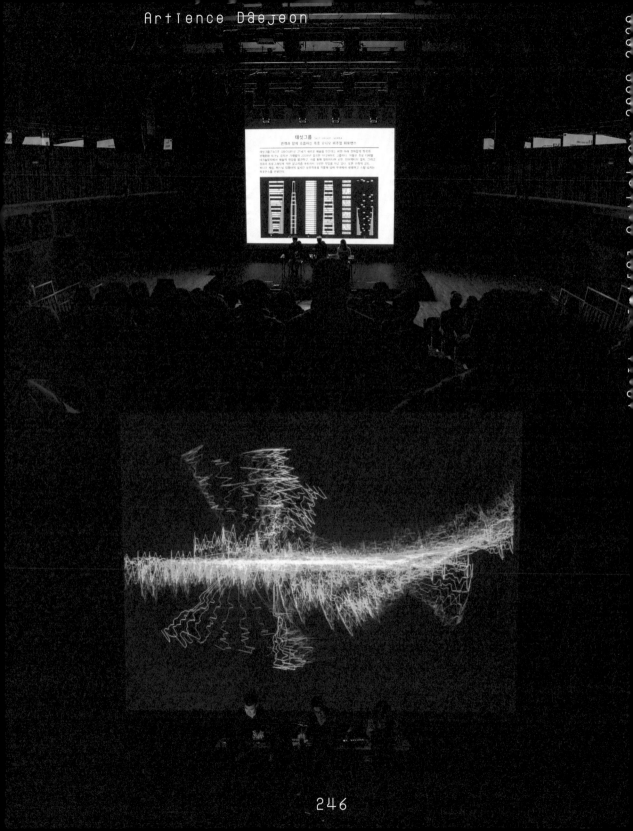

2 DEC, 2017

PLUMS
FESTIVAL

러시아 모스크바에서 매년
열리는 Plums Festival을
위한 오프닝 공연.

Opening performance at
the annual Plums Festival
in Moscow, Russia.

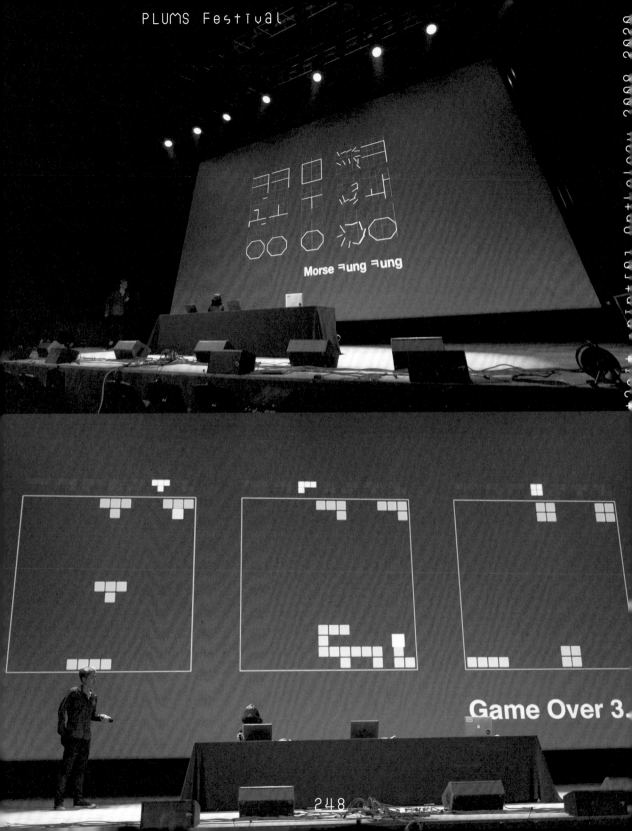

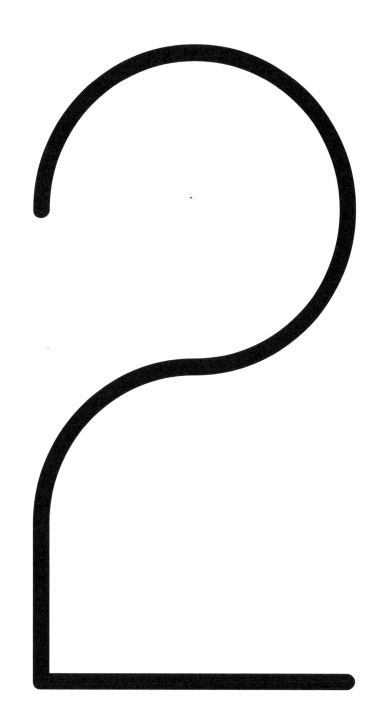

249

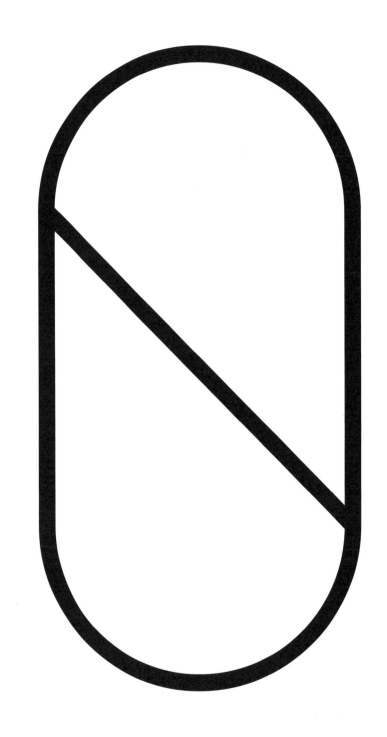

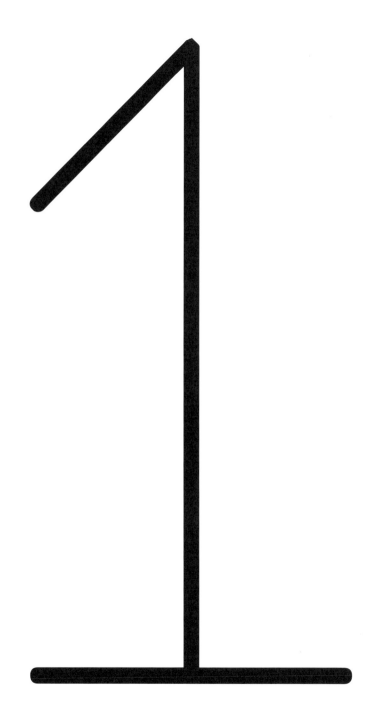

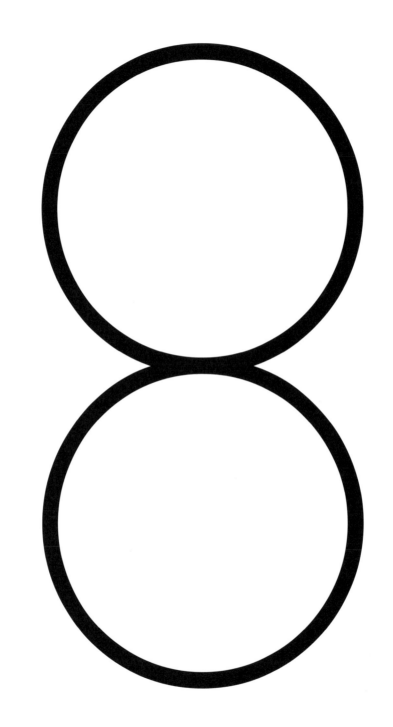

17 NOV, 2018

tacit.perform[6]
_10th
Anniversary

태싯그룹의 10주년
기념공연이자 일곱 번째
단독공연.

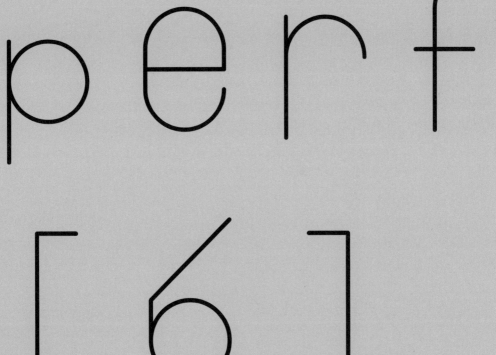

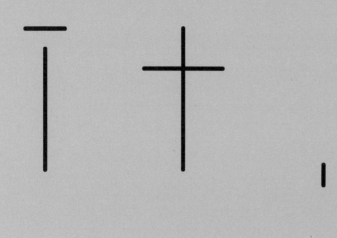

첫 공연부터 연주됐던
〈훈민정악〉부터 신작인
〈System 2〉까지 여섯 편의
주요 작품을 공연했다. 10년에
걸쳐 발표한 작품들을 통해
태싯그룹의 인식과 작품관의
변화, 시선과 태도를 확인하는
자리였으며, 동시에 10년을
자축하는 자리이기도 했다.
'소리와 영상의 자유로운 소통
속 탄생하는 구성과 해체,
소멸과 재구성, 경쟁과 화합
등의 과정을 관객이 자유롭게
떠올릴 수 있게 제시했다'는
평을 받았다.

Tacit Group's 10th
anniversary performance
and seventh solo
performance. Tacit
Group performed six
major works, from
Hunminjeongak, their
initial launch project, to
System2, our latest work.
Exploring the work
released over the past
10 years, it was an
opportunity to confirm
the insightfulness of
the Tacit Group, and
the evolution in the
perception, gaze and

attitude toward the work.
Simultaneously, it was
also an opportunity
to celebrate ten years,
having been criticized
for exploring the process
of composition and
dismantling, extinction
and reconstruction,
competition and
harmony. A journey
which has been
validated through the
free communication of
sound and video, allowing
the audience to freely
consider.

playing the sounds that move within the system, and ultimately creating a piece that corresponds in real time seems almost like building an 'Independent world'. It must require a considerate amount of time, with lots to ponder.

Jinwon Lee So we are going to do one work a year. (Laughs)

Jaeho Chang Because it's coded one by one, the internal systems of every works are quite complicated. Usually 3 or 6 performers are involved, so we need to bring the signals together from those computers and create sounds and visuals. The visuals differ slightly for every pieces but since it's hard to recognize the system only by listening to sounds, the most important principle of making is to visually present the works and make them understandable for the audiences. So we tend to make it as minimal as possible.

Yeseul Shin Sounds and visuals are always linked together, which is input and output?

Jinwon Lee In the case of <Morse ㅋung ㅋung> and <System 1> image came first.

Kyuwon Park <Hun-min-jeong-ak> has different sounds depending on the characters, and <Game over> also has different sounds depending on the structure of Tetris blocks. I think <Analytical> is the work that sound comes first.

Yeseul Shin Then, what is the most important thing in the process of building the system?

Jaeho Chang It's not the most important thing, but I think stability is the most stressful. Computers should not stop during the performances. Recently, we are focusing more on sounds. Because stabilizing the system took most of the time, we hadn't really cared about the sound, even though we majored in sound. We always felt somewhat sorry for that.

Jinwon Lee Stability, sounds and visuals each has to be good, but the completeness as a whole is a big part. We need to give the audiences details

58

we're looking for in a clear manner and it has to go smoothly from the beginning to the end, so completeness is one thing I care a lot.

Yeseul Shin When this system comes to the actual performing venue, things happen. There are always laptops on stage, performers standing in front of them, typing something over and over. What is going on inside that laptop screen?

Jinwon Lee Everyone is curious about the scene. Screen we are looking at is different from the screen that audiences see. On our screens, there are Max/MSP and C programming language program which we often use to create our works, and chatting program we use to communicate during the performance. We're creating something with a bunch of programs on our screens and typing data in. Nevertheless the performance is improvisatory, so we really need a chatting program. We have to make some adjustments between us through it. Sometimes we are like, "Enough, guys."

Yeseul Shin If it's improvised, I wonder to what extent an agreement is made beforehand.

Jinwon Lee Usually the running time is set. In special cases, we have prepared lines for the show. In case of <Hun-min-jeong-ak>, there is a well-designed sequence to present our intend clearly. We start by typing simple shapes such as circles, squares and vertical lines, and at one point, we draw a square and a vertical line to show the audiences the letter 'ㅁ', and then we type 'hello' in Korean and talk to the audiences, and then we ask for some kind of a reaction from the audiences by typing "Give us a round of applause." As we slowly expand the boundary of the work from shapes to letters, to words, and to conversations, players talk to each other and continue making agreements on what's going to happen next.

Kyuwon Park <Drumming> has more of a detailed plan for the performance, and it sounds better finishing the piece all together, so there's a timer for the end. During the performance, when someone decides that it's time to finish the performance,

믹스 깔끔 - J.w - 크기 변화(Volume) 사용.
　　　　 - J.h - 빠르게서서히 변화하는 거 (timbre) - 아떠

아날로디가 - J.w - 멜로디에 따라 EQ 넣기
　　　　　 - J.h - 두껍게 ~ - ~ 아래 위로 ~
　　　　　 - J.w - 0~12n / 0~s (~12) 로 씨오,너네
　　　　　 - J.h - 개들을 중요하는 방식에서 Random 으로 둔

Stem - Amb - J.w - 사운드가 같이 잡혀야됨 거.
　　　　　 - J.h - filter 값을 계속 배게 반대
　　　　　 - J.h - 빌드업 조여 질때 위치, 정보 등이 문어져
　　　　　 - J.h - 경이도 위험

257

제가   태씻   태씻   1 0   영영영영
연주   처음   주년   영   영
봤을   영   영

Six Pacmen

Steve Reich → Tacit Group
Six Pianos → Six Pacmen
1973 → 2013
의식지 → 미로
연주 → 게임

Drumming
Steve Reich → Tacit Group
작곡 → Design
1970 → 2013
악보 → Geometry
Music → Audio-Visual

17 Nov, 2018 Seoul

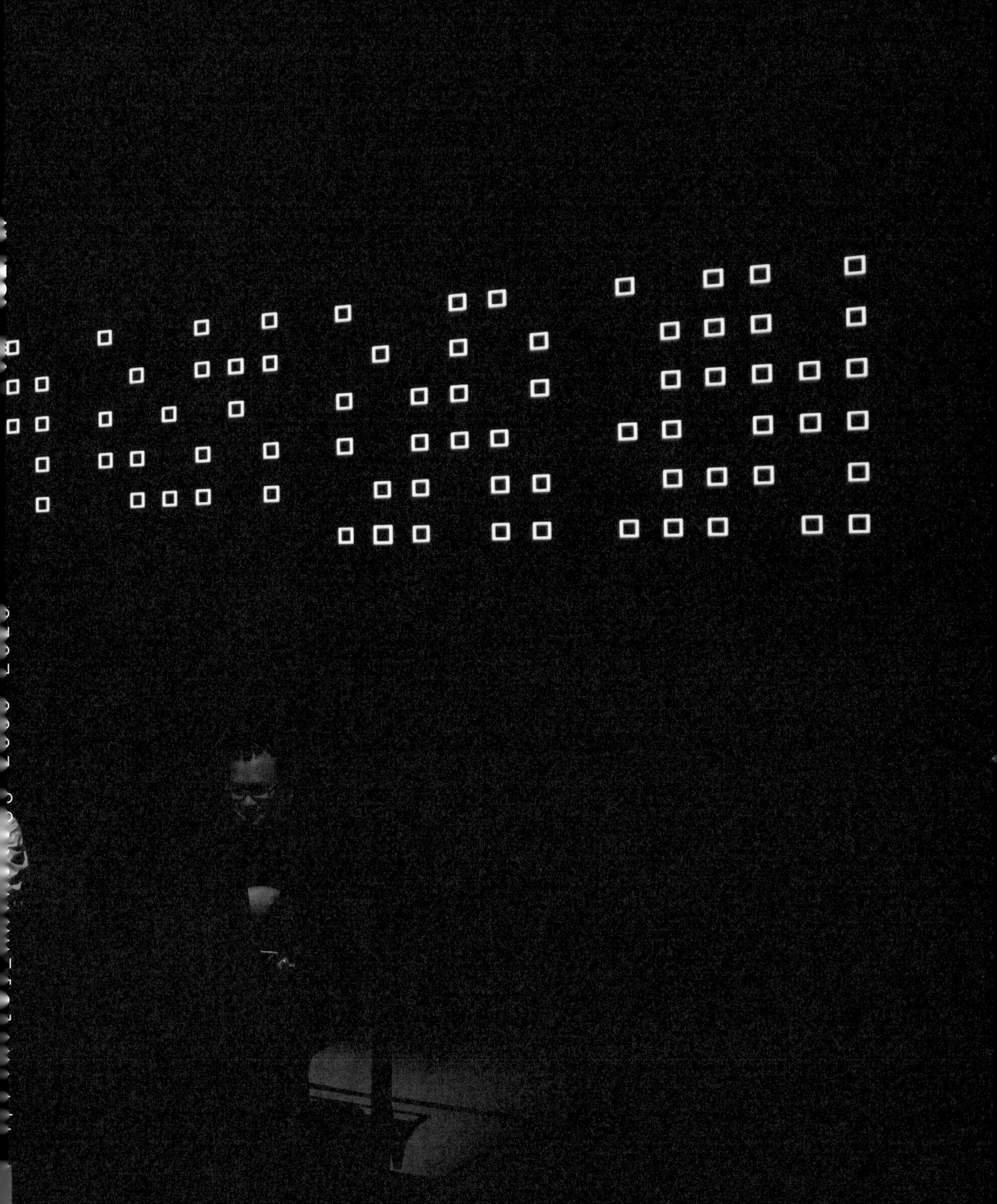

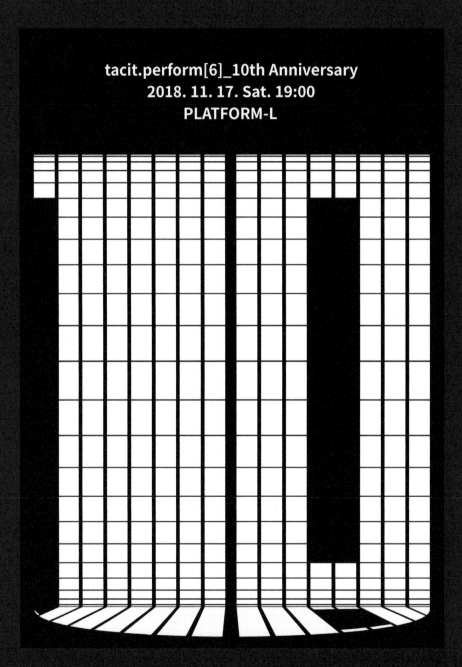

30 NOV, 2018

MEDIA ART FESTIVAL, GWANGJU

현대사회의 다양한
특성과 문제점을
미디어아트로 풀어낸
광주미디어아트페스티벌
2018에서 태싯그룹은
‹훈민정악›과 ‹System 1›
‹System 2›를 공연했다.
'대화'가 음악으로 변환되는
퍼포먼스라는 평을 들었다.
페스티벌의 주제는 '알고리즘
소사이어티 기계-신의
탄생'이었다.

At the Gwangju Media
Art Festival 2018,
which addressed a
variety of problems
and issues presently
faced by modern
society with media art,
Tacit Group performed
Hunminjeongak,
system 1 and *system
2*. Tacit Group received
reviews that suggested
'conversation' is a mode
of performance that can
transform into music. The
theme of the festival was
'The Algorithm Society
Machine-The Birth of
God'.

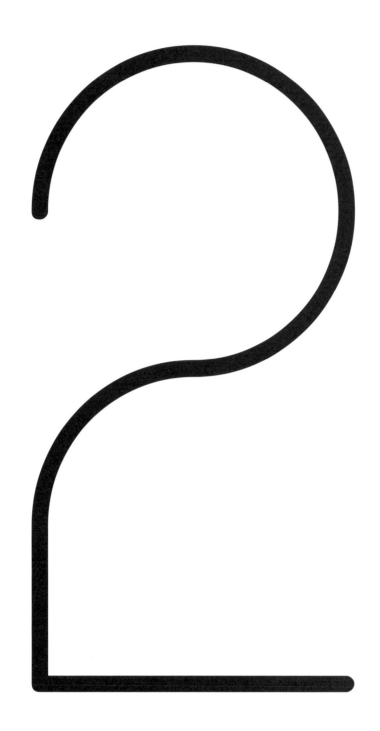

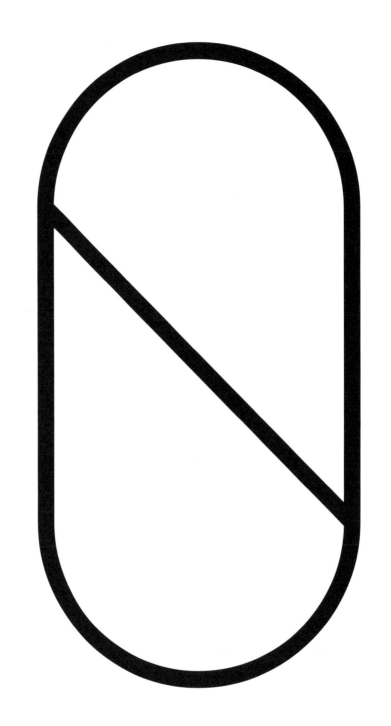

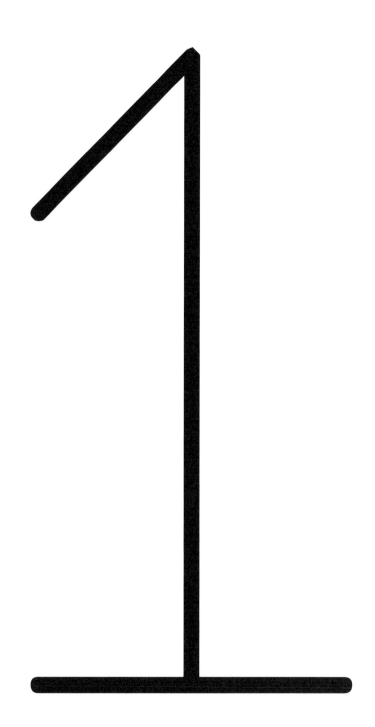

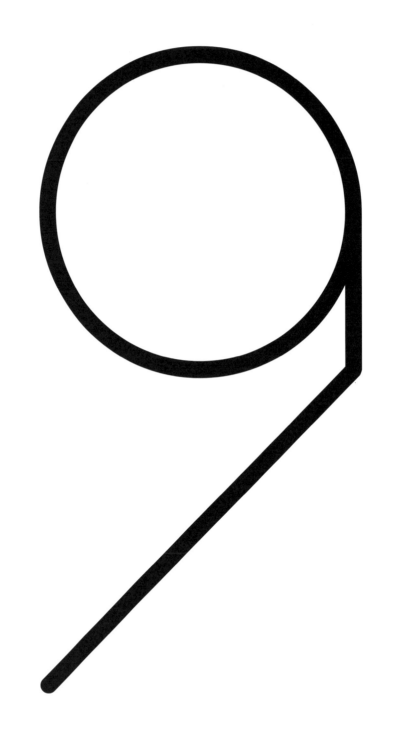

FESTIVAL
DE MÚSICA
ASIÁTICA
AVANZADA

스페인 마드리드에 있는
Naves Matadero에서 초청
공연을 펼쳤다.

Invitational performance
at Naves Matadero in
Madrid, Spain.

pasarela

ALTURA 4.35m

FESTIVAL DE MÚSICA
ASIÁTICA AVANZADA

NAVES
MATADERO
CENTRO INTERNACIONAL DE ARTES VIVAS

FANuaves

10 MAY
Nave 10. Precio 8€
TACIT GROUP 20:30h.

11 MAY
Nave 10. Precio 8€
TACIT GROUP 19:00h.
Nave 11. Precio 15€
YOSI HORIKAWA 21:00h.
FAUXE 22:05h.
SOTE 23:15h.
KYOKA 0:20h.
PAN DAIJING 1:30h.
HITO (PLAY
differently, OTO) 2:15h.
KOICHI SHIMIZU 3:25h.
YOUSUKE YUKIMATSU 4:20h.
HAN XIAOHAN 5:30h.
Horario sujeto a cambios.

Abono todo el festival 20€

naves.mataderomadrid.org

JUEGO
GRATIS

MADRID

271

DERO MADRID

Madrid Río

ENTRADA GRATUITA AL RECINTO

HORARIO
APERTURA RECINTO
De lunes a domingo: 9–22h

HORARIO GENERAL
DE ACTIVIDADES

1 MAYO–31 OCTUBRE
De martes a viernes: 16–22h
Sábados, domingos
y festivos: 11–22h

1 NOVIEMBRE–30 ABRIL
De martes a viernes: 16–21h
Sábados, domingos
y festivos: 11–21h

HORARIOS TAQUILLAS
NAVES MATADERO

11:30–13:30h y 17h hasta
el comienzo de la función
Lunes cerrado
Tel. 914 730 957
Venta anticipada:
naves.mataderomadrid.org

CINETECA

30 minutos antes del inicio
de cada sesión, hasta el
inicio de la última sesión
Venta anticipada:
cinetecamadrid.com

s Matadero
Matadero

cias

🏛 | MADRID   naves.mataderomadrid.org

FESTIVAL DE MÚSICA ASIÁTICA AVANZADA

NAVES MATADERO

FAN Naves

10 MAY
Nave 10. Precio 8€
TACIT GROUP 20:30h.

11 MAY
Nave 10. Precio 8€
TACIT GROUP 19:00h.

Nave 11. Precio 15€
YOSI HORIKAWA 21:00h.
FAUXE 22:05h.
SOTE
Feat. Tarik Barri 23:15h.
KYOKA 0:20h.
PAN DAIJING 1:30h.
HITO (PLAY
differently, OTO) 2:15h.
KOICHI SHIMIZU 3:25h.
YOUSUKE YUKIMATSU 4:20h.
XIAO HAN 5:30h.

Horario sujeto a cambios.

Abono todo el festival 20€

JOBO GRATIS*

🏛 | MADRID   naves.mataderomadrid.org

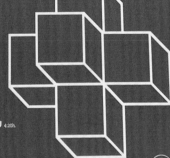

PROGRAMACIÓN
ABRIL y MAYO

MARÍA SIEBALD
TRASUNTO #2
Pequeños poemas bailados que integran danza y lengua de signos
5, 6 y 7 ABR
Nave 10. 20:30h.

30 ARTÍCULOS DE LOS
DERECHOS HUMANOS
Videoinstalación que muestra los ADH adaptados en lengua de signos
5 – 21 ABRIL
Nave 10. Azotea. Entrada libre

ITZIAR BARRIO
ALL OF US WANT TO WORK LESS
(TODOS QUEREMOS TRABAJAR MENOS)
Instalación
5 – 21 ABRIL
Nave 10. Sala de bombeo.
Viernes de 17h a 20h. Sábados, domingos y festivos de 12h a 20h.

ROBOTA MML
Rodaje en vivo
12, 13 y 14 ABRIL
Nave 11. 20:30h. 10€

VA WÖLF / NEUER TANZ
VON MIT NACH T: NO 2
Estreno en España de una de las últimas trabajos de una de las figuras
emblemáticas de la danza alemana.
26, 27 y 28 ABRIL
Nave 11. 20:30h. 15€

FAN NAVES
FESTIVAL DE MÚSICA ASIÁTICA
AVANZADA
10 y 11 MAY
Nave 10 y 11.
Consulta horarios y artistas en naves.mataderomadrid.org

STÉPHANE GLADYSZEWSKI
CORPS NOIR
Una obra de arte escénica donde el cuerpo del propio artista, los objetos
y las imágenes proyectadas generan nuevas emociones.
30, 31 MAY y 1 JUN
Nave 11. 20:30h. 15€

🏛 | MADRID   naves.mataderomadrid.org

1   How does it work to create music with algorithms?

A common way of composition is to imagine the results first, and then to find the appropriate method to produce the results. But we first think of a new method and use it to see what results can come out of it. The reason we use the algorithm is not to make any particular result, but to make a new way of composing.

2   How do you create mathematic codes to do music?

We are inspired by theories of physics, tools of mathematics, and digital technology. When new ideas come up, try it out through computer programming and get a variety of results there. If we do not like the results, go back to the original idea and change it until we get the results we like.

3   Through this process, everything is worth the same, no matter the result?

Some algorithmic artists say that the algorithm itself becomes art, regardless of the result. However, the algorithm is important, but the results are also important for us. Almost everything on the stage is played improvisingly, but we always make the system not get too far out of the certain boundaries.

4   We have passed by Napster, boom of online music stores, iTunes legal downalod... where is your place in this scene?

The result of our work is different every time, so it does not fit well with the existing distribution scene. Artists such as Brian Eno and Tristan Perich have released their recordings through Floppy Diskette or electronic circuitry, and Tacit Group is considering a similar approach.

5   What differences you from the other groups trying to do similar music?

The basis for creating a system varies from game to genetics. And unlike most audiovisual works, we use visuals to help the audience understand our system.

6   Your works never are completed. You update underlying systems all the time. What does it mean?

The important thing in our works is the system, not the result. It means the results of our works should not be fixed. Therefore, the system can be changed or evolved depending on various situations to make various results.

7   What does innovate means for you?

We prefer the word 'discovery' more than the word creation or innovation. I think that to create art is to discover jewels that someone has not seen from something of the existing.

8   Any advice for entrepreneurial people in the field of music innovation?

(no comment)

9   How do you programme a computer to get a musical process?

It depends on idea. We use various software such as Max, Abelton Live, openFrameworks(C++), and Processing(Java) to make prototypes and to realize the final system for stage.

10   What artistic possibilities can be discovered in technology?

All arts have always been related to science, mathematics, and technology. The results of new scientific theories and technologies have always attracted the attention of artists, and artists have found a new world of art from them. So is today's technology such as A.I. Artists will create a new form, genre, and style of art that has been difficult to imagine until before A.I. technology.

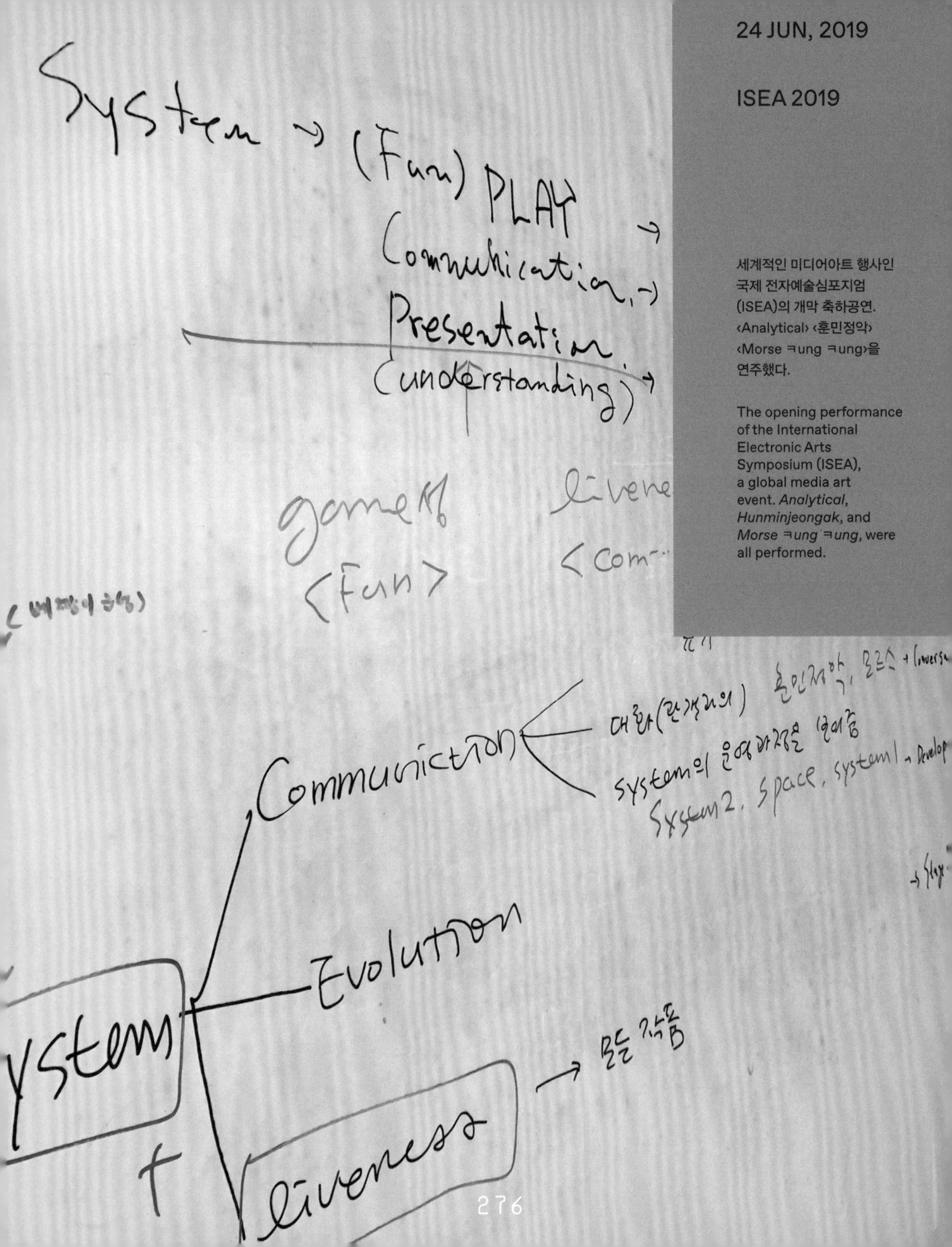

System → (Fun) PLAY →

Communication, →

Presentation

(understanding) →

game성 livene

< Fun > < Com···

< 예술에 능함 >

Communication ← 대화(관계맺기) 훈민정악, 모스 + Convers

system의 운영과정을 보여줌

system2. space, system1 → Develop

→ Syst

Evolution

system

+ liveness → 모든 간격들

세계적인 미디어아트 행사인
국제 전자예술심포지엄
(ISEA)의 개막 축하공연.
‹Analytical› ‹훈민정악›
‹Morse ㅋung ㅋung›을
연주했다.

The opening performance
of the International
Electronic Arts
Symposium (ISEA),
a global media art
event. *Analytical*,
Hunminjeongak, and
Morse ㅋung ㅋung, were
all performed.

ystem → (Fun) PLAY → Game Over

Communication. → 홍인정악. Morse

Presentation. → Analytical

(understanding)

game썼   liveness

$\langle$ Fun $\rangle$ $\langle$ Com--- $\rangle$

듣기   In C

Communication $\leftarrow$ 대화(관객과의) 홍인정악, 도

system의 운영과정을 협의중

System2. space. system

em → Evolution

↑

liveness → 모든 것는 B

NORDTALKS

덴마크를 비롯한 북유럽
대사관이 기후변화와 녹색
전환을 주제로 개최한 행사.
태싯그룹은 축하공연으로
초대됐다.

An event held by the
NORDIC Embassy , on the
theme of climate change
and Green transition. Tacit
Group was invited to a
celebratory performance.

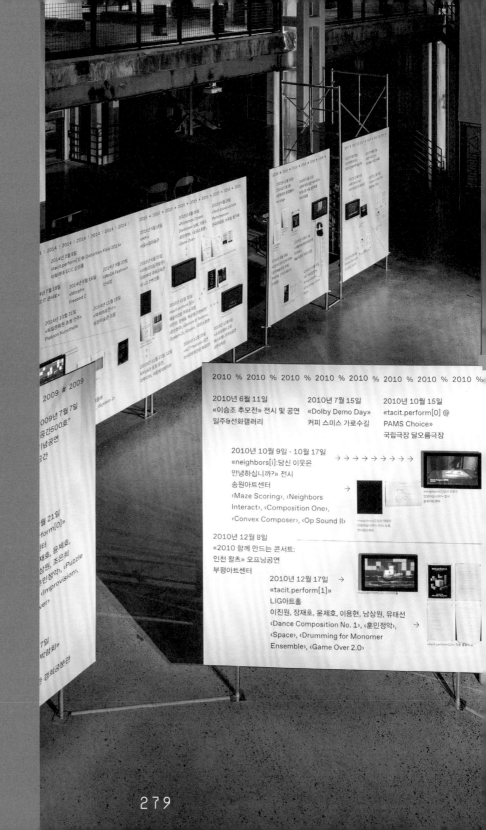

31 AUG–20 OCT,
2019

NO LIVE

오디오비주얼 아티스트의
활동을 조망하는 전시 ‹No
Live›에 참여했다. 10여
년의 활동 면면과 더불어
전시장인 코스모40의 공간적
특성(벙커)을 이용해 ‹op.
sound› 시리즈를 전시
작품으로 변형해 선보였다.

Participated in the
exhibition *No Live*, an
encompassing umbrella
of audiovisual artist's
activities. *op.sound II*
was transformed into
an exhibition piece by
employing the spatial
characteristics (bunker
venue) of the exhibition
hall Cosmo 40, in addition
to documenting ten years
of Tacit projects.

전시기획: 신은진
Curated by
Eunjin Regina Shin

op.sound[cosmo40]
테크니션: 정창균
Technician:
Changgyun Jung

사진: 타별
Photography: tabial

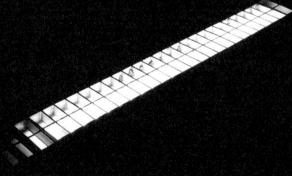

Installation Anthology 2008 2020

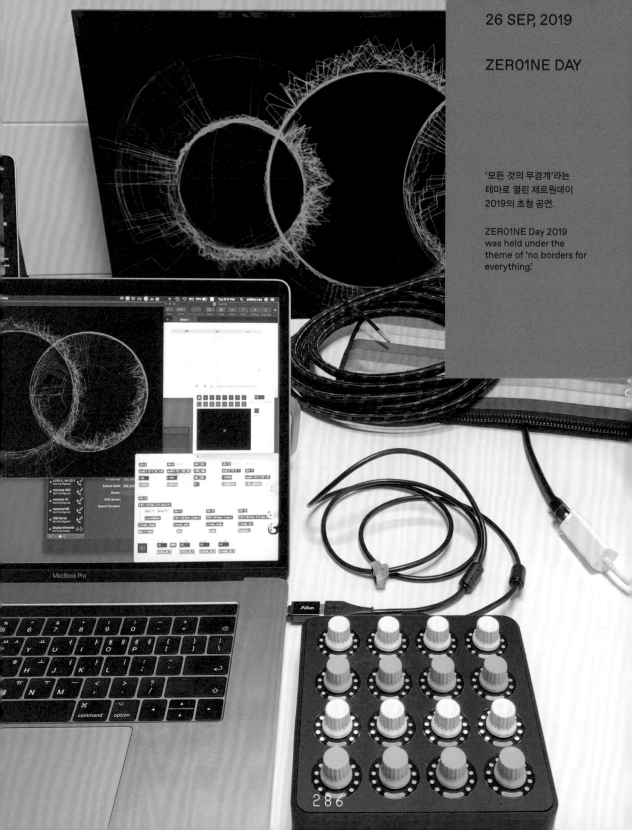

'모든 것의 무경계'라는
테마로 열린 제로원데이
2019의 초청 공연.

ZERO1NE Day 2019
was held under the
theme of 'no borders for
everything.'

28 SEP, 2019

**WESA
FESTIVAL 2019**

6회째를 맞은 WeSA
페스티벌에서 ‹Bilateral
Feedback›을 공연했다.
페스티벌을 기획하고
아티스트를 선정, 초청하는
데 참여해왔지만 태싯그룹이
정기 페스티벌에서 공연을
펼친 것은 1회인 2014년 이후
최초이다.

At the 6th WeSA Festival,
Tacit Group performed
Bilateral Feedback.
Tacit Group have been
involved in planning
festivals, selecting and
inviting artists, but it is
the first time since 2014,
that the Tacit Group has
performed.

SEJONG
EXHIBITION

'세종대왕과 음악 치화평'을
주제로 열린 전시회.
태싯그룹은 원곡을 알 수 없는
작품인 '치화평'을 한글과
모르스 부호를 연결해 21세기
음악을 재해석한 ‹Morse
ㅋung ㅋung›을 전시 형태로
출품했다.

An exhibition held
under the theme of
'Sejong the Great and
Music Chihwapyeong'.
Tacit Group exhibited
Morse ㅋung ㅋung, a
reinterpretation of 21st
century music, linking
Hangul and Morse code
to Chihwapyeong, a work
of unknown origin, in the
form of an exhibition.

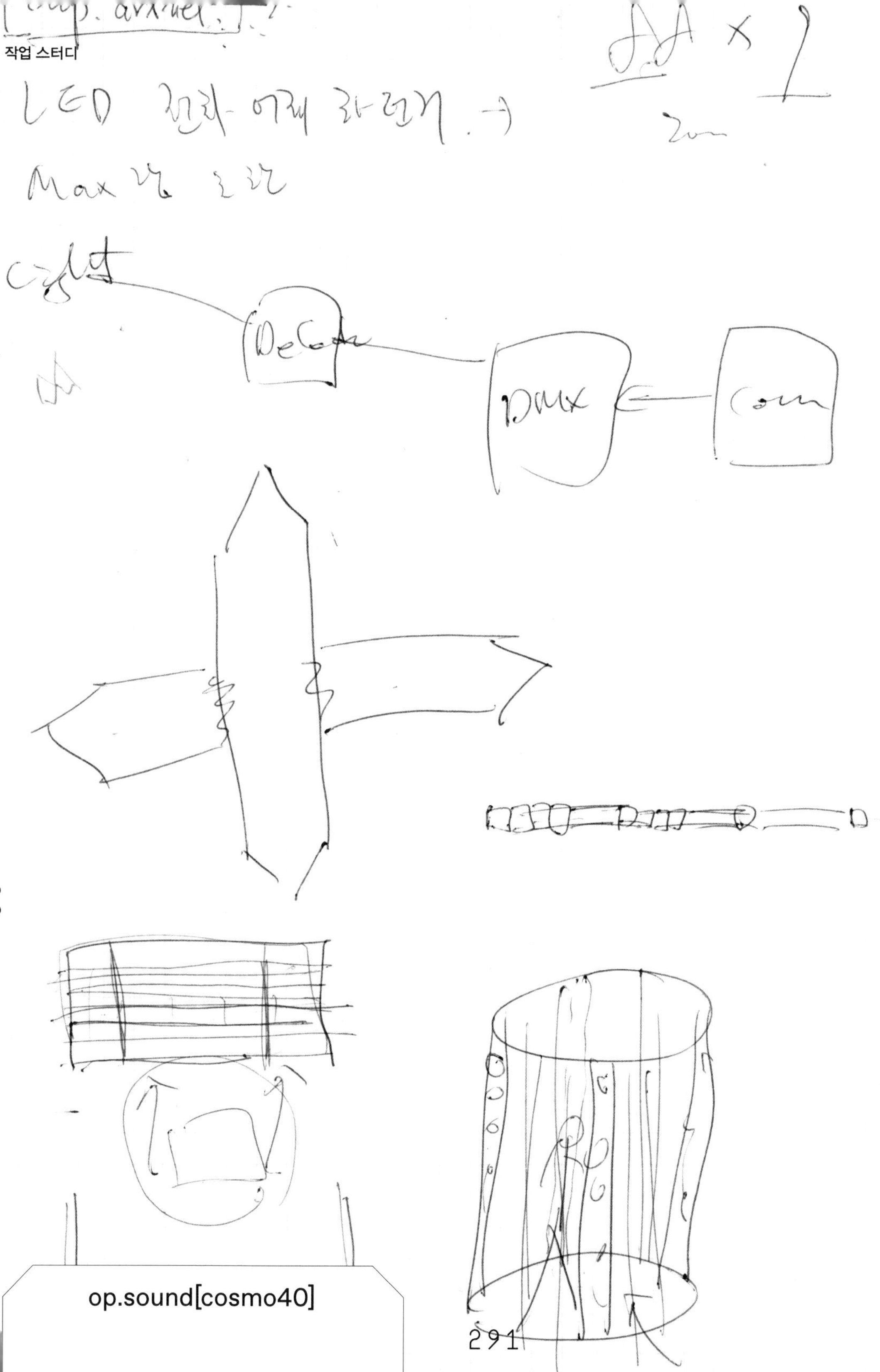

LED 전체 어레 라밀기 →

Max값 조절

Cylist

DeC

DMX

Con

op.sound[cosmo40]

1. 녹음 실

3. 재생공간 — software .

$$1000$$
$$6 0000 \text{ uA}$$
$$6 0000 mA$$
$$60000 mA = 60A$$

"Noise" + op. sound. $\longrightarrow$ 또 Human

humanized sound

(1.2m)

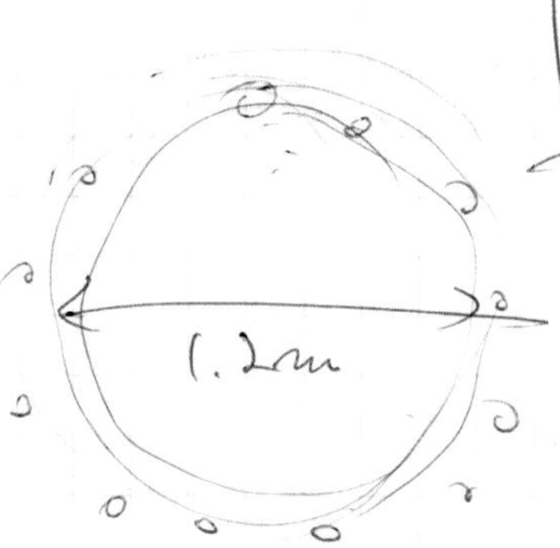

Instrument (Listening Room)

Chaos $\longleftrightarrow$ Deterministic
(prepared)

"Metric Clarity"

↑?

Noise $\longleftrightarrow$ Sinusoid

trapped Sound.

Lighting 느낌

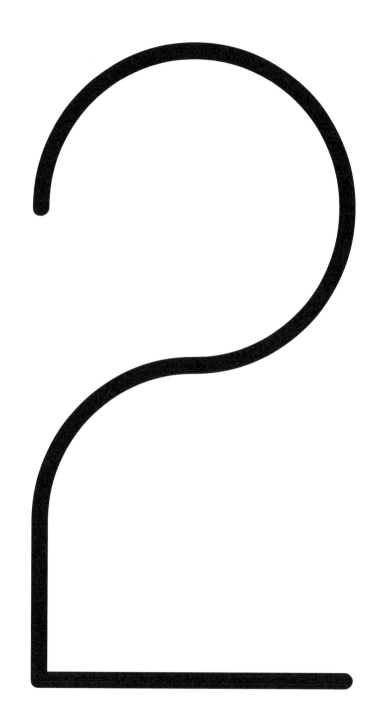

293

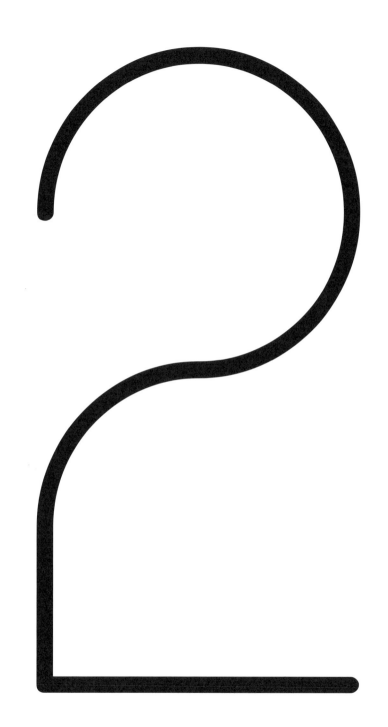

295

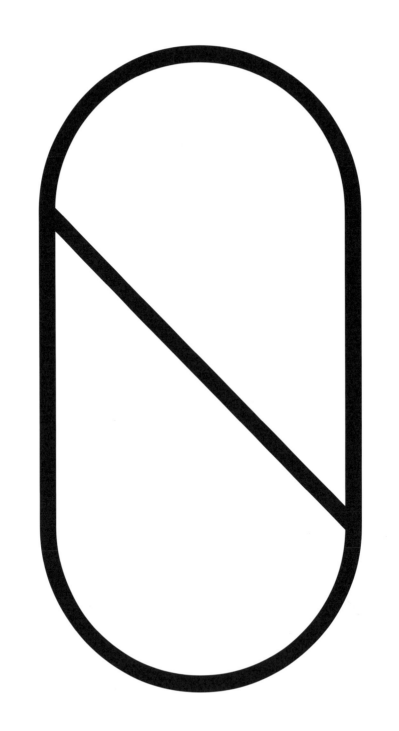

17 JAN-2 FEB, 2020

tacit.install[1] _ op.sound [piknic]

복합문화공간 피크닉에서 열린 전시. ‹op.sound› 시리즈의 네번째 버전인 ‹op.sound[piknic]›을 발표했다.

An exhibition held at a multi-cultural space picnic. *op.sound[piknic]*, the fourth version of *op.sound*, was released.

테크니션: 정창균
Technician:
Changgyun Jung

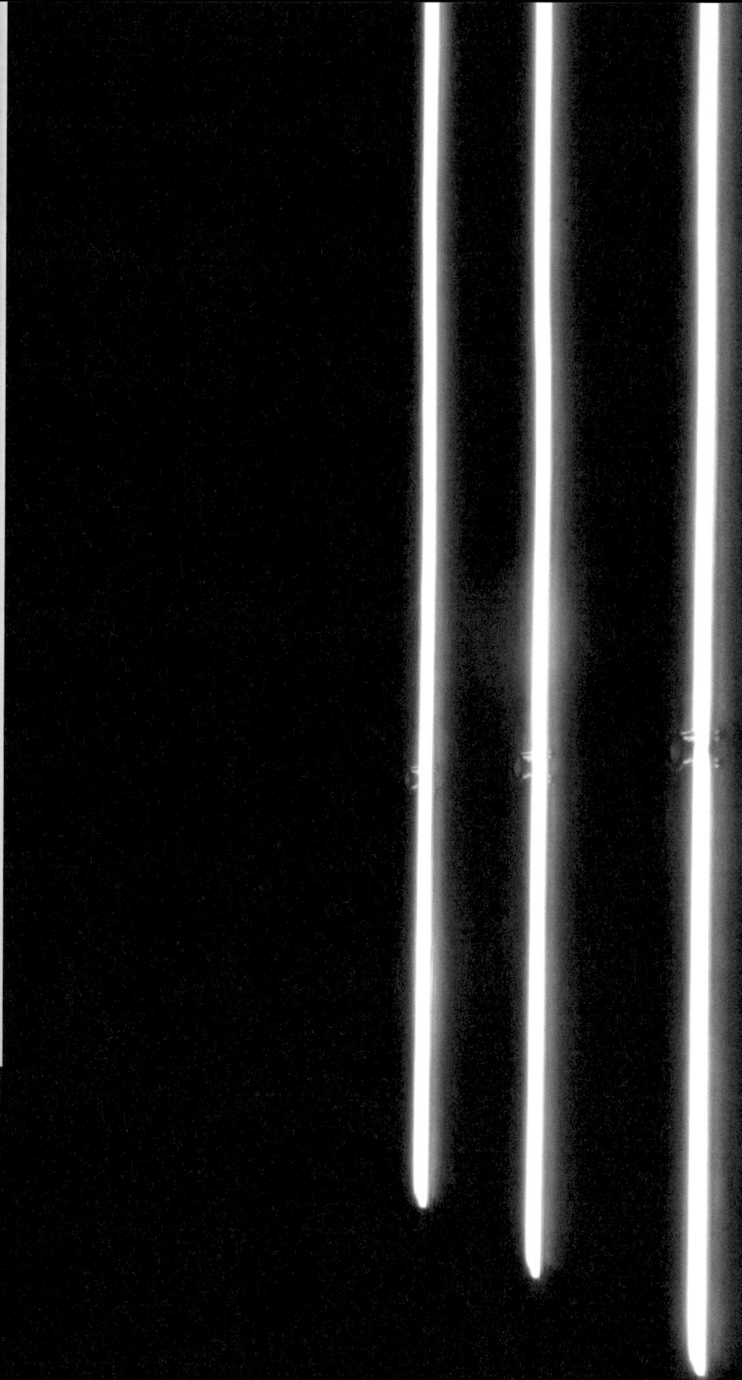

ANTHOLOGY

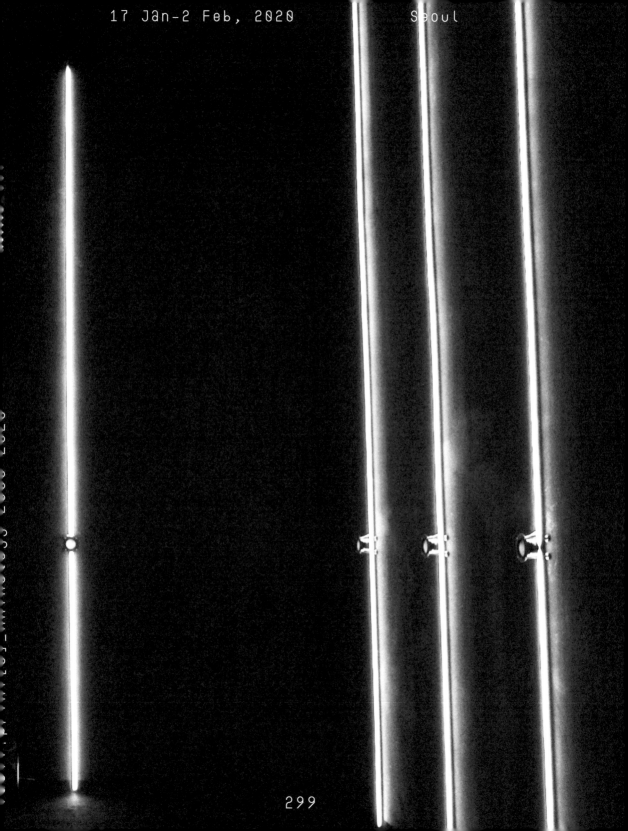

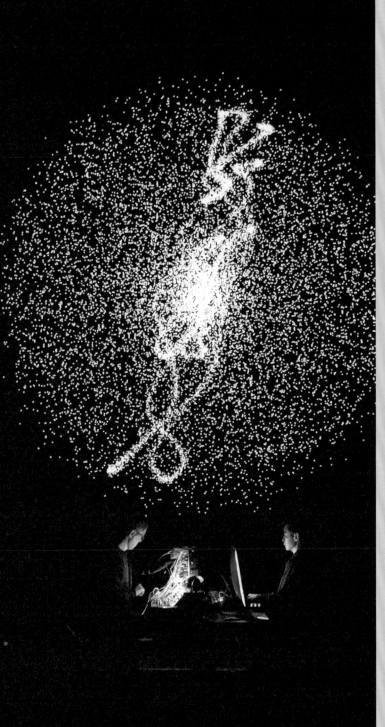

2020
PARADISE ART
LAB FESTIVAL

기술과 예술이 융합된 작품을
지원하는 파라다이스 아트랩
페스티벌. 태싯그룹은
오디오비주얼 부문에
선정돼 신작인 ‹Bilateral
Feedback›을 공연했다.

Paradise Art Lab Festival,
which supports work that
combines technology
and art. Tacit Group was
tasked with leading the
audiovisual division and
performed their new work
Bilateral Feedback.

사진: 타별
Photography: tabial

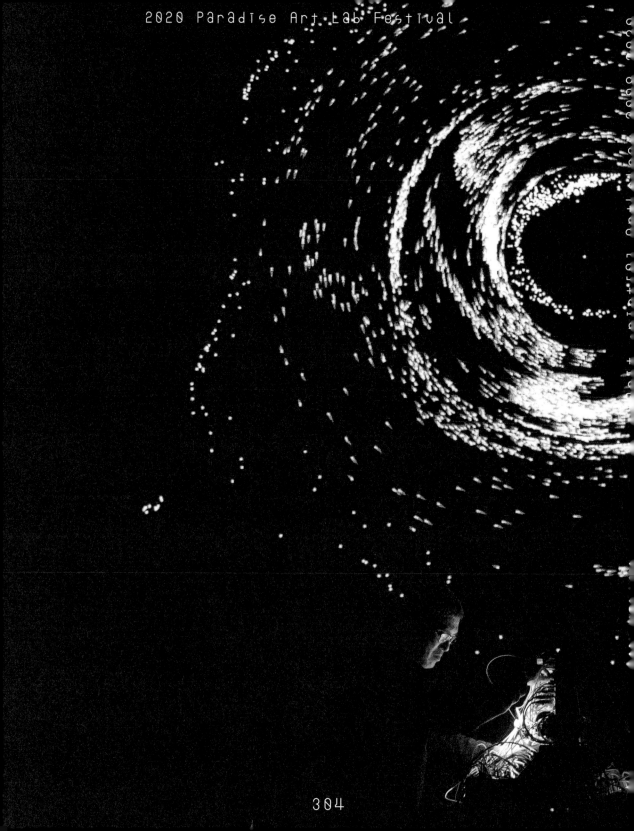

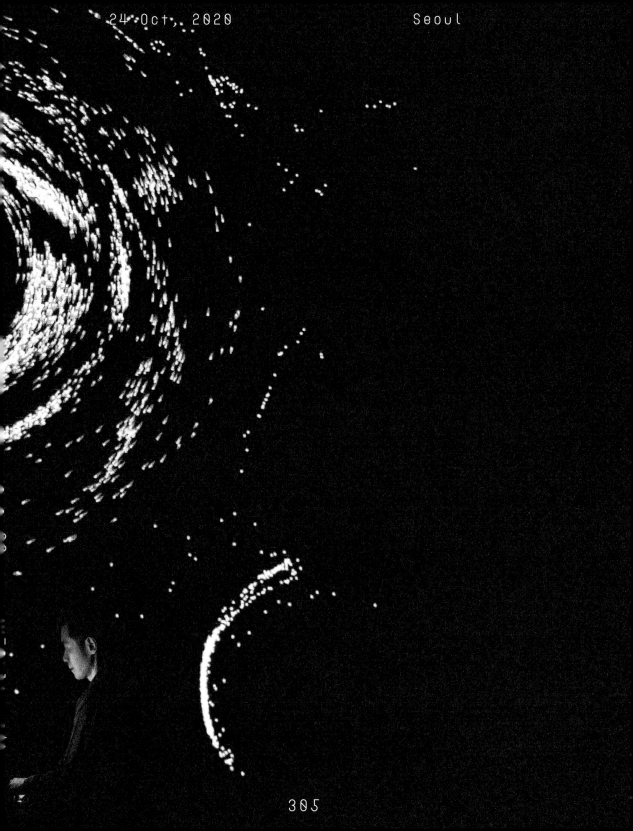

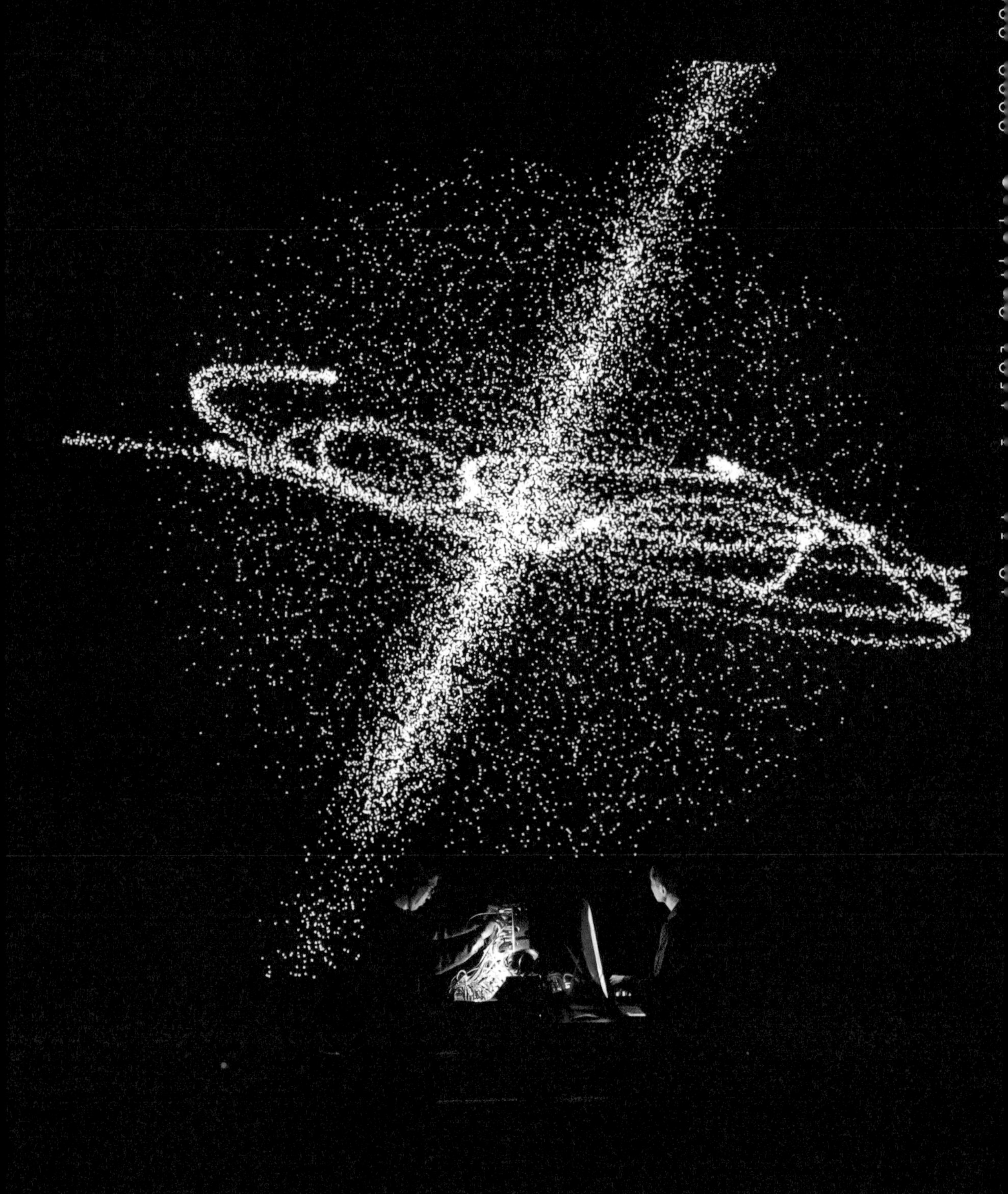

12 NOV, 2020–
28 FEB, 2021

THE MOMENT
OF GIEOK

조선일보 창간 100주년 한글
특별전. 한글 관련 역대 최대
규모로 열린 미술 전시 행사로
태싯그룹은 ‹Morse ㅋung
ㅋung›을 세 대의 LED 패널로
변주한 작품을 선보였다.
끊임없는 분해와 재창조
과정을 통해 한글이 추상성과
조형성을 시청각으로 동시
전달하는 예술 매개체임을
보여주었다는 평을 받았다.

A special exhibition in
Hangul, for the 100th
anniversary of the
Chosun Ilbo. As an art
exhibition event held
on the largest scale
ever related to Hangeul,
Tacit Group presented a
work that transformed
Morse ㅋung ㅋung into
three LED panels. It was
criticized for interpreting
Hangeul as an art medium
that simultaneously
conveys abstraction
and formativeness with
audio-visual, through
the process of constant
decomposition and re-
creation.

프로듀서: 신은진
서체 디자인:
홍은주 김형재
구조물 제작: 팀에이든
테크니션: 정창균

Producer: Regina Shin
Type Design:
Hong Eunjoo,
Kim Hyungjae
Fabrication: team Aidan
Technician:
Changgyun Jung

사진: 타별
Photography: tabial

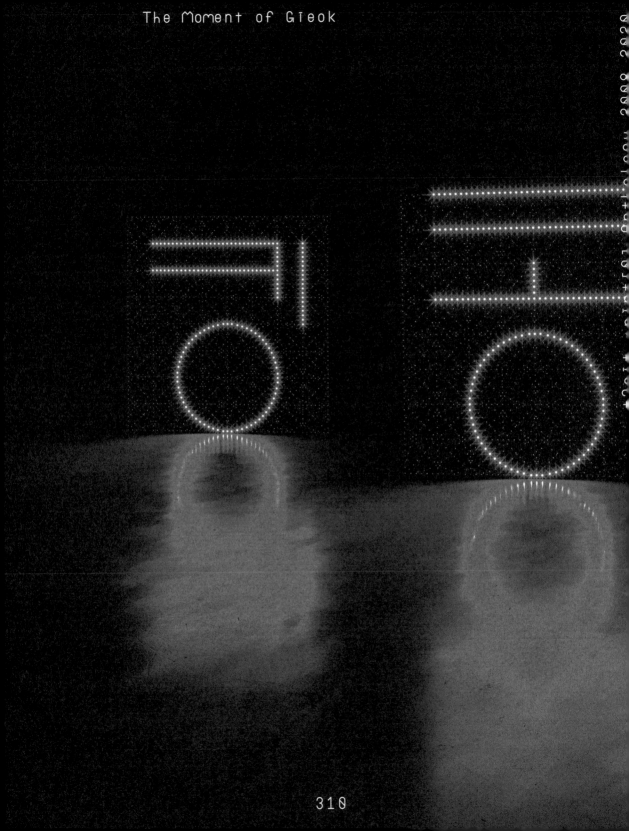

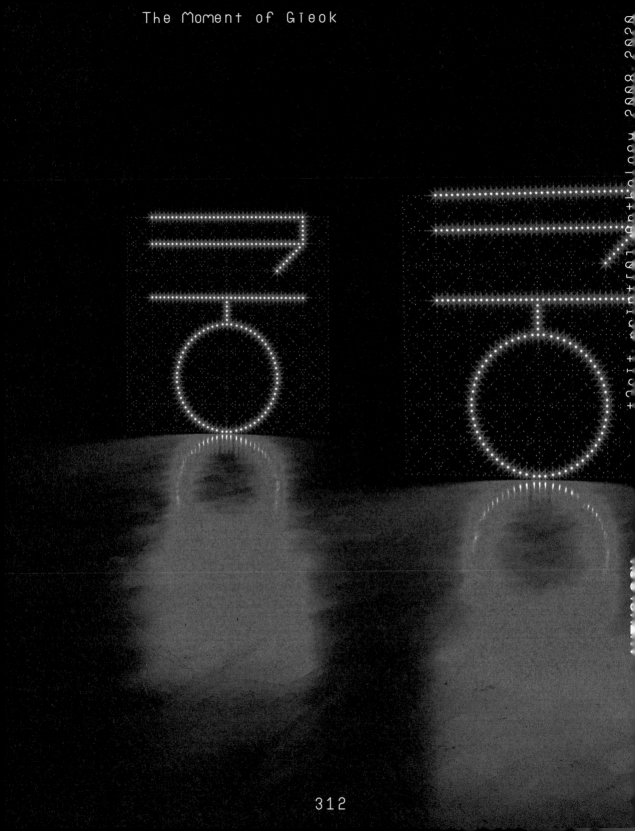

tacit.install[2] _
tacit group
@church

교회였던 공간을
전시관으로 개조한 'THIS
IS NOT A CHURCH'에
개최된 태싯그룹 단독
전시회. ‹op.sound›
연작 시리즈에 교회라는
공간적 특성을 부여한
‹op.sound[3671240]›와
신작 ‹61/6 speakers›를
전시했다.

Tacit Group's exclusive
exhibition held at THIS
IS NOT A CHURCH,
which was converted
from a space of worship
into an exhibition hall.
Tacit Group exhibited
op.sound[3671240]
which gave the *op.sound*
series the spatial
characteristics of a
church and a new work *61
speakers*.

사진: 타별
Photography: tabial

‹61/6 speakers›

프로듀서: 신은진
구조물 디자인 및 제작: 정성윤
테크니션: 정창균

Producer: Regina Shin
Design & fabrication:
Jung Sungyoon
Technician:
Changgyun Jung

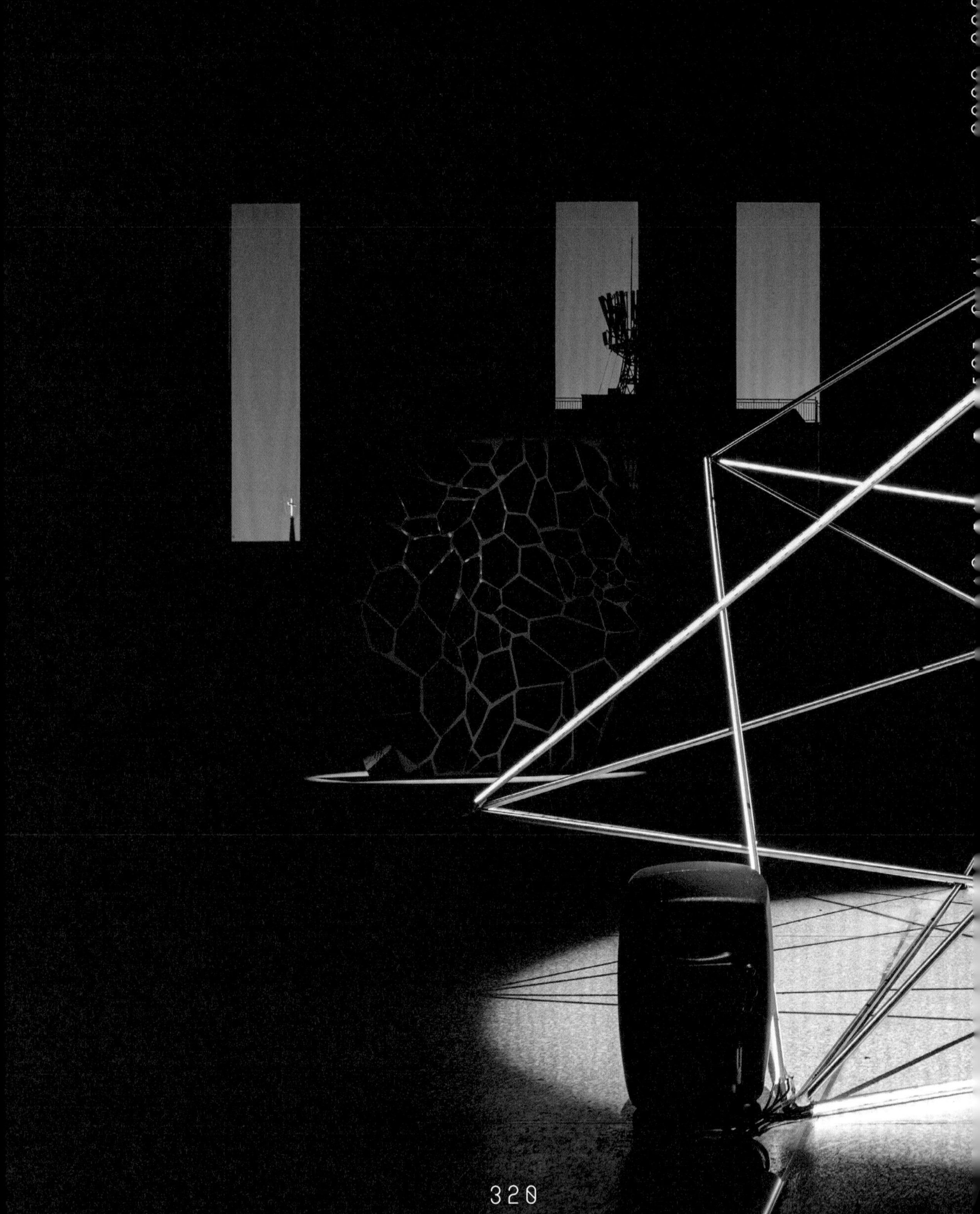

‹op.sound[3671240]›

프로듀서: 신은진
구조물 디자인 및 제작: 팀에이든
테크니션: 정창균

Producer: Regina Shin
Design & fabrication:
team Aidan
Technician: Changgyun Jung

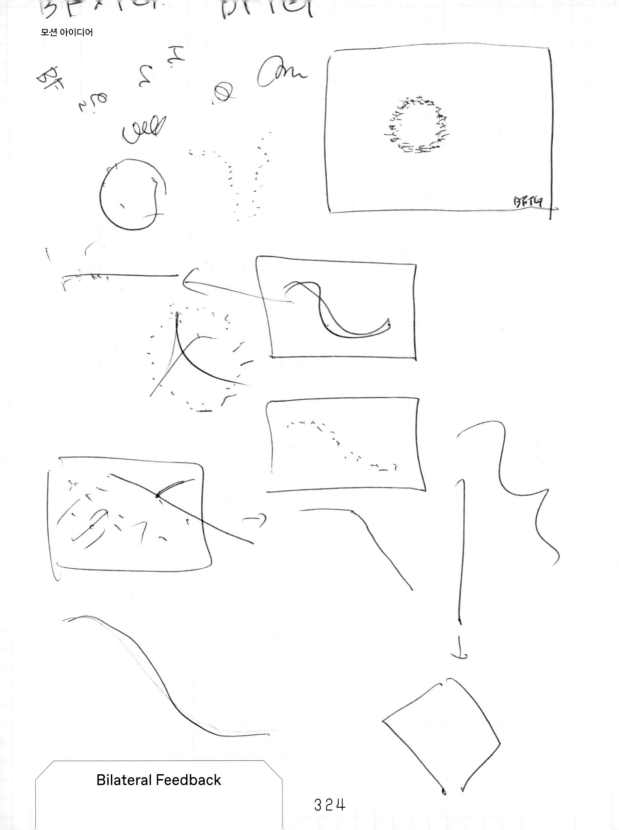

Bilateral Feedback

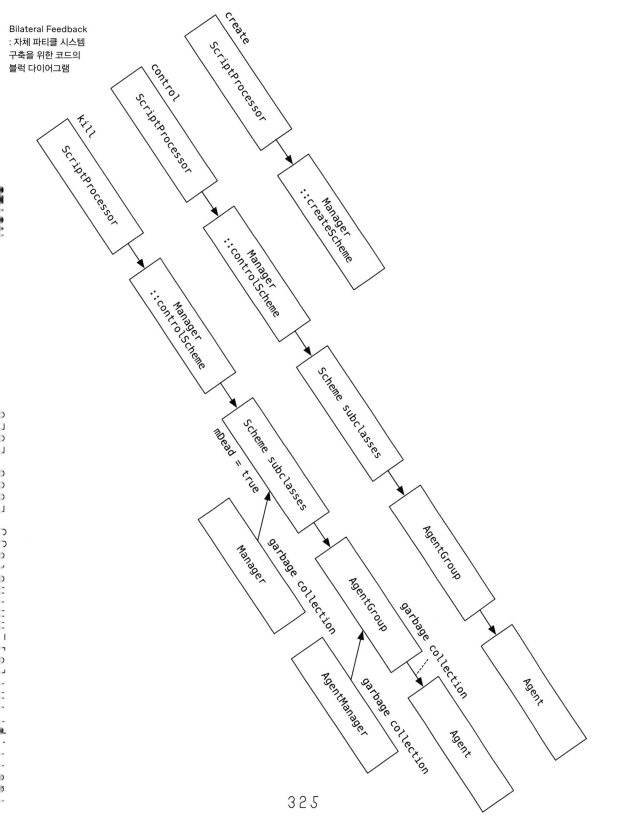

Bilateral Feedback
: 자체 파티클 시스템
구축을 위한 코드의
블럭 다이어그램

325

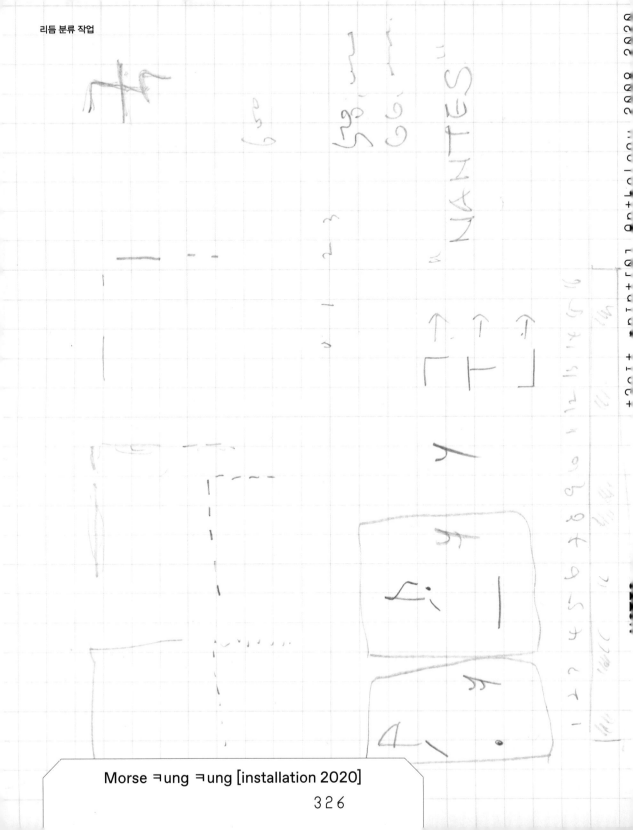

Morse ㅋung ㅋung [installation 2020]

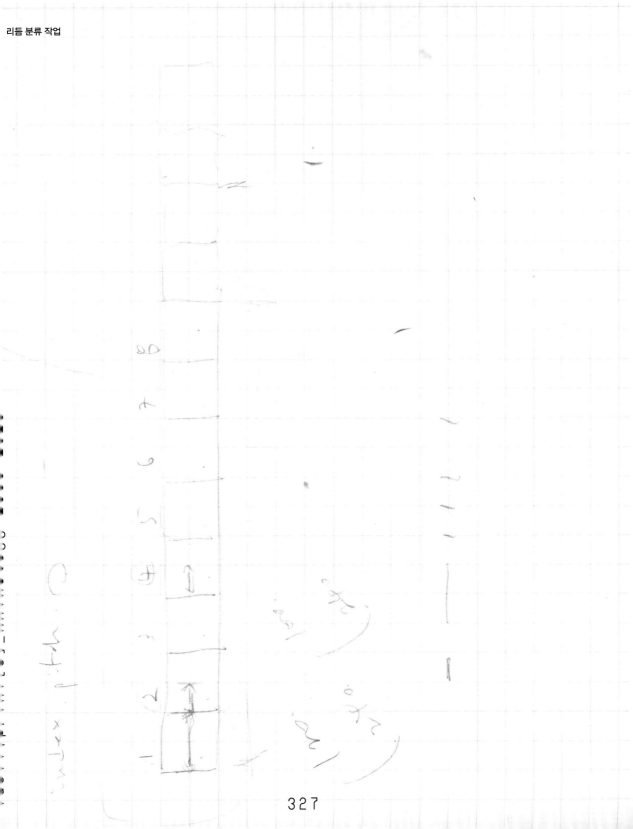

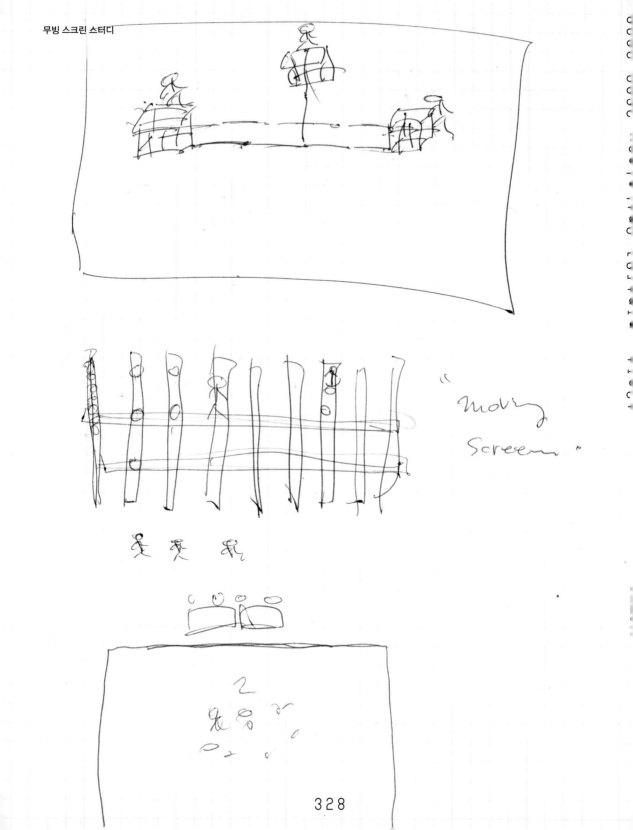

"Moving Screen".

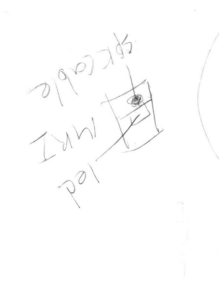

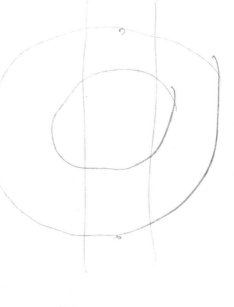

1. 출력음
2. Amp
3. AUB.

데이터 플로우
디자인

$$\sin\theta = \frac{y}{z}$$

$$\cos\theta = \frac{x}{z}$$

$$y = \sin\theta \times z$$

$$x = \cos\theta \times z$$

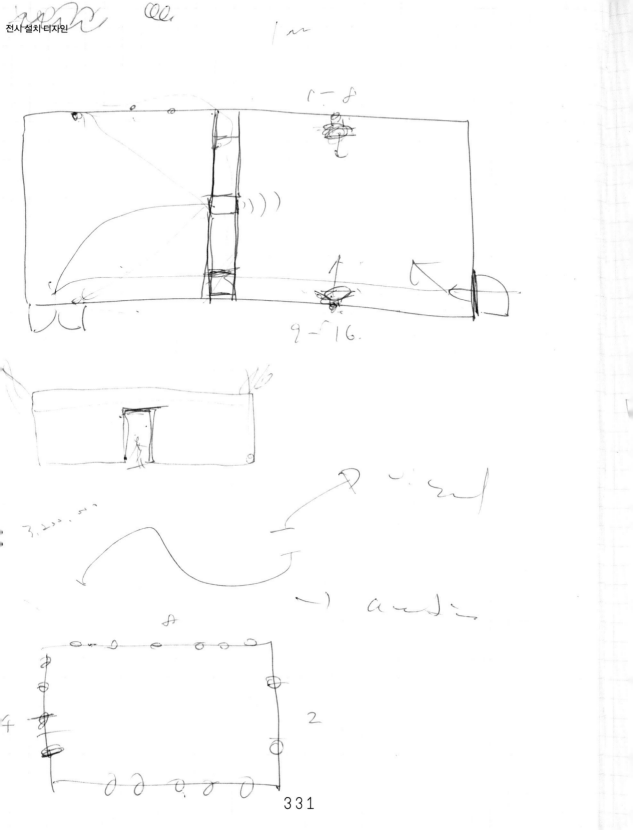

ESSAY

미디어 아트는
X-예술이다

박영욱 연세대학교 미디어아트연구소 HK교수

1895년 뢴트겐(Röntgen)은 진공관 실험을 하던 중 우연히 이상한 빛을
발견했다. 매우 짧은 파장의 이 빛은 보통의 빛과 달리 상대적으로 밀도가 낮은
물체들을 투과해버렸다. 예컨대 사람의 인체 중에서 살이나 수분처럼 밀도가
낮은 물체는 통과하지만 뼈처럼 밀도가 높은 물체들은 반사되는 것이다.
지금도 병원에서 흔히 사용하는 X선이 바로 이 이상한 빛이다. 그런데
이 광선이 X광선이라 불리는 이유는 이러하다. 당시로써 이 빛의 실체를
명확하게 규정할 수 없었다. 사람의 몸이나 밀도가 낮은 물건들을 그냥
통과해버리는 빛이 있다는 것은 도무지 설명이 되지 않았던 것이다. 그래서
뢴트겐은 이를 '엑스' 광선(X-Ray)이라고 불렀다.

　　기존의 학설이나 범주로는 설명할 수 없었기 때문에 이러한 명칭으로
불리는 것은 어쩌면 당연한 일이다. 하프 파이프를 타고 아슬아슬한 묘기를
펼치는 인라인 어그레시브 경기나 레슬링도 아니고 권투도 아닌 더군다나
유도도 아닌 말 그대로 이종 격투기가 '엑스' 스포츠라고 불리는 이유도
똑같다.

　　'엑스' 스포츠는 단순히 새로운 스포츠가 아니다. 그것은 기존의 스포츠
범주나 장르 자체가 마구 섞여 존재하는 규정할 수 없는 이질적인 스포츠다.
말하자면 레슬링의 특성을 지니면서도 동시에 레슬링의 규칙을 위반하고
있으며, 권투의 특성을 지니면서도 동시에 권투의 규칙을 위반하고 있는
것이다.

미디어 아트는 엑스 광선이나 엑스 스포츠처럼 처음부터 기존 예술의 규칙을
위반하는 것이었다. 백남준의 경우만 하더라도 그가 텔레비전을 전시하였을
때 그것은 위반이었다. 텔레비전은 뒤샹의 변기처럼 단순한 기성품(레디
메이드)의 의미만 지니는 것은 아니다. 텔레비전은 이미지를 담고 있기
때문이다. 그렇기 때문에 그의 전시는 조각도 아니다. 그렇다고 회화는 더더욱
아니다. 텔레비전은 이미지를 담고 있는 틀이기 때문에 오히려 캔버스와
흡사하다고 볼 수 있다. 백남준의 예술은 근본적으로 기존 예술의 규칙들을
위반하고 있다.

　　미디어 아트가 위반적일 수밖에 없는 이유는 그것이 바탕으로 하는

뉴미디어 자체의 특성과 관련이 있다. 과거의 매체는 단일한 장르에 국한이 된 것이었다. 가령 유화나 캔버스는 오로지 시각적 이미지를 담는 매체였을 뿐 그 속에 소리를 담을 수는 없었다. 음악의 경우도 악기는 오로지 소리라는 청각 현상만을 만들 뿐이었다.

그러니 음악은 오로지 귀를 위한 예술이었을 뿐이다. 하지만 텔레비전이나 다양한 영상기기 혹은 컴퓨터와 같은 디지털 매체는 이미 처음부터 이미지와 소리가 결합이 되어있다. 그것은 소리만을 위한 매체이거나 시각 이미지만을 위한 매체가 아닌 것이다. 미디어 아트는 당연히 이미지와 소리의 엄격한 구분에 바탕을 둔 기존의 예술 규칙을 위반할 수밖에 없다.

고전음악 작곡이론을 전공하고 네덜란드에서 전자음악을 공부한 장재호 교수와 테크노 음악으로 대중가요계에 널리 알려진 가재발이 함께 하는 태싯그룹(Tacit Group)의 작업은 사운드 아트로 분류된다. 하지만 사운드 아트로 분류되는 사실 자체가 매우 역설적이기도 하다.

사운드 아트는 '엑스 '광선이나 '엑스'스포츠처럼 여러 개의 장르가 혼합된, 더 정확하게 말하자면 어떤 장르에도 가둘 수 없는 이질적인 예술이기 때문이다. 태싯그룹의 공연을 보면 이런 상황이 더욱 실감나게 이해된다. 연주자들은 연주라기보다는 게임을 즐기거나 채팅을 하기도 하며, 실시간 카메라로 관객을 비추고 관객의 이미지를 음악과 함께 변형시키기도 한다. 따라서 이들의 작업을 단순히 컴퓨터 전자음악으로 분류할 수 없다.

이들의 작업에서도 알 수 있듯이 사운드 아트는 음악의 한 부류가 아니다. 전통적인 음악이나 회화가 아닐 뿐더러 단순한 퍼포먼스도 아니다. 이 모든 것이 하나의 작업으로 연결되어 있으며, 음악은 소리의 예술이며 회화는 시각 이미지의 예술이라는 도식을 거부한다.

물론 이러한 도식을 거부하고 들리는 그림을 그리려거나 보이는 음악을 만들려는 시도는 예전부터 존재하였다. 괴상하게 들릴지 모르지만 고흐나 뭉크도 여기에 포함된다. 가령 뭉크의 그림 '절규'는 단지 보는 그림이 아닌 듣는 그림이다. 뭉크는 그 그림을 통해서 결코 절규하는 사람의 모습을 재현하고자 한 것이 아니다. 그의 그림은 절규하는 사람의 비명을 생생하게 전달한다. 말하자면 그 그림은 절규하는 모습이 아닌 절규의 비명 자체를 전달하는 것이다. 드뷔시 또한 음악을 통해서 단지 소리가 아닌 하나의 장면 혹은 인상을 전달하고자 하였다.

음악과 회화, 퍼포먼스 등의 다양한 결합이 본격적으로 시도된 것은 20세기 이후의 일이다. 칸딘스키의 회화는 노골적으로 음악을 모델로 삼았으며, 피에르 셰페르의 구체 음악은 일상적인 소리들을 사용하여 구체적인 상황의 이미지를 떠올리게 만들었다. 한 마디로 소리와 이미지를 뒤섞어 회화를 음악으로, 음악을 회화로 만들려 한 것이다. 이들이 이런 작업을 시도한 것은 그저 기존의 장르를 섞어서 퓨전의 장르를 만들려는 의도 때문이 아니다.

세상에 존재하는 모든 이미지들이나 현상들은 원래부터 섞여 있다. 어떤 색을 볼 때, 사람마다 다를 수는 있지만, 따뜻함을 느끼거나 차가움을 느끼며, 우울함 혹은 경쾌함을 느낀다. 형태를 볼 때도 형태만이 아닌 리듬감을 느낀다. 일상생활에서 우리는 이미지를 듣고 소리를 보고 있다.

원래부터 모든 이미지와 현상은 소리, 색깔, 형태, 맛, 감촉 등이 어우러져 존재한다. 어느 것 하나만을 떼어놓을 수는 없다. 이제껏 장르화된 예술은 이것들 각각을 떼어놓으려 하였다. 그러다 보니 각각의 예술 장르는 어느 한 감각만을 기형적으로 극대화하려는 경향으로 나타난다.

사운드 아트는 바로 기존의 예술이 단일 감각의 기형적 생산만을 낳는 경향에 저항하여 실험되는 예술의 한 형태이다..따라서 사운드 아트는 기존의 서양음계에서 사용하던 매끈한 음들에만 집착하지 않으며, 고상한 화음의 나열이 곧 좋은 음악이라는 전통적 도식도 거부한다. 사운드 아트는 매끈한 음과 소음의 경계도 허물며, 나아가 소리가 단순히 귀를 위한 청각적 현상일 뿐이라는 도식마저도 거부한다.

사운드 아트는 음이 하나의 시각적 이미지로 표출되거나 문자로 나타나기도 한다. 그리고 음악은 단순히 악보를 연주하는 것이 아니라, 그것을 수행한다. 이런 면에서 사운드 아트의 공연은 존재하지 않는다. 단지 사운드 아트의 퍼포먼스만이 있을 뿐이다. 말하자면 즉흥적이고 우발적인 하나의 사건을 창출하는 것이다.

그러한 우발적 사건으로서의 퍼포먼스는 태싯그룹의 작품 ‹Game Over›에서 테트리스 게임과 같은 오락으로 수행된다. 이들의 연주는 단순히 정해진 악보를 연주하는 것이 아니라 게임이라는 퍼포먼스를 행하는 것이다. 이 작품에서 이들이 강조하는 또 하나의 측면은 ‘생성음악’(generative music)이라는 것이다. 포괄적인 맥락에서 생성예술은 예술작품의 창작자가 하나의 시스템만을 만들 뿐 작품 자체의 결과를 모두 다 총괄할 수 없는 것을 의미한다.

축구에서 감독의 역할을 생각해 보자. 감독은 하나의 전술 체계, 가령 4-4-2시스템을 구축할 수 있다. 이는 미드필드의 역할을 강화하는 체계이다. 하지만 이 체계는 상대편의 전술에 따라서 혹은 그날의 상황에 따라서 어떠한 방식으로 실현될지 모른다. 과거 고전주의 시기에는 세세한 연주진행 상황을 모두 악보에 새겨서 작곡가가 모든 것을 통제하고 연주자가 자신의 명령에 따라 연주하게 하였다. 하지만 디지털 음악에서는 작곡가가 기본적인 알고리즘만 제시하고 시스템을 구성하면, 연주는 임의적으로 상황에 따라서 다양하게 수행될 수 있다. 즉 상황에 따른 퍼포먼스가 될 수 있는 것이다.

디지털 악기는 매우 정교한 알고리즘에 의해서 만들어지는 기계론적인 음악이지만, 오히려 디지털은 그러한 퍼포먼스를 만들어내기에 매우 적합한 악기이다. 왜냐하면 디지털 매체의 장점은 얼마든지 변형이 가능하기 때문이다. 디지털 음악이 전통적인 음악과 달리 퍼포먼스적인 성격이 강하게 나타날 수 있는 것은 바로 디지털 악기의 특성 자체에서 비롯된다.

태싯그룹의 연주는 바로 그러한 우발적 퍼포먼스의 특성을 최대한으로 활용한다. 또한 음악 자체로 볼 때는 마치 재즈음악에서의 잼과도 같이 매우 자유롭고 독립적인 연주를 통해서 강제적 질서가 아닌 하나의 자율적이면서도 느슨한 질서를 추구한다.

태싯그룹의 작품 〈In C〉는 미국의 작곡가 테리 라일리의 곡을 디지털 악기로 연주한 것이다. 이 곡은 C장조로 이루어진 간단한 멜로디를 모티브로 계속 변형하여 반복되는 미니멀리즘 곡이다. 미니멀리즘의 가장 큰 특징은 최소패턴의 '토톨로지'(동어반복)이다. 이는 어느 세세한 것에 반복적으로 집착하는 편집증 혹은 강박적인 패턴이다.

음악에서 미니멀리즘의 대표적인 형태는 바로크 시대의 오스티나토인데, 이 말의 의미만 봐도 강박적인 것과 연결되어 있음을 쉽게 알 수 있다. 그런데 이러한 세세한 것에 대한 강박적 집착은 마치 사이코패스적인 것처럼 보일지 몰라도 실은 현상이나 이미지에 대한 새로운 이해를 낳는다.

가령 동일한 색을 미묘한 변화만 주면서 반복해 보자. 지금껏 느끼지 못했던 파란색의 따스함을 발견할 수 있다. 말하자면 색 자체에서 단순히 색이 아닌 온갖 소리와 감촉 혹은 감칠맛을 발견하는 것이다. 그것은 색이 시각 이미지라는 고정 관념에 대한 위반하고 미지의 X 세계로 들어가는 길이다.

Media Art is
X-Art

Young-wook Park, HK Professor at Yonsei University Media Art
Research Institute

In 1895, Röntgen accidentally discovered a strange light while
experimenting with a vacuum tube. This very short wavelength of light,
unlike ordinary light, can be transmitted through relatively low density
objects. For example, in the human body, objects with low density such
as tissue or fluid allow this light to transit through, whereas objects with
high density such as bones reflect it.

At that time, the nature of this light could not be clearly defined;
there was no obvious explanation for why light could simply pass
through a person's body or low density objects. That's why Roentgen
deemed it the 'X-Ray'. In present day, X-rays are commonly used in
hospitals, utilizing this remarkable light. It is only natural that it be called
by such a name because it could not be explained by existing theories or
studies of the day

'X' sports are not just new sports, but a hybrid of sport that cannot
be defined, in which existing recreational categories and pursuits
are combined together. In other words, a sport can possess the
characteristics of wrestling and at the same time violate the rules of
wrestling, or resemble the attributes of boxing while at the same time
violating the rules of said sport.

Media art, like X-rays and X-Sports, violates the rules of existing
artforms beginning from its inception. To reference Nam June Paik, it
was a violation when he created and displayed his television array. The
television didn't just represent and utilize a static manufactured product
like Duchamp's toilet, but could also display moving images. Therefore,
his exhibition cannot be categorized as sculpture. Nor could it be
classified as a painting: though television possesses a canvas like quality,
its technological capabilities defy the nature of a painting. Nam June
Paik's art fundamentally violates the existing rules of art.

The reason media art is contravening is related to the properties of
the new media it is based upon. In the past, media was limited to a single
genre; oil paintings and canvas for example, were the only media that
contained visual images, but could not incorporate sound. In terms of
music, instruments could only be used to create an auditory curiosity
known as sound, meant only for the ears.

However, digital media such as television, video devices, and
computer technology have been used to combine images and sounds
from their inception, and they are not just a medium for only sound and
visual images. To be sure, media art is destined to violate existing art

rules based upon the strict distinctions between image and sound.

The project Tacit Group (Professor Jang Jae-ho, who majored in classical music composition and theory and studied electronic music in the Netherlands, and Gazaebal who is widely known in the popular music industry for his techno music) can be classified as 'Sound Art'. However, that it is described as sound art is somewhat paradoxical.

This is because sound art is a heterogeneous artform in which several genres are combined like 'X' rays or 'X' sports, or to be more precise, cannot be confined to any one genre. Tacit Group's performance verily illustrates this situation. As opposed to simply playing, these performers enjoy games and conversation, using real-time cameras to illuminate the audience which transmute images of the audience with music. Consequently, their work cannot simply be classified as computer electronic music.

As can be witnessed in their work, sound art is not a classification of music. Sound art is neither traditional music nor painting nor a simple performance. As all these elements are interconnected as a single work, rejecting the dogma that music is the designated art of sound and painting is the authorized domain of visual images.

Of course, attempts have been mounted since antiquity to challenge these distinctions by drawing pictures to be heard or create music visible to the eye. It may sound unorthodox, but these assays include Gogh and Munch. For example, Munch's painting 'Scream' is not just a painting to be seen, but a statement to be heard.

Munch did not try to reproduce the figure of a screaming person through the painting. His painting vividly conveys the sentiment and sound of a person who screams. That is to say, the painting communicates the scream itself, not the appearance of screaming. Conversely, Debussy delved to impart a scene or impression, and not solely sound through music.

It was after the turn of the 19th century that various combinations of music, painting, and performance were sought in earnest. Kandinsky's paintings explicitly modeled music, and Pierre Sheper's Musique Concrete invoked everyday sounds to evoke images of specific situations. In essence, he tried to translate painting into music and music into a painting by combining image and sound. This kind of work was not attempted due to some frivolous desire to indulge in fusion or mixed genres.

All images and phenomena that exist in the world are inherently mixed. When assessing color, it may vary according to the individual; it may feel warm or cool, or evoke depression or good cheer. When looking at a shape, I feel a sense of rhythm, not just the geometrical schematic of

339

form. In everyday life, we hear images and see sounds.

Fundamentally, all images and phenomena exist in harmony with sound, color, shape, taste, and texture. You cannot distinguish only one element. Art history thus far has insisted upon the separation of each of these. Accordingly, the respective genres have seemingly pursued the grotesque maximization of only one sense.

Sound art is a form of expression that is tested against the disposition of existing art that produces only a myopic distortion. Therefore, sound art does not adhere to the svelte tones of preexisting Western scales, and rejects the accepted dogma that only the arrangement of elegant harmony produces good music. Sound art breaks the linear path between sound and noise, and even refutes the assumption that sound is simply an auditory sensation for the ear.

In sound art, sounds are expressed as an independent visual image or as characters. Music does not simply play along with sheet music, it is performed. In this respect, there is no actual sound art performance. There is only the performance of sound art. Which is to say it creates an improvised and spontaneous episode. Such an instinctual performance is exemplified in Tacit's work *Game Over* which is performed as an entertainment through a game of Tetris. Their performance does not simply play to a musical score, but functions as performance as game. Another aspect they emphasize in this work is that of 'generative music'. In a comprehensive context, generative art suggests that the creator of an artwork yields only one system and cannot manage all the results of the work itself.

To further illustrate, consider the manager's role in football. The coach can establish a tactical system, such as a 4-4-2 configuration. This is a strategy that strengthens the role of the midfield. However, this system may be realized several ways depending on the opponent's tactics or the conditions of the day. During the Classical Period, detailed minutiae were inscribed on the score, guiding the composer who controlled everything with the performers playing in accordance.

Conversely, in digital music if a composer inputs only basic algorithms and constructs a system, performances proceed arbitrarily with a multitude of possibilities depending on the situation. In other words, the performance evolves according to the situation.

The advantage of digital media is that it can be transformed any number of times, and unlike traditional music, digital music can be enhanced by characteristics native to digital instruments. Digital instruments not only produce mechanistic music with very sophisticated algorithms, but are also very suitable for creating such performances such as those presented by Tacit Group.

The Tacit Group's performance capitalizes on the characteristics constitutive of spontaneous or accidental performance. Also, in terms of the music itself, it is freeform and independent. Similar to that of an improvisational jazz music session, it pursues an autonomous and non hierarchical order as opposed to a compulsory framework.

The work *In C* is a digital piece performed by American composer Terry Riley. This is a minimalistic song that is repeated by continuously transforming a simple melody played in C major into a motif. The outlying feature denoting minimalism is the 'tautology' of the minimal pattern (synonymous repetition). This is a compulsive or obsessive pattern of repeatedly obsessing over details.

One representative form of minimalism in music is the Ostinato of the Baroque era, and it is easy to see how it is connected to the obsessive just by observing the meaning of the word 'obsessive'. While the compulsive obsession with these details may seem pathological, it in fact gives birth to a new understanding of the image or phenomenon.

For instance, let's repeat the same color but with only subtle changes. You may discover the warmth of blue that you have never felt before. In other words, in the color itself lay not just color, but all manner of sound, texture, and taste. It challenges the notion that color is only a refracted visual image, opening a door to the unknown world of 'X'.

태싯그룹의 소리가 암시하는 것들: 알고리듬 역사의 시작

이영준 기계비평가

태싯그룹의 소리설치작업 ‹Morse ㅋung ㅋung›을 보고 다음과 같은 온갖 소리에 대한 생각이 떠올랐다.

1

미국 사람 중 최초로 사진을 본 사람은 전신을 발명한 새뮤얼 모스였다. 그가 본 사진의 형태는 다게레오타입이었는데, 그는 또한 미국 최초의 사진가이기도 했다. 그가 발명한 모르스 코드는 소리를 디지털로 표기하는 방식이었는데 다게레오타입은 아날로그식 사진이었다는 점이다. 모르스 코드의 특징은 꼭 소리로만 나타낼 필요가 없다는 것이다. 어떤 신호이든 긴 것과 짧은 것을 구별할 수만 있으면 모르스 코드를 나타낼 수 있다. 즉 돌이나 망치로 두드리는 소리든 불빛이든 긴 것과 짧은 것을 구별할 수만 있으면 모르스 코드를 만들 수 있다. 한편, 사진이 디지털식이 된 것은 모르스 코드의 출현 이후 160년은 더 지난 후였다.

2

창밖에서 좋은 음악이 들리길래 더 잘 들으려고 창문을 열었는데 이상하게 음악은 들리지 않고 온갖 소음만 들렸다. 창이 닫혀 있는 동안에는 창이 고음을 막아서 저음만 들렸는데, 창을 열자 차 소리, 사람 소리 등 온갖 소음이 뒤섞인, 고음과 저음이 뒤섞인 소리가 한꺼번에 들어온 것이다. 그리고 이런 다양한 소리의 다이내믹이 애초 들으려 했던 음악 소리를 지워버린 것이다. 그런데 애초의 음악과 창문을 연 다음 들린 소리 사이에는 어떤 차이가 있는 걸까? 소리에도 위계가 있어서 어떤 소리는 들을 만한 소리이고, 어떤 소리는 잡소리로 치부돼도 되는 걸까? 분명히 그런 것 같다. 어떤 소리는 엄청난 돈을 들여 재현해내는 데 반해 어떤 소리는 돈을 들여 못 들어오게 막으니 말이다. 음반으로 재현되어 고급 하이파이 오디오로 재생되는 소리가 전자이며 방음 시설을 하여 바깥의 소리가 못 들어오게 하는 것이 후자이다.

3

파동을 연구하는 전자공학 교수가 모는 차를 타고 가면서 파장과 매질의 밀도에 대해 얘기를 하고 있었는데 그는 자동차의 속도를 통해 그 관계를 직접 보여줬다. 차가 느리게 갈 때는 진동의 파장이 크므로 노면의 요철이 차체 하부를 뚫고 실내로 들어왔다. 차의 속력이 빨라지자 파장은 짧아졌고 진동은 전달되지 않았다. 즉 진동은 자잘해져 차체를 뚫고 들어올 수 없었다. 이게 가능한 이유는 파장과 주파수는 서로 반비례하는 관계에 있기 때문이다.

4

박테리아가 소리를 낼까, 나무가 자랄 때도 소리를 낼까 하는 의문을 가져본 적이 있다. 혹은 지구의 자전에서 나는 소리도 있을까 하는 의문도 가져봤다. 아마 소리가 나긴 하는데 사람의 귀에는 안 들릴지도 모른다. 그렇다면 사람의 귀는 그리 정밀하고 신통한 감각기관은 아니다. 그런데 그 못난 귀를 위하여 몇억 원이나 하는 비싼 오디오 시스템이 있다는 것은 아이러니한 사실이다. 오디오 시스템이 비싼 이유는 생리적인 귀를 위해서가 아니라 문화적인 귀를 위해 만들어져 있기 때문일 것이다. 카라얀이라는 사람은 문화적 현상이지 생리적 현상이 아니니까 말이다.

5

이 세상에 악기가 꼭 바이올린이나 피아노같이 비싼 것만 있는 것은 아니다. 소리를 내는 것은 무엇이든지 악기가 될 수 있다. 1983년쯤 세종문화회관에서 캐나다의 타악기 그룹 넥서스가 공연을 했는데 그들은 손에 잡히는 것은 무엇이든 악기로 바꿔버렸다. 한 연주자가 세면대에 연결하는 주름 진 파이프를 크게 원 모양으로 휘둘렀더니 윙위잉 하는 기묘한 소리가 났다. 또 한 연주자는 못이 잔뜩 박혀 있는 것 위를 손으로 부드럽게 쓸자 슈르르릉 하는 신묘한 소리가 났다. 나는 대형화물선을 타고 여행한 적이 있는데 배 자체는 엄청나게 두꺼운 강철로 만들어져 있어서 아주 튼튼했고 비틀림 강도가 세서 웬만해서는 선체가 휘는 일이 없었다. 그런데 실내는 보통의 사무실이나 아파트의 방을 만들 듯 적당한 목재로 돼 있었던 것 같다. 바다의 상태는 매 순간 다르고 배에서 나는 엔진소리도 rpm의 변화에 따라 계속 변한다. 바다와 엔진의 변화는 목재로 된 방을 매 순간 다른 방향, 다른 각도, 다른 강도로 뒤틀어 놓았고 거기 맞춰 다른 소리가 났다. 배는 롤, 피치, 요(roll, pitch, yaw)의 세 가지 방향의 운동을 하는데 바다는 계속 움직이며 변하기 때문에 어떤 한 운동도 다른 운동과 같은 것이 있을 수 없다. 거기 맞춰 비틀리는 방도 항상 다른 소리를 냈다. 그 조합의 수는 무한대였다. 방이 내는 소리의 가짓수도 무한대였다. 어떤 때는 씰그럭씰그럭, 어떤 때는 삐걱삐걱, 또 어떤 때는 끼익끼익 등. 한 달의 항해는 방이 내는 다양한 소리의 변주를 듣는 시간이었다.

6

MBC라디오는 1991년부터 〈우리의 소리를 찾아서〉라는 방송을 하고
있는데, 각 지역의 민요를 짤막하게 들려주는 스팟 방송이다. 대한민국의 인구
대다수가 사는 도시와는 멀리 떨어진 농사나 어업에 종사하는 분들의 민요기
때문에 낯선 에스닉 음악처럼 들리는데도 불구하고 이 방송의 임팩트는 커서,
많은 사람이 민요는 낯설어해도 〈우리의 소리를 찾아서〉는 익숙하게 알고
있다. 심지어는 개그 프로그램에서도 이를 패러디 했을 정도다. 그런데 과연
이런 민요가 '우리'의 소리일까? '우리'를 대한민국 사람 전체라고 하면 '우리의
소리'는 누구에게나 익숙한 소리다. 그러나 대한민국에는 더 이상 민요를
부르거나 듣지 않는, 도시에 사는 인구가 훨씬 많음을 고려하면 민요 소리로 전
국민을 하나로 묶는 것은 불가능해 보인다. 사람들이 이념, 종교, 세대에 따라
극심하게 분열된 지금 소리에 대한 취향도 극심하게 분열돼 있다. 트로트를
좋아하는 사람도 있지만 싫어하는 사람도 있고, 고상한 클래식 음악이라고
해서 모든 사람 귀에 고상하게 들리는 것도 아니다. 농사짓는 시골에 가보면
들일 할 때 트로트 등 가요 틀어 놓지 민요 틀어 놓는 집은 없다. 민요는
기록에나 남아 있는 소리 중 하나인 것이다. 결국 〈우리의 소리를 찾아서〉의
'우리'는 민요를 듣던 시절의 과거의 우리, 혹은 잊힌 민요를 방송국에서
나와서 한 번 해보라니까 옛 기억을 더듬어 불러볼 수 있는 나이 든 시골
분들로 구성된 '우리'이다. 결국 소리를 통해 하나로 묶일 수 있는 '우리'란
존재하지 않는 상상의 공동체일 뿐이다. 그런데도 〈우리의 소리를 찾아서〉는
'청취의 우리'를 만들어내는 절묘한 작용을 하고 있다. 민요를 즐기던 공동체에
한 번도 속해 본 적이 없는 사람도 〈우리의 소리를 찾아서〉를 들으면 자신이
한때는 민요를 즐겼었다는 가상의 사실을 가상적으로 기억해 내고 애잔한
감흥에 젖는다. 지금 '우리의 소리'는 더 이상 민요가 아니라 핸드폰 벨 소리,
골목길을 누비는 오토바이 소리, BTS의 노랫소리 등 동시대를 구성하는
소리다. 이 각각의 소리는 좋아하는 사람과 싫어하는 사람으로 극명하게
나누어져 있어서, 더 이상 소리의 '우리'란 존재하지 않는다. 수많은 청취의
파편적 주체만이 있을 뿐이다.

7

에디슨은 어릴 적 화물차 한 칸을 빌려서 화학실험을 하다가 불을 내는 바람에
차장한테 뺨을 맞은 후 귀가 먹어서 소리를 들을 수 없게 됐다. 에디슨은
수술을 받을 수 있으나 일부러 받지 않았고 평생을 농아로 살았다. 하지만 그는
세상의 잡소리를 듣지 않고 책에 몰두할 수 있어서 좋다고 했고, 그의 직원들은
에디슨이 평소에는 귀가 안 들리는 것처럼 행동하지만 자기가 듣고 싶은
말을 할 때면 잘 듣는다며, 에디슨이 듣고 싶은 소리만 듣는다고 불평했다.

불행하게도 우리는 에디슨과 달라서, 우리를 괴롭히는 소음을 선택할 방법이 없다. 아파트의 층간소음은 사람을 꼼짝없이 피해자로 만들며, 길거리를 걸을 때 온갖 소음을 피할 수 없다. 강의 시간에 교수의 목소리가 마음에 안 든다고 목소리를 바꿔 달라고 할 수도 없다. 우리는 소음의 주체가 아니다. 만일 주체적으로 소리를 걸러낼 수 있으면 그것은 이미 소음이 아니므로 어떤 소리가 소음이라는 사실은 우리가 꼼짝 없이 그 소음의 포로가 됐다는 뜻이다.

8

안현필의 영문법 책에는 한 유머가 나오는데, ghoti가 피쉬로 읽힌다는 것이다. laugh에서 끝의 gh는 f로 읽힌다. women에서 o는 i로 읽힌다. nation에서는 ti가 sh로 읽힌다. 그러니 ghoti가 fish로 읽힌다는 것이었다. 이는 영어에서 글자와 소리가 얼마나 일치하지 않고 불규칙적인지 보여주는 우스개 사례였다. 한국 사람은 누구나 훈민정음은 목에서 소리 나는 구조를 토대로 만들어진 가장 과학적인 글자라고 귀에 못이 박이게 배웠다. 글자와 소리가 일치하는 것이라면 왜 전 세계의 의성어는 다 다를까. 개 짖는 소리도 다르고 개구리 우는 소리도 다르고 폭탄 터지는 소리도 다르다. 나라마다 개와 개구리의 종류가 다르고 폭탄의 성분이 달라서일까. 소리는 글자로 나타낼 수 없다. 소리란 온갖 물질들이 떨리면서 공기도 따라서 떨리고 그 떨림이 사람 귀에 전달된 것인데 물질의 떨림이란 몇 가지 글자로 나타낼 수 있을 만큼 간단한 현상이 아니기 때문이다. 글자는 소리의 표현이 아니라 입으로 말하는 언어의 소리를 극히 제한적인 조건에서만 대표해주는 약속의 부호일 뿐이다. 그런 글자를 가지고 언어도 아닌 온갖 소리를 나타내려고 하니 제대로 될 리가 없는 것이다.

이런 생각들을 하다가 태싯그룹의 이전 작업을 봤다. 다양한 글자와 소리의 조합을 시험하는 작업이었다. 소리는 글자를 표상하는 것 같은데 살짝살짝 빗겨 간다. 관객은 언제 소리에 맞는 글자가 나오나 기다리지만 기대하는 결합은 영 나타나지 않는다. 대신 소리와 글자는 서로 미끄러지며 쫓고 쫓긴다. 그래서 tacit인가. tacit이란 소리 없음이란 뜻이니 어떤 소리도 기대하지 말란 뜻인가. 그렇다면 소리의 한계를 시험해 보자. 그것이 듣는 쪽의 한계이든 소리 내는 쪽의 한계이든 말이다. 태싯그룹이 2020년 12월 명성교회에 설치한 최근작 ‹61/6 speakers›는 양쪽의 한계를 모두 시험하는 작업이다. 61개의 스피커가 사람의 가청주파수 이하의 진동수로 떨리는 모습은 138억 년 전 우주가 처음 생길 때 저런 소리가 나지 않았을까 싶게 숭고미를 풍겼다. 매일 뻔한 소리를 듣고 사는 사람에게 이런 소리 아닌 소리를 듣는 것, 몸으로 겪는 것은 귀한 체험이다. 그것은 흡사 바위가 떨리거나 나무 뿌리가 뻗어 나가는 소리를 듣는 것처럼 조심스러운 대지의 메시지를 받아들이는 일이다.

이런 감각적인 것의 뒤에서 모든 것을 조종하는 것은 보이지 않는
알고리듬이다. 모든 소리의 원천은 물질의 떨림이다. 그것이 목청이건 기타
줄이건 공기건 말이다. 그런데 근원은 한 겹이 아니다. 그 원천의 뒤에, 혹은
밑에 또 한 겹의 근원이 있다. 사람의 경우 목청을 떨리게 하는 것은 특정한
음절을 만들어 그것들을 분절화하여 어떤 생각을 전달해야겠다는 의지다. 그
생각은 철학사상일 수도 있고 이데올로기일 수도 있고 요리 레시피일 수도
있다. 사람이 아닌 존재에게는 그 근원은 좀 더 넓고 다양하다. 동물의 목소리
뒤에 숨어 있는 것은 생존본능이며 바람 소리 뒤에 숨어 있는 것은 기압의
차이를 만들어내는 자연의 원리. 정보과학의 시대에 소리의 근원은 다른
데 있다. 그것은 알고리듬이다. 태싯그룹은 알고리듬을 이용해 작곡하며, 그
절차는 기존의 작곡과 다르다. 태싯그룹은 알고리듬을 이용해 특정의 소리를
만들어내는 것이 아니라, 어부가 그물을 던지듯 던져 놓는다. 태싯그룹의
장재호는 어느 인터뷰에서 알고리듬을 풍경 소리에 비유한 적이 있다. 풍경은
사람이 만들었지만 그 소리는 자연이 내는 것이다. 사람의 의도는 풍경을
어떤 재질과 크기로 만들어서 어디에 매달 것인지까지만 적용된다. 그다음은
자연이 알아서 하게 놓아둔다. 알고리듬은 사람이 만들었지만 그것의 작동은
사람이 일일이 통제할 수 없다. 케이지의 ‹4분 33초›에서 아무도 4분33초
동안 발생하는 소음을 통제할 수 없다. 태싯그룹의 알고리듬 음악 역시
태싯그룹이 의도하며 연주하는 게 아니다.

이는 18세기 말 증기기관으로 대표되는 산업기계가 등장한 이래 점차 기계가
자율적으로 작동해온 역사의 연장선에 있다. 그 연장선의 끝은 둘로 갈라져
있는데 하나는 알고리듬에 모든 것을 맡겨놓으면 인간의 주체성과 창의성,
자유의지는 어디로 간 것이냐고 걱정하는 사람들이다. 기계적으로 보면
인간은 자동차의 법적 소유자일지 몰라도 작동의 주체가 아니라 오류의
원천일 뿐이다. 그리고 대부분의 사람은 창의성이나 자유의지와는 상관없이
상품 세계가 정해놓은 감각과 생각의 통로를 따라가며 살아간다. 따라서 그런
걱정은 기우일 뿐이다. 연장선의 또 다른 끝은 어차피 이렇게 된 거 알고리듬의
세계를 즐기고 보자는 태도다. 진작부터 알고리듬에 영혼과 신체를 내맡기고
있으면서 그런 사실을 부정할 것이 아니라 알고리듬이 우리를 어디까지 끌고
가는지 보자는 게 태싯그룹의 생각이다. 알고리듬은 인간이 만들었지만
알고리듬이 만들어내는 소리가 인간을 어디로 끌고 갈지는 아무도 모른다.
그 소리를 듣는 청자( )는 기존의 음악을 듣는 이와 다르다. 기존의 청자가
음악을 듣는 방식은 머릿속에 미리 입력된 멜로디와 리듬을 귀로 듣는 소리의

그것과 비교해 가면서 일치 혹은 불일치를 즐기는 식이다. 태싯그룹의 청자는 알고리듬이 만들어가는 그때그때 변하는 소리에 자신을 내맡기고 있기 때문에 언제 어떤 소리를 들을지 모르며 미리 입력해 둔 소리의 질서나 패턴은 이 경우 아무 소용이 없다. 어차피 태싯그룹이 만들어내는 소리는 기존의 어떤 음악 소리와도 상관이 없기 때문에 청자는 대조해 볼 수 있는 데이터가 없다. 그저 미지의 소리 세계를 더듬어 갈 뿐이다.

여기서 우리는 작지만 큰 역사적 변화를 마주 대하고 있다. 사실 알고리듬의 세상이 된 지는 이미 오래다. 유튜브를 볼 때, 구글 검색을 할 때 알고리듬이 길을 알려준다. 우리는 알고리듬이 어떻게 생겼는지, 어떤 메커니즘을 통해 우리에게 그런 길을 가르쳐 주는지 모른다. 그런데 일상에서 꼼짝없이 알고리듬의 영도 하에 살아가고 있다. 아무런 거부감 없이. 태싯그룹의 작업이 만들어내는 빛과 소리는 혹시 그런 사실에 대한 알레고리는 아닐지 생각해 본다.

Tacit Group's Sounds Imply: The Beginning of Algorithm History

Youngjun Lee, Machine Critic

After viewing Tacit group's sound installation work *Morse ㅋung ㅋung*, I reflected upon the following thoughts on the differing nature of sounds.

1

The first American to actually see a photograph was Samuel Morse, the inventor of the telegraph. The type of photograph he initially viewed was a Daguerreotype, and he was also the first American photographer. The eponymous code he invented was a digital representation of sound, but the Daguerreotype was actually an analog photo. Morse code's peculiarity lies in that it does not necessarily have to be represented by sound. Any signal can represent a Morse code as long as it can distinguish between long and short. In other words, you can create Morse whether it's the sound of striking something with a stone or a hammer, or emitting visible light. On the other hand, in order for photos to become digital, 160 years had to pass since the introduction of Morse Code.

2

I heard music that I liked outside the window, so I opened the window to be able to listen better, but strangely I couldn't hear the music, only all kinds of noise. While the window was closed, only the low tones were discernible as they seemed to block the high tones. However, when the window was opened, a mixture of high tones and low tones mixed with all matter of noises such as vehicles and people, all at once. The dynamics of these various sounds negated the totality of the musical sound that was originally intended. But what is the difference between 'original' music and the sound heard after opening the window? Since there is a hierarchy of sounds, is it possible that some be regarded as clearly audible and others as miscellaneous? It would seem evidently so. Some sounds require a great deal of money to reproduce, while others also cost money to be muted. The sound produced on a record and then reproduced with high-quality hi-fi equipment is the former, while the latter is a form of sound proofing to prevent external sound from entering.

3

While riding as a passenger in a car driven by an Electronics professor who studied waves, he was talking about the wavelength and density of the medium, and demonstrated the relationship by alternating the speed of the car. When the car reduced speed, the wave of vibration increased, so the irregularities of the road's surface affected the undercarriage of the vehicle and entered the interior. As the car increased speed, the wavelength shortened and the vibration became basically undetectable. Essentially, the smaller vibration was unable to penetrate the vehicle's body, due to the fact that wavelength and frequency are in inverse proportion to each other.

4

I have often wondered whether bacteria create noise, or if trees emit sound as they grow. I have also pondered whether the Earth's rotation creates sound. It may well do so, but it may not be audible to human ears. By this standard, the human ear is not a very precise or magical sensory organ. However, it is somewhat ironic that there are expensive audio systems that can cost hundreds of millions of dollars to develop, for the purpose of serving those less than perfect ears. Perhaps the reason certain audio systems are inordinately expensive, is because they are designed for the culturally attuned ear, and not the physiologically sensitive ear. Applying this logic, a philharmonic conductor such as Karajan appeals more to cultural phenomenon, as opposed to physiological phenomenon.

5

Many musical instruments are not necessarily expensive, such as violins and pianos. Anything that creates a sound can serve as an instrument. Around 1983, The Nexus, a Canadian percussive instrument group, performed at the Sejong Center for the Performing Arts, transforming anything they could hold into musical instruments. When a percussionist wielded a corrugated pipe connecting to a sink in a large circle, it emitted an odd buzzing sound. Also, as the player gently swept over a pile of nails, there was a strange shuddering sound. In the past I've traveled by large cargo ship. With the ship itself having been constructed with an incredibly thick gauge of steel, it is incredibly sturdy, and the torsional strength so strong that the hull never bends. However, many parts of the interior were constructed of suitable wood, as if creating a room for an ordinary office or apartment. Sea conditions change constantly, and the engine sound alternates with the rate of RPM. Changes in the sea and the engine's performance twisted the more pliable wooden room in different directions, angles, and intensity at every moment. This movement generated different sounds as the ship rolled, pitched, and yawed. Because the sea keeps moving and is ever changing, no one motion can replicate exactly as another. The room twisting to accommodate this movement in tandem always created a different sound, with the number of combinations and the number of sounds the room created being infinite; sometimes it was smooth, and sometimes it was squeaking. A month long voyage provided ample opportunity to observe and listen to the endless variations of the various sounds the ship's cabin and the ship itself created.

6

MBC Radio has been broadcasting *In Search of Our Voice* since 1991, and periodically features local folk songs. Although it seems like unfamiliar ethnic music originating with people who farm or fish far from major population centers where the majority of Koreans reside, the impact of this broadcast is sizable. Though many people are unfamiliar with these folk songs, *In Search of Our Voice* is now familiar to many and has even been parodied on a comedy program. But are these folk songs really 'ours'? When 'we' refers to all Koreans collectively, 'our voice' should be familiar to everyone. However, considering that there are far more people living in populous Korean city centers where they no longer sing or listen to folk songs, it seems impossible to unite the people of the entire country with the sound of folk songs. Currently, people are severely divided generationally and along lines of ideology and religion; taste in music is also fractious. Some people prefer 'trot' while some don't, and the nobility of classical music doesn't always seem elegant nor appeal to everyone's ears. If you visit rural farming areas, there is no house where songs of the trot or folk genres aren't played during fielding or harvest. Folk songs are one of the sounds that remain on record. Ultimately, the 'We' of *In Search of Our Voice* is the collective 'we' composed of aged rural people connecting with old memories, and not the 'we' who simply want to hear forgotten folk songs from the past on the broadcasting station. After all, 'we' that can be united through sound is just a nonexistent imaginary community. Nevertheless, *In Search of Our Voice* plays an important and effective role in creating a community of listeners. Even those who have never belonged to an actual community that enjoyed folk music listen to the program, and are transported hypothetically by the idea that they once enjoyed folk songs as some of the elders in the countryside do and did, and become immersed in a certain sorrow and wistfulness. Currently, 'Our Voice' is no longer that of folk songs, but the sounds that comprise the contemporary era, such as the ringtones of mobile phones, motorcycles speeding through alleys, and BTS songs. Each of these sounds is clearly divided into those who enjoy and those who do not like them. Hence, the collective enjoyment of a certain sound no longer exists, and only fragments each with a multitude of listeners remain.

7

Edison conducted experiments in a makeshift chemistry lab in a train boxcar as a youth, but after being struck by an angry train conductor following a fire during a chemistry experiment, Edison fell deaf and was unable to hear. Edison could have had surgery, but deliberately chose not to, and lived his whole life hearing impaired. He was said to have preferred this state of hearing loss as it allowed him to focus and immerse himself in books without distraction. Edison's staff complained that he only feigned deafness, yet could hear perfectly well when someone said what Edison wanted to hear. Unfortunately we are different from Edison, so we don't have the right to choose or ignore the noise that bothers us. The noise between floors in an apartment victimizes people, and all types of noise while walking on the street cannot be avoided. You can't ask for a change if you don't like the professor's voice during a lecture. We are not the focal point of noise. If we can filter out the sound independently, it is no longer noise, so the fact that a certain sound is a noise means that we have become captive to it.

8

There is a degree of humor in Ahn Hyun Pil's English grammar book, where 'ghoti' reads as 'fish'. The humor lies in 'gh' appearing as 'f'. For the word 'women', 'o' is read as 'i', and in the word nation, 'ti' is substituted with 'sh'. With ghoti being read as fish, it uses humor to demonstrate how regular and irregular letters sound in English. All Koreans have been taught that Hunminjeongeum is the most scientific letter system, based on a structure that originates in the throat and connects to the ear. If letters and sounds match, why do onomatopoeias differ around the globe? The sound of a barking dog, the cry of a frog, and the sound of bombs falling and detonating are all verbally described differently. Is it because the kinds of dogs and frogs vary from country to country, and the composition of bombs deviates? Sound cannot simply be expressed by letters alone. Sound is created when multiple elements resonate along with air, thereby transmitting a vibration to the human ear. The vibration of an element is not a simple phenomenon that can be expressed solely with a few letters. Letters are not an expression of sound, but an indicator that represents the sound of a given language emitted through the mouth under extremely specific conditions. It couldn't possibly be universally executed correctly when trying to express all manner of sounds using different alphabet and lettering systems in multiple languages.

While reflecting upon these things, I had the opportunity to observe Tacit Group's previous work, which tested and challenged the combinations of various letters and sounds. The sound seems to represent the letters, but it is somewhat skewed. The audience always looks for the correct letters to appear, but the expected combination does not always emerge. Instead, sounds and letters move and interact, as does tacit. The word tacit means unspoken, so does that mean no sound should be expected? If so, let's test the limits of sound; whether it be the limits of the listener or the limitations of the speaker. Their most recent project *61/6 Speakers*, which Tacit Group presented at Myungsung Church in December 2020, is a work that tests both sets of limits. The assembly of 61 speakers resonating at frequencies below those audible to the human ear exudes a sublime beauty, leaving one to wonder if such a sound was created when the universe first appeared 13.8 billion years ago. It serves as an invaluable and precious experience for those people who live hearing obvious sounds every day, to be exposed to sounds other than what is normally apparent, and then experience them kinetically. It's about accepting the message of the earth with careful observance, like listening to the sound of a rock's tremor or a tree's roots spreading out.

It is an invisible algorithm that manipulates everything behind these sensations. The source of all sounds is the resonance of matter. Whether it's wood, guitar strings, or the air around us. However, the root is not a single layer: there is another layer behind or below that source. In the case of humans, what makes the voice tremble is the will to create certain syllables and divide them in order to convey a thought or idea, which could be philosophical, an ideology, or a cooking recipe. For other sentient beings, the source is wider and more diverse. What is hidden behind the voices of animals is rooted in the survival instinct, and what is hidden behind the sound of the wind is the principle of nature that creates variables in atmospheric pressure. In the age of information science the source of sound is different, It's an algorithm. The Tacit Group composes using an algorithm, but the procedure veers from existing methods. The Tacit Group does not employ an algorithm to produce a specific sound, but casts an algorithm like a fisherman would a net. In an interview, Jaeho Jang of Tacit group compared the algorithm to the sound of a landscape. The landscape is shaped by man, but the sound is created by nature. People's intentions can be applied only to what materials and size the landscape offers and where to attempt to place them. After that, nature will take its course. The algorithm was created by humans, but its operation is beyond human control. As in Cage's *4 Minutes 33 Seconds*, no one can control the noise generated during the course of 4 minutes 33 seconds, and so it is in this spirit that Tacit Group's algorithmic music is not in fact played or controlled by the members of Tacit Group.

The performance is an extension of history in which machinery has operated somewhat autonomously since the emergence of the industrial age, represented by the steam engine at the end of the 18th century. The end of the extension is divided into two parts, where people contemplate what happens to human subjectivity, creativity, and free will if everything is left to the algorithm. Mechanically, although humans may be the legal owners of automobiles, they are not the subject of its operation, but a source of operational errors; most people live by following the pathways of sensations and beliefs ascribed by the marketplace and consumerism, irregardless of creativity and free will.

Upon reflection, all of those people's worries are superficial. Another end of the extension is the attitude of simply enjoying the world of algorithms regardless. Tacit Group believes that from the beginning, we have surrendered the body and soul to the algorithm, and as opposed to denying that fact, see and explore how far the algorithm will take us. Though the algorithm was created by humans, no one knows where the sound produced by the algorithm will take humans. The listener who hears sound is different from the one who simply listens to the existing music. The conventional way for listeners to listen to music is to enjoy conformity or disagreement while comparing the melody and rhythm presupposed in the brain with that of the actual sound heard through the ear. Since the Tacit Group's listeners are entrusted with the changing sounds created by the algorithm, they do not know what sounds they will hear, nor when they will hear them. The order or pattern of the sound entered in advance is of no use in this case. Consequently, the sound produced by the Tacit Group has no relation to any existing musical sound, so there is no comparable data immediately available to the listener. It simply travels through the unknown world of sound.

So here we are facing seemingly small, yet in essence, large historical changes. In fact, it's been a relatively long time since the advent of the current world of algorithms. When one views YouTube or performs a Google search, the algorithm guides you. We don't know what the algorithms look like, or what mechanisms teach or lead us in any given direction. However, in everyday life, I live in the spirit of.algorithms without any reluctance. I wonder if the light and sound produced by Tacit Group's work may be an allegory for this fact.

354

INTERVIEW : JAEHO CHANG + GAZAEBAL

모호하고 뾰족한 예술의 경계를 향해
인터뷰: 장재호 + 가재발

ARTIST

음악의 시작

가재발　　　　철들면서부터 음악을 하고 싶었다. 하지만 적극적이진 않았는데, 좋아만 했을 뿐 특출한 재능을 보였다거나 한 건 아니었기 때문이었다. 아무도 알아주지 않는데 음악을 하겠다고 나서고 싶지 않았다. 그래서 그냥 밤에 라디오 듣다가 카세트테이프에 녹음해서 친구들한테 들려주었다. 나름대로 고민해서 노래를 뽑고 순서를 정하고 곡과 곡 사이의 간격을 조정해서 만들었는데, 친구들이 좋아했다. 그래. 내가 음악을 좀 잘 알지. 이런 기분이었고 그게 좋았다.

장재호　　　　어렸을 때 꿈이 아주 확실했다. 기계공학이었는데, 초등학교 때부터 세운상가를 내 집같이 드나들었다. 전자 회로를 사다가 라디오를 만들고, 집에 있는 텔레비전을 뜯었다가 다시 조립하는 게 그 시절 나의 일상이었다. 당시 '마이크로 마우스'라고 해서 미로를 찾아가는 로봇을 만드는 경연 대회 같은 것들이 붐이었다. 너무 재미있어 보여 대학에서 꼭 이걸 전공으로 해야겠다고 생각했다. 그런데 당시에는 그런 걸 배울 수 있는 학과가 별로 없었다. 서울대와 한양대 정도였던 것 같은데 점수가 엄청 높았다. 내 성적으로 들어갈 수 있을까? 고민하지 않을 수 없었다.

가재발　　　　본격적인 시작은 미국에서였다. 단돈 200만 원을 들고 뉴욕으로 갔는데, 비행기 안에서조차 음악을 할 생각은 없었다. 그런데 녹음과 프로덕션을 가르치는 학교가 있다는 얘기를 듣는 순간, 바로 이거라는 생각이 들었다. 돌이켜 생각해도 이상한 일이었다. 학업을 마치고 뉴욕의 음악 스튜디오에 인턴으로 들어갔다.

하루는 크리스털 메소드라는 일렉트로닉 밴드와 우 탱 클랜, 르자의 세션에 들어갔는데, 컴퓨터 프로그램만 가지고 음악을 만들었다. 너무 신기해서 작업하는 걸 계속 지켜봤다. 갑자기 어, 저건 나도 할 수 있겠는데 생각이 들었다.

한국에 들어와서는 음악 엔지니어 일과 작곡 일을 병행했다. 작곡가라기보다는 언더그라운드 테크노 뮤지션이라고 해야 할 것 같다. 그때부터 '가재발'이라는 예명을 쓰기 시작했다. 치기 어린 네이밍이었다. 랍스터의 발처럼 센 음악이라는 뜻도 있고, 다 가 버려라, 나 혼자 있게(GO AWAY PLEASE) 하는 뜻도 있다.

그때가 2000년 무렵이었다. 세기말이다. 도리도리 테크노다. 온 나라가 다 시끄러웠고, 홍대에서는 클럽 씬이 시작됐다. 서울발 힙합과 테크노가 태동하고 있었다. 그런데 그 씬을 만들어 온 음악가, 기획자들에게는 미국에서 온 가재발이라는 인간이 이질적이었던 것 같다. 데뷔 음반이 나왔는데 홍대 씬에 받아들여지지 않았다. 그게 몹시 화가 났다. 대중적 히트는 기대하지 않았지만 홍대 씬에서는 인정받고 싶었던 것 같다. 오기가 생겼다. 그래? 어디 한번 해보자 싶었다. 지하 작업실에 틀어박혀서 미친 듯이 홍대 사람들이 좋아한다는 스타일을 팠다. 그렇게 2집을 발매했는데 역시나 반응은 그저 그랬다.

그렇다면, 외국에서 인정을 받는 수밖에 없겠다고 생각했다. 매일 8마디 만들기 프로젝트를 시작했다. 사실 음악이란 건 8마디에서 다 끝난다. 그걸 매일 만든다는 것은 하루에 한 곡을 만든다는 거다. 크리에이티브가 샘물처럼 솟아야 가능한 거디. 그걸 몇 달을 계속했다. 괜찮은 모티브가 나오면 한 곡이든 두 곡이든 완성해 외국 레이블에 보냈다. 오래 걸리지 않아 몇몇 레이블에서 긍정적인 답변이 왔고 결국 영국에서 EP가 나왔다. 듣보잡 한국 뮤지션의 뭘 보고 그랬는지 레이블에서 엄청나게 밀어줬다. A면의 'MULL'이라는 곡이 발매 첫 주에 바로 테크노 음악 차트 tunein에서 1위를 했다. 한국인으로서는 처음이었는데 갈증 같은 게 해소되는 기분이었다. 유럽과 남미의 유명 DJ들이 리믹스도 하는 등 인기를 누렸지만 그렇다고 내가 유럽 클럽 씬을 종횡무진했던 건 아니다. 나를 서울에 눌러 앉힌 건 아이러니하게도 상업적인 성공이었다.

동시에 진행하고 있던 바나나걸이라는 프로젝트가 놀랍게도 홍대 클럽 씬이 아닌 전국의 나이트클럽 씬을 석권하는 바람에 국내에 눌러앉게 돼 버렸다. 여기서 한가지 이야기해두고 싶은 게 있는데, 바나나걸의 '엉덩이'가 얼핏 흔한 댄스곡이라고들 생각한다. 하지만 가재발 오리지널 트랙을 들어보면 생각이 달라질 거다. 나름 전략적으로 장르의 난해함을 쇼킹한 가사와 달콤한 멜로디로 위장해서 그렇지 묵직하고 지금 들어도 매력적인 트랙이다.

장재호   중학교를 졸업할 무렵 형이 LP 한 장을 사 왔다. 아쉬케나지(Vladimir Davidovich Ashkenazy)라는 피아니스트가 연주한 쇼팽의 피아노 소나타였다. 당시 피아노를 배우고 있긴 했지만 좋아하지는 않았다. 그런데 그 음반을 듣는 순간 꿈이 바뀌었다. 아, 피아노가 이런 거구나 싶었다. 그때까지 알던 것과는 전혀 다른 음악의 세계가 거기 있었다. 클래식 음악을 해야겠다고 생각했다. 부모님의 반대는 있었다. 기계공학을 하겠다던 아이가 갑자기 클래식이라니, 아마도 공부하기 싫어 그런다고 생각하셨던 것 같다. 지난한 투쟁 끝에 겨우 허락을 받아냈고 작곡 쪽으로 진학을 했다.

돌이켜보면 나 자신도, 부모님도, '음악을 좋아하는 장재호'와 '기계와 컴퓨터를 좋아하는 장재호'가 연관이 없다고 생각했던 것 같다. 사실 그때 서양에서는 전자음악이나 컴퓨터 음악이 상당히 큰 발전을 이루고 있었다는데도 나는 별 관심이 없었다.

대학에 들어간 후 아직도 기억에 남아 있는 인상적인 일이 있었다. 대학교 첫 레슨을 들어갔는데, 교수님이 숙제를 하나 주셨다. 선율을 쓰는데 2도와 5도로만 진행해라. 2도와 5도 진행이란, 한 음에서 다음 음으로 진행할 때, 예를 들어 '도'라면 '레'나 '시'로는 갈 수

있어도 '미'나 '라'로는 갈 수 없는 거다. 혹은 5도 진행은 '도'에서 '솔'이나 밑으로 '파'는 갈 수 있어도 다른 진행을 못 하는 것. 굉장히 제한된 룰을 주고 곡을 써보라는 게 첫 번째 과제였다. 정말 황당한 기분으로 돌아와서, 밤새도록 고민을 하고, 도대체 이래서 무슨 음악을 만들 수 있나? 좌절도 했다. 그런데 계속 시도를 하다 보니까 결국 멜로디가 만들어졌다. 그때까지 들어보지도, 상상하지도 못했던 방식으로 음악을 만든 것이다.

그때부터 작곡의 방식이란 매우 다양하고, 그 방식이 결과를 끌어내는 하나의 길을 보여준다는 인식을 갖게 됐다. 개인적으로 수학을 굉장히 좋아하는데, 숫자를 통해 작곡하는 것에 관한 약간 집착이 생긴 것도 그때다. 이후 다른 사람들은 아름다운 음악을 만들려 노력하는데 나는 이상한 음악들을 만드는데 심취했다. 미로를 이용한 음악도 만들고, 말도 안 되는 짓들을 정말 많이 했다.

태싯그룹이 만들어진 계기

가재발   Max/MSP 라는 프로그램으로 만든 작품을 봤는데 정말 멋있었다. 이걸 배울 방법을 찾다가 장재호 선생님을 만나게 됐고 한예종 뮤직 테크놀로지 학과까지 들어갔다. 학교에서는 선생님을 무지하게 괴롭혔다. 이거 가르쳐 달라. 저거 해보자. 학생 주제에 교수님한테 밑도 끝도 없는 제안을 했다. 눈치챘겠지만, 내가 무언가 시작하면 정신 못 차리고 밀어붙이는 타입이다. 공부도 미친 듯이 했다.

당시 장재호 선생님은 사운드를 생명체로 보는, 알고리드믹한 작업을 하고 있었는데 내가 관심이 있던 것과 접점이 많았다. 내 관심사는 랜덤을 컨트롤 할 수 있을까. 컨트롤 할 수 있는 랜덤을 만들 수 있을까 하는 것이었다. 그래서 제안을 했다. 우리도 플럭서스(fluxus)같은 스쿨을 만듭시다! 어처구니없을 정도로 거창한 말이지만, 모든 위대한 것들이 다 그렇게 시작하는 거 아닌가. 그렇게 태싯그룹이 만들어졌다.

장재호   사실 컴퓨터 음악에 관심을 두게 된

건 군대에서였다. 군대에 가면 사람이 단순해진다. 나의 미래는 무엇인가? 이런 고민을 하다가 이런 생각이 들었다. 내가 좋아하는 것 두 가지, 음악과 컴퓨터를 합쳐보자. 그렇게 컴퓨터 음악을 시작했고, 네덜란드에서 5년 정도 공부를 했다. 한국으로 돌아온 후에는 가톨릭대학교에 계시는 이준 교수님을 통해 미디어아트를 접하고, 함께 작업을 많이 했다. 그러다 이준 교수가 유학을 가면서 혼자 남아 방황 아닌 방황을 좀 했는데, 그 무렵 가재발을 만나게 됐다.

사실 알고리듬 작곡이라는 게 창작자의 입장에서는 흥미롭지만, 듣는 사람들은 냉담한 경우가 대부분이다. 이게 무슨 음악이야 하는 거다. 공감대를 끌어내기가 쉽지 않다. 나도 즐겁지만 관객도 즐거워할 수 있는 음악을 만들 수 없을까 고민하게 됐다. 알고리듬 아트를 버리지 않으면서도 사람들이 공감할 방법을 모색하던 차에, 가재발과 마음이 맞았다.

그래서 알고리듬 학파를 만들어 보자는 생각에서 2008년 태싯그룹을 시작하게 됐다. 그때부터 지금까지 알고리듬 아트라는 큰 주제가 우리에게는 가장 중요한 영감의 원천이 되고 있다.

WORKS

영감, 알고리듬과 시스템

가재발　　　이런 질문을 많이 받는다. 오디오를 먼저 만드는지, 영상을 먼저 만드는지. 둘 중 누가 오디오를 만들고 누가 영상을 만드는지. 그런데 사실 그런 생각을 해본 적이 거의 없다. 항상 시스템이 먼저였다. 시스템은 태싯그룹에겐 가장 중요한 요소이고, 가장 많은 영감을 주는 요소이다. 그래서 어떤 작품은 제목이 아예 ‹System 1› ‹System 2›인 경우도 있다. 우리가 시스템을 얼마나 중요하게 생각하는지 알리고 싶은 거다.

장재호　　　현대 전자음악의 디테일한 사운드와

스펙트럼을 온전히 관객에게 공감시키기는 쉽지 않다. 하지만 작품의 근간을 이루고 있는 시스템의 규칙을 알아내는 즐거움 같은 건 전달하고 싶다. 얼핏 보기에는 숫자 퍼즐 같았는데 그 안에서 규칙성이 찾아내는 쾌감이 작품과 관객 사이의 다리 역할을 해 주지 않을까 기대한다.

어떤 작품은 친절하고 어떤 작품은 좀 불친절하기도 하지만, 기본적으로는 동일하다. 시스템을 보여주는 것이다. 조금 구체적인 예를 들면, ‹훈민정악›은 한글이라는 특별한 체계를 이용한 작품이다. 한글은, 하나의 소리와 그 소리를 만들어 내는 구조가 매칭되는 독특한 문자다. 다시 말해 하나의 시스템인 것이다. 그리고 한국 사람이라면 그 시스템을 모두 알고 있다. ‹훈민정악›은 바로 그 점을 이용한 작품이다. 예를 들면, 초성으로는 기본적인 파형을 만들고, 중성(모음)으로는 그 파형을 필터링한다. 그러곤 종성(받침)을 이용해 소리의 길고 짧음을 컨트롤한다. 그런 규칙들을 프로그래밍해 놓고는 타이핑을 해보는 거다. ‘안녕하세요’를 치면 무슨 소리가 만들어질까? 그런 식으로 접근을 했다.

‹Game Over›는 테트리스의 게임판을 하나의 악보로 보는 작품이다. 쌓여 있는 블록의 모양새가 음악의 모양새가 되도록 한 거다. 그런 식으로 작품마다 비주얼과 사운드 간의 관계를 다양하게 만들어 놓았다.

가재발　　　이렇게 작품의 시스템을 알게 되면 정말 재미있는데, 모르면 엄청 지루해진다. 느낌이긴 하지만 20-30% 정도의 관객이 시스템의 존재와 작동 원리를 알고 쫓아오는 것 같다. 최근에는 작품 중간중간에 설명을 띄우기도 했다. 세팅을 바꾸는데 빠르면 3-5분 정도 걸리니까 막간에 다음 작품의 시스템을 파악할 방법을 알려줬다. 예를 들면 이런 거다. ‘자, 이 빨간 막대기가 오른쪽에 있으면 피치가 높은 소리고, 왼쪽에 있으면 낮은 소리고, 두꺼우면 소리가 크고, 얇으면 소리가 작은 겁니다’ 그러니까 공연 때는 사진을 안 찍던 사람들이 오히려 그 설명 사진은 찍는 거다. 그걸 토대로 작품을 더 열심히 감상했다. 그때 약간 안도했다. 사람들이 시스템을 알면 이걸 즐길 여지는 있구나 하고. 생각해보면, 기술 전체가 우리에겐 영감인 것 같다. 예를 들어, 베지에 커브(Bézier Curve)라는 알고리듬이 있다. 포토샵이나 일러스트 프로그램에 사용되는 곡선 알고리듬인데, 우리는 그 알고리듬에 포토샵과는 다른 변수를 적용해 본다. 그런 과정 자체가 엄청난 영감이 되곤 한다. 기존에 만들어져 있는 영상이나 회화, 컨셉, 사운드, 음악, 심지어 우리가 좋아하는 음반 같은 것보다는 기술에서 훨씬 큰 영감을 받는다.

장재호 　　　수학 공식도 마찬가지다 베지에 같은 수학과 테트리스 같은 게임 알고리듬도 영감이 된다.

사운드 소스와 프로그램

가재발 　　　처음에는 원더걸스의 〈텔 미〉 멜로디를 사운드 소스로 사용해서 공연을 하기도 했다. 그런데 별로 마음에 들지 않았고 점차 그런 시도를 하지 않게 됐다. 사실 기존의 음악이나 자연의 소리를 사용하면 장점이 분명 있다. 사람들이 그 소리에 익숙하고, 그 소리가 의미하는 바를 알고 있어 친숙하기 때문이다. 그런데 결국 중요한 건 작품과 사운드 아닌가? 그게 마음에 들지 않으니 다른 장점은 아무 소용이 없는 거다.

장재호 　　　기존 소스를 사용하는 건 우리와 맞지 않았다. 존 케이지는 '빗소리나 트럭 소리를 캡처해서 악기로 쓰고 싶다'라고 이야기한 적이 있고, 프랑스의 뮤직 콩크레트(Musique concrete) 같은 경우도 그런 소리로 작업을 많이 하는데, 우리는 별 흥미를 못 느낀다. 손쉽게 풍부한 소리를 얻어낼 방법이긴 하다. 하지만 한편으로는 우리 마음대로 컨트롤하기에는 어렵다. 그래서 태싯그룹은 아주 로우 레벨부터 하나하나 만들어가는 편을 선택했다.

가재발 　　　〈라이프 오브 사운즈(Life of Sounds)〉

라는 작품이 있다. 소리의 삶이라는 뜻인데, 만약 이 작품에 채집한 소리를 이용한다면 한계가 생겨버린다. 소리를 생성하는 것부터 하나하나 직접 만드는 게 우리의 의도를 훨씬 제대로 반영하는 거다.

작품을 할 때 사용하는 프로그램에 관해 얘기하자면, 지금은 Max를 많이 사용하지 않는다. Max를 제일 많이 사용했고 잘하기도 하지만 사실 Max를 사용하면 불편한 점들이 있다. 간단한 작업은 상관없는데 객체를 아주 많이 사용하는 작업일 경우, 그 객체들을 개별적으로 컨트롤하기에는 무리가 있다. 예를 들어 객체가 만 개 있다고 생각해보자. 모두 다 빨간색으로 변해 라고 명령하는 건 쉽다. 하지만 만 개의 색깔을 모두 다른 색으로 하려면 너무 힘들어진다.

그래서 C++를 시작했다. C++를 사용하면 만 개가 아니라 컴퓨터의 능력이 허용하는 만큼의 개수를 개별 컨트롤할 수 있다. 지금은 예전에 Max로 했던 작업도 웬만하면 C++로 옮기고 Max를 꼭 써야 한다면 Max 내부에서 사용이 가능한 JavaScript라는 언어도 많이 사용한다. 사운드는 지금도 MSP를 많이 쓴다. 사용이 쉬운 프로그램도 여럿 있는데 거의 다 전통적인 음악에 기초한 방식이다. 예를 들어, 도와 도# 사이의 음을 하나 만든다고 생각하면, MSP를 사용하면 그 두 음 사이에서 수천, 수만 개의 음을 만들 수 있다. 그런데 전통적인 음악에 기초한 프로그램들은 그런 음을 만드는 게 아예 불가능한 경우도 있다. 자유도가 떨어진다.

장재호 　　　C++은 Object-oriented이기 때문에 사용하기 편리한 것 같다. Task-based의 코딩이 아니라, 스크린에 등장하는 객체들을 하나하나 디자인하는 식이다. 그러다 보니까 작업자가 디테일하게 신경 쓰지 않아도 자동으로 만들어지거나, 랜덤하게 생성되는 결과물들이 있다. 의도하지 않은 결과이기 때문에 우리가 매우 재밌게 지켜보는 부분이다.

장재호　　　　　태싯그룹이 10년이 되면서 돌아보는 시간을 가졌다. 그때 우리가 텍스트를 이용한 작품을 꽤 했다는 걸 깨달았다. 왜 그런지 생각하다 '관객들에게 뭔가 말을 하고 싶구나' 하는 결론에 다다르게 됐다. 우리에게 가장 중요한 건 '소통'이었던 거다. 그게 텍스트처럼 노골적이든, 비주얼이나 시스템을 통해서든 말이다.

가재발　　　　　〈훈민정악〉이 좋은 예인 것 같다. 〈훈민정악〉을 공연할 때 도입부에는 'ㅇ', 'ㅁ' 같이 도형처럼 생긴 자음을 타이핑한다. 그러면 관객들은 '네모가 나오는구나, 동그라미가 나오는구나' 생각할 거다. 그런데 동그라미 옆에 줄을 하나 딱 그으면, '이'가 된다. 아무 의미가 없던 도형이 갑자기 문자가 되고, 관객들도 '아, 저거 글자였잖아.' 하게 된다. 우리는 그 순간을 노려 문장을 타이핑한다. '안녕하세요' 그렇게 관객과 우리 사이에 커뮤니케이션이 계속된다. 사실 우리는 커뮤니케이션의 시작이 '안녕하세요'가 아니라, 'ㅇ'에서 '이'가 되고 그게 '안녕하세요'가 되는 과정 전체라고 생각한다. 그다음은 우리끼리 채팅으로 이야기를 한다. '오늘 관객분들 수준이 높으시네', '그러게 말이야' 이런 식이다.

　　　숨어 있는 또 하나의 커뮤니케이션은 컴퓨터와 퍼포머 사이에 존재한다. 우리는 인풋을 넣고 컴퓨터는 그것에 반응해 아웃풋을 내준다. 이렇게 〈훈민정악〉에는 다양한 층위의 커뮤니케이션이 존재한다. 그래서 개인적으로는 〈훈민정악〉이 지금까지는 태싯그룹이 하고자 하는 작업을 제일 잘 보여주는 작품인 거 같다.

장재호　　　　　돌아보면 저는 아카데믹하고 작가적인 관점에서만 작업을 하는 편이었다. 관객을 신경 쓰지 않았다. 태싯그룹을 시작하고는 완전히 바뀌었다. 우리가 좋아하는 것을 관객도 좋아해 줬으면 좋겠다는 생각이 처음으로 들었다. 작품은 '우리가 하는 건 이런 거야'라고

알리는 과정이고 진짜 목적은 '우리랑 같이 가자, 이거 되게 재밌어'라고 하는 거다.

가재발　　　　　내가 고등학교 때 믹스테이프를 만들어서 친구들에게 줬던 것과 일맥상통하는 것 같다. 태싯그룹을 하면서 좋았던 것 중 하나가 마음대로 음악을 만들 수 있다는 거였다. 바나나걸이나 가재발 음악을 할 때는 리스너나 유행을 의식할 수밖에 없었다. 태싯그룹하면서는 상대적으로 자유롭다.

장재호　　　　　태싯그룹 작품 중에는 게임을 이용한 것이 셋 있다. 〈Six Pacmen〉과 〈Puzzle 15〉, 그리고 〈Game Over〉.

　　　〈Six Pacmen〉은 스티브 라이히의 〈Six Pianos〉라는 음악을 이용한 작품이다. 여섯 명의 연주자가 팩맨 게임을 해서 모두 할당된 아이템을 다 먹으면 다음 마디로 넘어가는 건데, 고스트들이 나타나서 팩맨을 방해한다. 게임으로 보면 고스트는 재미를 주는 요소다. 그런데 연주자의 입장에서 보면 연주를 컨트롤하는 장악력이 약해지는 면이기도 하다. 그 부분을 어떻게 풀어내는지가 남은 과제다.

　　　반면, 〈Game Over〉는 밸런스가 딱 맞는다. 테트리스는 최대한 블록을 평평하게 쌓아야 하는 게임이다. 그런데 그러면 음악이 굉장히 단조로워지고 재미없어진다. 음악이 다채로우려면 테트리스 블록이 울퉁불퉁하게 쌓여야 되는데. 그러면 게임이 어려워진다. 게임을 하는 연주자들은 게임 오버가 되지 않게 고군분투해야 한다. 그게 관객으로서는 아슬아슬하고 재밌다. 동시에 음악도 복합적으로 된다. 결론적으로, 연주자가 게임오버가 되지 않도록 벌이는 즉흥성이, 좋은 게임과 좋은 음악이라는 두 가지 목적을 달성하는 거다.

가재발　　　　　〈LOSS〉라는 작품은 2013년 국립현대미술관에서 한번 공연하고 더 이상 하지 않았다. 이 작품은 사운드가 태어나고 성장하고 결혼하고 아이를 낳고 죽는 과정을 담은 것인데, 연주자의 역할은

하나다. 처음에 사운드를 태어나게 하는 것이다. 그러면 '사운드'들이 알아서 살아간다. 첫날 공연에서 웃지 못할 해프닝이 있었다. 애네들이 계속 먹고, 커지고, 자기들끼리 결혼도 하고, 아기도 낳으면서 작품이 끝도 없이 계속 이어진 거다. 관객들은 지루해지고 나가 버리기 시작해 어쩔 수 없이 컴퓨터를 꺼버렸다. 다음날 공연을 위해 작업실로 돌아와 '네오'를 만들었다. '네오'는 바이러스 같은 걸 퍼뜨려서 작품을 끝내게 하는 일종의 변종 사운드다. 또다시 작품이 너무 길어지면 네오를 투입할 작정이었는데, 결국 사용하지는 않았다.

PLAN

전시, 최근의 작업

가재발   우리가 관심을 가지고 추진하고 있는 것들이 있다. 하나는 오디오 비주얼 인스톨레이션 작업인데, 2020년에 진행한 작업은 〈Bilateral Feedback〉을 제외하고는 모두 인스톨레이션이었다. 음반을 내는 것도 고려하고 있고, 물론 WeSA 페스티벌도 확장해 나가려 한다.

장재호   전시에 대한 이야기부터 시작하자면, 2019년에 cosmo40에서 했던 전시가 계기가 됐던 것 같다. 〈NO LIVE〉라는 전시 중 태싯그룹 앤솔로지로 참가했는데 그동안 우리가 발표한 작업을 전시했다. 사실 태싯그룹은 그동안 공연 중심으로 작품을 발표해왔기 때문에 전시를 통해 인상적으로 보여줄 수 있는 것이 그다지 많지는 않았다. 그런데 그중 〈op.sound[cosmo40]〉를 지하 벙커 같은 장소에 설치의 형태로 업그레이드했다. 〈Op Sound II〉를 발전시킨 작품이었는데, 소리가 많이 울리는, 어두컴컴한 장소에 설치하니 굉장히 몰입감이 있었다.

가재발   〈Op Sound II〉는 2010년에 발표한 작품이다. 우리가 〈Neighbors[i]〉라는 제목으로, 첫 전시를 했을 때였는데, 그때 이후로는 전시 작업을 한 적이 없었다. 사실 〈Neighbors[i]〉도 지금 돌이켜보면 전시가 뭔지 잘 모르고 했던 것 같다. 그때는 우리는 공연하는 아티스트라고만 생각했다. 그런데 알고리듬에 관심을 가지고 공부를 하면서 전시의 형태로만 풀어낼 수 있는 작업이 많았고 그런 흥미와 욕구를 펼치고 싶었다. 말하자면 그때는 우리가 알고 있는 지식, 우리가 알게 된 것을 한번 해본 것이었다.

사실 〈op.sound〉 시리즈의 첫 작품도 공연의 형태였다. 2009년 처음 발표했을 당시에는 평면 스크린에 플레이 되는 영상을 관객이 앉아서 보는 방식이었다. 이 작품을 전시장소의 특성을 살려 새롭게 재해석했다. 우리가 의도한 그대로의 빛과 사운드를 전달할 수 있는 공간이다. 공연과는 좀 다른 경험을 전달할 수 있을 것 같다.

장재호   〈NO LIVE〉 전시에서 〈Op Sound II〉 작업을 하면서 태싯그룹의 콘텐츠가 보편적인 음악의 범주를 벗어난, 그러니까 공연이 아니라 전시의 형태로도 가능하다는 것을 발견했다. 그동안 너무 당연하게 '우리는 공연 그룹'이라고 생각했던 것이 깨진 것이다.

이제는 태싯그룹의 작품이 공연의 형태로만 나올 수 있다고는 생각하지 않는다. 지금까지는 연주자들이 무대에서 공연을 하고 관객들은 객석에서 앉아 감상하는 형태의 공연을 해오긴 했다. 하지만 작품의 핵심이 시스템이라는 점을 생각해보면, 그건 혼자서 작동하게, 다시 말해서 스스로 연주를 하게 할 수도 있다. 이런 맥락에서 늘 전시의 형태도 생각은 해왔는데 실천이 어려웠다.

태싯그룹의 전시는, 공연에서 체험하는 시청각적 경험을 전시의 형태로 제공하는 것이라서, 기존의 전시와는 조금 다를 거로 생각한다. 어쩌면 사운드아트와 비슷할 수도 있는데 차별 지점은 있다. 사운드 아트는 음악이나 음향보다는 컨셉추얼한 부분이 강조되고, 미술적이고 비주얼이 강하다. 우리가 중요하게 생각하는 음악적, 음향적인 체험과는 맥락이 조금 다르다. ‹op.sound› 시리즈는 전시라기보다는 공연의 체험을 공간적으로 제시하는 시도이다.

가재발 　‹op.sound[picnic]›과 ‹op.sound[3671240]›는 매우 음악적인 컨셉의 전시 작품이다. 이미 설치돼 있는 작품을 눈으로 감상하는 것이기도 하지만, 일정한 시간을 들여 작품이 만들어내는 소리를 들어야 한다. 그 과정에서 시각적, 공간적, 청각적 몰입감을 끌어내는 것이 목적이다. 사실 이런 작업, 그러니까 사운드를 하는 사람들이 인스톨레이션 형태의 작품을 하는 게 자연스러운 상황이기도 하다. 문화 예술적으로 그런 요구가 있는 것 같다. 료지 이케다, 로버트 헹케 같은 아티스트도 그런 경우다. 사운드가 음반이나 공연의 형태로만 전달되는 시대는 이제 아닌 것 같다.

장재호 　그러니까 우리의 작품 세계가 공연에서 전시로 변했다거나 한 게 아니다. 물론, ‹NO LIVE› 전시가 계기가 되긴 했다. 하지만 아까도 이야기했듯 우리 작품 속에 잠재돼 있던 전시의 가능성을 발견해낸 것이지, 방향을 선회한 것은 아니다. 우리는 자신을 오디오비주얼 아티스트라고 규정하는데, 우리가 만들어내는 작품이 일반적인 음악의 범주에서도, 미술의 범주에서도 벗어나 있다는 뜻이다. ‹Op Sound II›는 몇 차례 업그레이드를 거쳐 2020년 12월에 ‹op.sound[3671240]›가 탄생했다. 예전에 교회였던 공간에서 성서의 숫자를 모티브로 진행했는데, 공간과 작품이 만들어내는 특별한 분위기가 있었다. 그 이에 ‹모르스 ㅋung ㅋung›의 경우는 전시 작품과 온라인 버전으로도 작업하고 있다.

장재호 　음반이라는 형식에도 관심이 있다. 1996년에 브라이언 이노(Brian Eno)가 ‹제너레이티브 뮤직 원(Generative Music 1)›이라는 앨범을 디스크 형식으로 낸 적이 있다. 컴퓨터에 꽂으면 프로그램이 실행되면서 음악이 만들어지는 앨범이었다. 또, 얼마 전에는 트리스탄 페리치(Tristan Perich)라는 작곡가가 전자 회로를 CD 케이스 안에 넣어 발표했는데, 스위치를 켜면 전자회로를 통해 리얼 타임으로 음악이 만들어진다. 우리는 이렇게 ‘음반’의 형태로 작품을 내는 실험을 지켜보고 있고 고민도 하고 있다.

어떤 문제의식인가 하면, 작품을 원래의 의도 그대로 전달하고 싶은 거다. 현실적으로는 작품의 코드가 OS 환경에 따라 다르게 작동되기도 하고, 유튜브나 비메오(vimeo) 같은 사이트에서 보면, 현장과는 다른 느낌이기도 하다. 외부 환경에 따라 우리의 의도가 왜곡되는 거다. 사실, 백남준의 작품들도 더 이상 브라운관이 만들어지지 않는 현실에서 자유로울 수가 없지 않나.

물론 아직 과제는 많다. 음반 형태의 작품을 만든다면 어떤 형태로 만들어야 할지도 고민이고, 사실 우리는 코드 자체도 의미 있는 작업이라고 보는데, 이걸 공개하는 게 맞을까도 고민스럽다.

WeSA 페스티벌

가재발 　WeSA 페스티벌은 우리가 큰 노력을 들여 지속해나가는 작업이다. ‘WeSA’는 ‘We are Sound Artists’라는 의미다. 매우 노골적이긴 한데, 그게 솔직한 마음이다. ‘우리는 사운드 아티스트예요!’ 하고 소리를 지르는 거다. 우리는 ‘사운드 아트’와 ‘사운드 아티스트’가 좀 다르다고 생각한다. 사운드 아트가 미술 쪽에서 시작된 건데, 그렇게 생각하면 사운드 아티스트는 사운드 아트 장르의 미술을 하는 사람이라고 정의할 수도 있다. 하지만 우리는 다른 뉘앙스를 제시하고 싶다. 사운드 아티스트는 ‘사운드를 하는 사람’이라는 것이다. 사운드를 가지고 작품을 하는 사람이라는 뜻이다. 그런 맥락에 놓인 사람들은, 사운드 아티스트이긴 하지만 사운드 아트를 하는 건 아닌, 그러니까 태싯그룹처럼 여기도 못 끼고 저기도 못 끼는 사람들이 된다. 그런 작가들이 모여 ‘우리는 사운드 아티스트입니다!’라고 외치는 게 바로 WeSA 페스티벌이다.

장재호   페스티벌은 오디오비주얼 장르의 현실 인식에서 비롯됐다. 태싯그룹이 처음 작품 활동을 시작했을 때는 환경이 매우 아카데믹했다. 관심을 가진 사람이나 관객은 대부분 클래식 기반의 컴퓨터 음악을 전공한 학생들이었고, 아티스트와 관객의 규모는 지극히 제한적일 수밖에 없었다. 그런데 2010년경부터는 클럽 씬의 디제이 중 아방가르드한 취향을 지닌 사람들이 한둘씩 아티스트로 유입되기 시작했다. 사실 컴퓨터를 비롯한 전자 장비로 작품을 만든다는 점에서 컴퓨터 음악과 클럽 음악은 비슷한 부분이 있다. 이런 상황을 지켜보면서, 아티스트가 넘어온다는 것은 관객도 넘어올 수 있다는 의미가 아닐까 생각하게 됐다. 아카데믹한 컴퓨터 음악 씬과 클럽 씬을 넘나드는 새로운 장을 만들 수도 있겠다는 생각이었다. 그때로부터 10년이 흘렀는데 이제야 겨우 그 실험을 본격화해 볼 수 있는 기반이 마련된 것 같다.

가재발   WeSA는 사운드 아티스트의 생태계 조성을 목표로 한다. 아티스트 스스로가 자신의 음악/예술 커리어를 끌고 나갈 수 있는 길을 만들고자 하는 것이다. 사실 위사 페스티벌은 관객에게 좋은 공연을 보여주기 위해서 개최하는 것이 아니다. 아티스트에게 기회를 제공하는 것이 더욱 중요한 목표라고 할 수 있다. 페스티벌에 참여한 아티스트가 레지던시에서 새로운 작업의 영감을 얻을 수도 있고, 아카데미에서 학생을 가르치면서 미래의 아티스트를 키워 낼 수도 있다. 아티스트의 음반 발매나 해외 진출 등을 서포트하는 다양한 프로젝트도 준비 중이다.

태싯그룹의 현재

가재발   태싯그룹 10주년 공연 당시 인터뷰에서도 이야기한 것처럼, '아무도 이야기를 안 하는 것 같다'는 기분이 들곤 한다. 우리 활동이 미약해서인지, 아니면 재미가 없는 건지 우리와 우리 작품에 관해서 이야기하는 사람이 거의 없다. 가끔은 우리가 음악인가? 미술인가? 그런 것조차 잘 모르겠는데, 누군가와 이런 이야기를 나누었으면 좋겠는데 그럴 기회가 거의 없다.

세미나 같은 걸 열어보기도 했다. 박영욱 선생님 모시고도 했고, 순수 미술 쪽분을 모시고 미학적으로 접근해보기도 했다. 물론 사람들이 좀 힘들어하긴 한다. 우리 작품이 어려운 건 사실이다. 한번은 큐레이터를 만났는데, 사실 음악 하는 사람들은 큐레이터를 만날 기회가 별로 없다. 그분이 '너는 왜 이걸 만들었냐?' 물었는데 말문이 막혔다. 그 '왜'를 설명하려면 우리가 만든 게 어떤 맥락인지 설명해야 하고, 그러려면 그 전엔 누가 뭘 했고, 앞으론 우리가 뭘 하고 싶고 이게 다 정리가 돼야 하는데, 쉽지 않았다. 그때 이런 생각을 했다. 우리가 뭘 하고 있는지 잘 설명할 수 있어야 하는구나.

가재발   사실 아직도 오디오비주얼이 무엇인지 설명하기 위해서는 수많은 예시와 설명이 필요하다. 얼마 전까지만 해도 세상에 존재하지 않았던 장르이고 아티스트도 그다지 많지 않다. 우리는 그냥 우리가 하고 싶은 것, 해온 것을 계속하는 거로 생각한다. 일례로, 우리가 공연 그룹이었던 것이 우리의 전시 작품에 고스란히 반영된다. 예를 들어 몰입감 같은 것이다. 공연은 아티스트가 관객을 작품 속으로 끌어들이는 과정이다. 같은 공간에서 같은 작품을 향유하며 같은 경험을 하는 것이다. 우리는 전시 작품을 할 때도 그것이 중요하다고 느낀다.

장재호   가재발은 테크노 아티스트 배경이 있어서인지 공연에서의 몰입감을 처음부터 즐겼던 것 같다. 나는 스스로가 그런 성향이 있다는 것을 알지 못했다. 그런데 공연을 거듭하면서 한 명의 아티스트로서 우리의 작품 속으로 관객들을 끌어들이고 나 자신도 그 속으로 들어가서 만나는 경험의 즐거움을 알게 됐다. 가재발이 '테크노 씬에서도 왕따였고, 가요 씬에서도 왕따였다'라는 얘기를 가끔 하는데 요즘은 나도 클래식 음악 쪽에서 왕따가 된 것 같다. 클래식 음악에 기반을 둔 작곡가들 그룹에서 멀어졌다. 물론 그들이 일부러 저를 왕따시킨다는 건 아니고, 내가 자신을 포지셔닝하는 방법이 달라진 것 같다.

태싯그룹이 음악 쪽에서도, 미술 쪽에서도 존재감이 잘 드러나지 않는 상태이긴 하다. 우리가 가는 길을 비평해주고, 분석해주고, 같이 협력할 수 있는 이론가들이나, 리서처 같은 사람들이 별로 없다는 것도 힘든 상황이다. 그래서 늘 고민을 한다. '우리는 대체 어디쯤 서 있는 걸까?'

장재호　　　 사실 이제는 음악과 미술이 더 이상 구별되고 분리된 개별 장르가 아닌 것 같다. 음악 하던 사람이 전시를 하고, 그림 그리는 사람이 음반을 내기도 한다. 장르 간의 벽 뿐 아니라 순수예술과 대중예술을 나누는 것도 촌스러운 일이 됐다. 기존의 악기만으로 작곡을 하고 연주를 하던 음악가들이 자신만의 악기를 만들고 개량하듯, 이제는 예술가들이 독자적인 장르를 만들어가는 것 같다. 태싯그룹의 작업도 그런 맥락이라고 생각한다. 음악도 아니고 미술도 아니고, 테크놀러지도 아니고 예술도 아니다. 그 경계가 만들어내는 모호하면서도 뾰족한 지점이 우리가 가고자 하는 방향이다. 그리고 현대의 많은 미디어 아티스트들이 함께 서 있는 지점인 것 같다.

ARTIST

MUSICAL BEGINNINGS

Gazaebal　　　I wanted to be involved in music from an early age. However, I was not initially active in it, because I believed I didn't demonstrate any discernible talent. Consequently, no one recognized any musical ability in me at the time, and I was not motivated to get involved with going out and attempting to become adept at playing any particular instrument. I chose instead to listen to the radio at night, creating recordings on cassette tape, which I would then share with my friends. I pursued this endeavour in my own fashion, curating the songs, deciding on the chronology, and adjusting the intervals between songs. My friends seemed to enjoy these tapes, which provided me with the impetus to continue. I realized that I knew a little about music, and that instilled a certain degree of confidence in me. I liked how that felt.

Jaeho Chang　　　When I was young, my dreams were very clear. My goal was to study mechanical engineering, and beginning in elementary school, I would visit Sewoon Arcade which was near my house. My daily routine was to visit there, where I would buy electronic circuits, building radios, and disassembling and reassembling the television at home. During the sixth grade of elementary school, I fell in love with computers, and at that time, there was a boom in popularity for competitions to create robots that could navigate a maze, dubbed "micro mouse." It appeared so enjoyable, and I was convinced that I must pursue this field of interest as my major in college. However, at the time there weren't many departments or programs available where you could study that. Maybe only Seoul National University and Hanyang University had available programs at the time, but the admission standards were incredibly high and the competition was fierce. What information would I include in my college application? I couldn't help but worry.

Gazaebal　　　My real beginning was in the United States. I went to New York with just two million won in savings, and I didn't know whether I was going to play music while travelling over on the plane. However, the moment I learned that there was an academy that taught recording and production, I was immediately intrigued. Even in retrospect, my focus and passion at that time seems somewhat strange. After studying, I was fortunate to gain an internship at a music studio in New York. On one particular occasion, I witnessed a session involving Crystal Method, Wu Tang Clan, and Leja. To my astonishment, there were no musical instruments of any kind, only computer programs for creating music. It was so amazing and I just kept watching them work, and I had the epiphany that I could do that as well.

　　　Upon returning to Korea, I worked as a music engineer and composer, probably more as an underground techno musician rather than a composer to be honest. I began using the stage moniker 'Gazaebal', which was a somewhat immature self title at the time. It was meant to evoke a sense of strong and tenacious music similar to the shell of a lobster's foot; it also roughly translated from Korean into a sentiment of wishing others to go away and leave me alone to work, as I often wished not to be bothered (GO AWAY PLEASE).

　　　This all took place around the year 2000. At the end of the century, the whole country was buzzing with Doridori - a type of Korean club dance - and the club scene was emerging in Hongdae, where Korean hip-hop and techno were born. However, to the musicians and pioneers who created this scene, it seems this individual coming back from the United States, who referred to himself as 'Lobster's foot' seemed like an alien. My debut album was released, but it was not readily accepted in the Hongdae scene and I was somewhat angered by this. While I wasn't expecting wide public recognition, I did expect to be acknowledged in the Hongdae scene.

Then my own stubborn determination surfaced and I realized I wanted to attempt a similar style, which involved being stuck in an underground studio and following a style that Hongdae people were incredibly enthusiastic about. I released my second album in that vein, but the reaction was also muted.

I realized I had no choice but to gain recognition from abroad and began a project to create eight measures every day. In fact, the eight measures are enough to compose a song. To achieve this every day means to create one song per day, and it is only possible when creativity bubbles up like a spring from the ground. This continued for several months, and when a good motif would emerge, it would result in one or two songs that I felt worthy of sending to a noteworthy reign label. It wasn't long before a few labels began providing positive feedback, and eventually my EP came out in the UK. The label was fairly influential in what global musicians saw and did. My song titled *MULL* on side A of the record topped the techno music chart 'tunein' right after the first week of release in the UK. It was my first time as a Korean artist, and I felt like my thirst had been quenched. Famous DJs in Europe and South America have remixed and enjoyed popularity with it, but that doesn't mean I've been prevalent on the European club scene.

It was, ironically, a commercial success that established my presence in Seoul. The project called Banana Girl, which was underway at the same time, and surprisingly, dominated the nightclub scene across the country, and not the Hongdae club scene, which was forced to take a backseat in Korea. One thing I want to clarify here, is I think Banana Girl's *Ass* is not a shallow, common dance song. However, listening to the original track of Gazaebal's may change your mind. Strategically, the inaccesibility of the genre is disguised with the juxtaposition of shocking lyrics and a cheesy melody, but it is a powerful and attractive track even now.

Jaeho Chang   When I graduated from middle school, my brother purchased an LP. It was a Chopin piano sonata, performed by a pianist named Vladimir Davidovich Ashikenazy. In fact, I was learning piano at the time, but it never really appealed to me. But the moment I listened to the album, my dream changed. It never occurred to me that the piano could be like this. There was a world of music completely different from what I had previously known or had access to, and I thought I then decided to pursue classical music with significant opposition from my parents. Suddenly the kid who wanted to pursue mechanical engineering was suddenly a classical composer, and perhaps just didn't want to study. After a difficult struggle, I finally convinced my parents, and ventured into composing.

In retrospect, it seems that neither myself nor my parents thought that the Jaeho Chang, who likes music and the Jaeho Chang who loves machines and computers, were compatible, when in fact electronic music and computer music were making a great deal of progress in the West at that time. Still, I wasn't yet interested in the merging of the two entities.

After entering college, there is still something impressive that remains in my memory. During my first university lecture, the professor assigned homework. I needed to compose a melody, only using intervals of 2nd and 5th. Progression to the 2nd and 5th degrees means that when progressing from one note to the next, such as 'do', you can go to 're' or 'ti', but you cannot go to 'mi' or 'la'. Or a 5th degree progression means that you can go from 'do' to 'sol' or 'fa' to the bottom, but you can't progress otherwise. The first task was to compose in a very limited structure. I returned in a really embarrassed state, having pondered all night, and was frustrated. 'What kind of music can I possibly create with this?' But as I kept trying, a melody finally emerged and I had created music in a way I couldn't have fathomed or imagined up until that point.

From then on, I came to the realization that the method by which music can be composed is varied, and that the method can lead to different results. Personally, I really love math, and it was through this realization that I became somewhat obsessed with composing music through numbers. Since then, others have heard some of the beautiful music I was trying to make. However, I was also so obsessed with making new and strange music going through the maze, that I did a lot of ridiculous things as well.

HOW AND WHY TACIT GROUP WAS CREATED

Gazaebal   I had seen a piece created with a program called Max/MSP and it was really impressive. While looking for a way to learn this, I met Jaeho Chang and entered the Music Technology Department of Korea National university of Art. At school, students never pestered the teacher thoughtlessly, asking him to teach this and do that. I made endless proposals to the professor within this particular subject as a student. As you may have noticed, when I start something, I'm the type that becomes very myopic and focused, studying incessantly

At the time, Jaeho Chang was working on an algorithmic project that viewed sound as an organism, and there were many commonalities with what I was interested in. I was interested in the possibility of controlling random entities at that time, Was it possible to create random entities that can be controlled? So I made him a proposal: to create a school similar to Fluxus. It was a ridiculously grandiose idea in hindsight, but don't all the great things begin with unrealistic expectations? And it was from that seed, that the Tacit group germinated.

Jaeho Chang   It was during my period of military duty specifically, that I became most interested in computer music. Entering into military service tends to simplify people and I began to ponder my future. I began considering the possibility of combining two things I most enjoyed: music and computers, and that resulted in my journey to Holland where I studied computer music for approximately five years. Upon returning to Korea, I was introduced to media art through Professor Zune Lee from the Daegu Catholic University, and we worked for a considerable time together.until Professor Lee left to study abroad, I remained in Korea and then met Gazaebal.

In fact, algorithmic composition is interesting from the point of view of the creator, but most of the listeners are indifferent. They ask themselves, what kind of music is this?

It is not easy to establish a consensus amongst an audience. I still enjoyed it, but I wondered if I could create music that the audience could also enjoy. So Gazaebal got in touch and we forged a new path, trying to look for a way to empathize with people without abandoning algorithmic art.

So, when we chose to inaugurate an algorithm school, Tacit Group formed in 2008. From that point on, the overriding theme of "algorithm art" has been the most essential source of inspiration for us.

WORKS

INSPIRATION, ALGORITHMS, AND SYSTEMS

Gazaebal   Two questions I'm frequently asked are whether we create the audio or the video first, and who makes the audio and who makes the video. However, when I think about this we've never given it much of a thought while working. Always the system comes first and it is the most important inspiration for the Tacit Group. Hence, certain works are entitled *System 1* and *System 2*, to show how much we value the system.

Jaeho Chang   It is not easy to always fully empathize with the audience while using the detailed sound and spectrum of modern electronic music. However, we believe there is reward in exploring and identifying the rules of the underlying system that supports the work? Initially, it seems similar to a numerical puzzle, but I hope that the pleasure found in the consistency and logic will serve as a bridge between the work and the audience.

Some works are more accessible and some less so, but they are essentially the same, as they demonstrate the system. To use a specific example, *Hunminjeongak* is a work employing Hangul, a unique system of characters in which a sound and the letters match. In other words, it is a system, and if you are Korean you know and understand the complete system. *Hunminjeongak* is a work that focuses on that point.

For example, we create a basic waveform with the initial voice, and filter the waveform with the neutral (vowel), which modulates the length and brevity of the sound by using the bell. It's about programming those instructions and then entering the data. What will be the result when you type "hello"? We approached it in this way.

GAME OVER is a work that appears similar to a Tetris' game board as one sheet of music. The form created by the stacked blocks became the shape of music. In this way, the relationship between the visual and the sound is varied for each work.

Gazaebal   It's really enjoyable when you understand the system like such, but otherwise it becomes quite boring, but it seems that only about 20-30% of the audience understand the presence and mechanism of the system in our works.

Recently, we've begun posting explanatory notes during the performance. It takes no more than about 3 to 5 minutes to change the set for the next performance, so we tried to let the audience know how to get a grasp of the system during the interlude. The explanatory notes say "if the red stick is on the right, the pitch is high, if it is on the left, the sound is loud, if it is thickened the sound is loud, and if it is thin the sound is low." Audience who weren't taking photos during the performance suddenly got their cell phones out and took the picture of the explanation itself Based on this information, the audience could understand and appreciate the work more, which ,to us, was a relief, that at least our works are enjoyable when systems are understood.

The whole technology seems to be an inspiration for us. For example, there is an algorithm named the Bézier Curve. It is a curve algorithm used in Photoshop and other illustration programs, and we attempt to apply a variable different from that used in Photoshop to the algorithm. That process in itself is a tremendous inspiration. Through this technology we get much more inspiration than from just sound, music, or even my favorite record.

Jaeho Chang   The same is true of mathematical

formulas. Mathematical algorithms such as Bezier and game systems such as Tetris are also an inspiration.

SOUND SOURCES AND PROGRAMS

Gazaebal   Initially, we used the melody of the Wonder Girls' Tell Me as a sound source. But we didn't particularly like it and gradually stopped using it. However, there is an advantage to using existing music or natural sounds, due to the audience's familiarity with the material. But we believe it's the entire work and sound that ultimately matters in the end, so we believe the advantage of being easily accessible through familiarity is negated.

Jaeho Chang   Using existing sound sources didn't suit us. John Cage once stated 'I want to capture the sound of rain or a truck and use it as an instrument', and in the case of the French music contest (Musique concrete), we worked in depth with many types of these sounds, but we didn't really feel much interest. It's an easy way to gain a rich sound, but it is difficult to control at will. Consequently, Tacit group chose to build a sound from the ground up.

Gazaebal   There is a work called Life of Sounds, which literally means the life of sound, but if you utilize the collected sounds in this work, there are limitations. By creating the sound oneself, it reflects our intentions much more accurately.

Regarding the programs that I currently use in my work, I don't really use Max a lot now. I used Max to a great extent in the past with positive results, but there are inconveniences involved when utilizing Max. Simple tasks are not a challenge, but when using objects a lot it becomes problematic as it is difficult to control the objects individually. For example, supposing there are several thousands of objects, it's fairly straightforward to command them all to turn red. However, it is very difficult to make multiple thousands of objects change to individual colors. Hence, I began programming with C++, as one is limited only by what the computer's capabilities will allow.Now, if you have to move to C++ and use Max, you also use a language called javascript that can be used inside of Max.

There are also a number of easy-to-use programs, almost all of which are geared towards traditional music. For example, if you think you are creating a note between do and do #, you can use Msp to generate thousands or tens of thousands of notes between those two notes. However, there are situations in which it is impossible to produce such a note with programs based on traditional music, so the degree of latitude in which to operate is limited.

Jaeho Chang   C++ is a convenient choice as it is an object-oriented programming language. Unlike task-based coding, C++ designs each object one by one, and sometimes I get unintended results, which we have a lot of fun with. Therefore, there are results that are automatically created or randomly generated without the operator paying attention to the details.

TACIT GROUP PROJECTS:
HUNMINJEONGAK TO LOSS

Jaeho Chang   As Tacit Group recently passed the ten year milestone, we've had time to look back and reflect. We realized that we had done quite a bit of text-based work. We considered the reasons for this, and came to the conclusion that we want to communicate something to the audience as the most important element for us was communication, whether it's through an explicit format such as text, or through visuals or systems.

Gazaebal   We think *Hunminjeongak* is a good example. When performing *Hunminjeongak*, typed consonants that appear as shapes such as 'ㅇ' and 'ㅁ' are seen in the introduction, and the audience thinks perhaps they are square and circle. However, if you draw a line next to the circle, it becomes 'ㅇㅣ'. Suddenly a shape that had no meaning suddenly becomes a character, and the audience then comprehends it as a letter. We then type words or sentences in that moment such as "Hello," and

communication continues between ourselves and the audience.

In fact, we believe that the beginning of communication begins not at 'hello', but when the process progresses from 'ㅇ' to 'ㅇㅣ' so as to evolve into 'hello', thereby initiating a dialogue and engaging the audience. In this way we communicate with each other and with the audience. After that, we chat with each other. It's as if the audience has reached a 'high level' on that day.

Another hidden communication exists between the computer and the performer; we input, and the computer responds by providing output. *Hunminjeongak* demonstrates examples of our best work operating on a multitude of levels.

Jaeho Chang   Looking back, I tended to work only from an academic and writer's perspective. I didn't concern myself with the audience. After helping to establish Tacit Group, my attitude changed drastically. For the first time, we thought about the audience also enjoying what I liked. The work involves the process of informing the audience in what we are trying to achieve and inviting them on the journey, with the purpose and aim of them enjoying it as much as we do.

Gazaebal   It seems to maintain a similar sentiment with what I shared with my friends by making mixtapes in high school. One of the things I really treasure about working with Tacit Group is the freedom to make music at will. When I was playing Banana Girl or Gazaebal music, I had to always be conscious of the listener or the contemporary trend. With Tacit Group, I am relatively unencumbered.

Jaeho Chang   Among the Tacit Group's collection of work, there are three that use games. *Six Pacmen Puzzle 15*, and *Game Over*.

Six Pacmen is a work using the music of *Six Pianos* by Steve Reich. When six players play the Pac-Man game and consume all the assigned items, it moves on to the next bar, and ghosts appear randomly and interfere with Pac-Man. In terms of the game, these ghosts are part of the fun factor, but from the perspective of the performer, it weakens control over the performance. This challenge remains an incomplete task.

Conversely, *Game Over* strikes a perfect balance. Tetris is a game where you have to stack blocks as flat as possible, but then the music becomes very monotonous and boring. In order to counteract this,Tetris blocks need to be piled up unevenly for music to become colorful, and the game increases in difficulty. Players must struggle to avoid elimination, which can be exhilarating and fun from the audience's point of view, with the music graduating in complexity. In conclusion, the improvisation, which prevents ejection of the player, achieves two aims: a well played game and good music.

Gazaebal   A work called *LOSS* was performed once at the National Museum of Modern and Contemporary Art, After 2013 it was not performed again. This work is about the process of how sound is born, grown, married, gives birth, and ultimately dies. In the beginning, the sound is born. Then the 'sounds' take care of life. On the first day, there was an unbelievable occurrence at the performance. The work continued endlessly kept eating, getting bigger, getting married, and having babies. The audience became bored and began to leave at which point we were forced to turn off the computer. The next day, we returned to the studio for a performance and created 'Neo'. 'Neo' is a kind of 'sound' that spreads something like a virus and ends the work. If the work carried on for too long again, we intended to insert Neo, but we ultimately did not use it.

PLAN

EXHIBITIONS AND RECENT WORKS

Gazaebal   There are several things we are interested in promoting. One is the installation of audio visuals. All of the work we completed in 2020 was installation oriented with the exception of *Bilateral Feedback*. We are also considering

publishing a record, and of course, we are in the process of expanding the WeSA festival.

Jaeho Chang   To explain the story of the exhibition, it would appear that the exhibition held at Cosmo 40 in 2019 was definitely an opportunity. Among the exhibitions presented was *No Live*, in addition to an anthology of work Tacit Group Anthology has presented. In fact, the Tacit Group has been releasing mainly performance oriented work thus far, so there have not been many opportunities to present work in an impressive manner through exhibitions. However, *op.sound[cosmo40]* was refitted to be installed in a venue that previously served as an underground bunker. It was a work that was developed in the *Op Sound II* series, and became very immersive when it was installed in a dimly lit space with incredibly dynamic acoustics.

Gazaebal   *Op Sound II* is a work released in 2010, when we introduced our first exhibition under the header Neighbors[i], and we haven't worked on an exhibition since that time. In retrospect, Neighbors[i] seemed to possess an exhibitory DNA without knowing what an exhibition was. At that time, we thought of ourselves as mainly performing artists. However, while developing our interest in algorithms, we discovered there many works that could only be presented in the style of an exhibition, and delved to explore those interests and desires; we had only done what we knew up until that time.

In fact, the first presentation of the *op.sound* series was also presented in the form of a performance. When the work was first performed in 2009, the audience was able to sit and watch videos displayed on a flat screen. This work was then reinterpreted by utilizing the characteristics of a new exhibition space. It is a space where we can deliver light and sound as intended. It seems to be able to deliver a somewhat different experience from the original performance.

Jaeho Chang   While working on *Op Sound II* for the *No Live* exhibition, we came to the realization that the Tacit Group's body of work lay outside the scope of universal music, so the work actually lent itself relatively well to the form of an exhibition as opposed to a performance. Our former beliefs and assumptions about us only being a performance group were challenged and perhaps broken.

We don't believe Tacit Group's work can only appear in the form of a performance. Until now, performers have performed on stage and audiences have been occupying the role of sitting in an auditorium. But considering that at its core the work is a system, it can actually operate by itself. With this in mind, we have always considered presenting in the form of an exhibition, but it was difficult to put into practice. The purpose of Tacit Group's exhibition is to provide the audiovisual experience from the performance, in the form of an exhibition, so I think it will be somewhat different from the existing production. Perhaps it's similar to sound art, but there is a noticeable difference. In sound art, the conceptual is emphasized as opposed to music or sound, and artistic and visual elements are strengthened. The context is a little different from the musical and acoustic experiences we traditionally consider important. *op.sound* series is an attempt to spatially present the experience of a performance in the form of an exhibition.

Gazaebal   *op.sound[picnic]* and *op.sound[3671240]* are exhibitions that are very musical in orientation. They invite the audience to approach the work visually, but they also have to take a certain amount of time to listen to the sounds the work creates. The purpose is to draw the individual visual, spatial, and auditory immersive experience in the process. In fact, it is a natural progression for artists who engage in sound performance to do installation-type work. There seems to be great demand for it in cultural and artistic terms, as artists such as Ryoji Ikeda and Robert Henke have demonstrated. It would seem that this is no longer an era in which sound is expressed only in the form of records or performances.

Jaeho Chang   So it's not as if our world of arts has shifted entirely from performance to exhibition, the

No Live exhibition was simply a great opportunity. However, as previously mentioned, we discovered the potential of the exhibition that was evidently latent in our work, and did not hesitate to pursue this journey. We define ourselves as audiovisual artists, which means the works we produce are outside the realm of mainstream music and art. *Op Sound II* was retooled several times, and *op.sound[3671240]* was born in December 2020. In a space that previously served as a church, Biblical numbers served as a motif, resulting in a unique and special atmosphere created by the artwork and the space. Additionally, we are working on an installation as well as an online version of *Morse ㅋung ㅋung*.

Jaeho Chang   I am also interested in the long playing album format. In 1996, Brian Eno released an album called *Generative Music 1* in disc format. It was an album where music was created as the accompanying program ran on a computer. Also, not long ago, a composer by the name of Tristan Perich announced he was placing an electronic circuit in each CD jewel case. When the switch is activated, music is created in real time through the electronic circuit. We continue to observe and contemplate experiments that produce work in the form of innovative 'records' such as these.

When it comes to acknowledging problems of exhibiting, I always want to convey the work as it was originally intended. In reality, the code of the work differs depending on the OS environment, and when viewed on sites such as YouTube and Vimeo, it feels and appears different from the actual presentation. This results in our intentions being distorted through these external environments. For example, can work such as Nam June Paik's really be free in the reality of CRTs obsolete technology?

Of course, there are still many tasks ahead. If we create work in the form of a record, we are worried about what form it will take, when in fact we believe the code to be meaningful unto itself; so we worried about whether it is right to disclose this.

Gazaebal   The WeSA Festival is an ongoing endeavor that we put a great amount of effort into. WeSA stands for 'We are Sound Artist'. It's very definitive, but it comes from an honest heart. We are 'sound' artists! And boisterously so!. I think the terms 'sound art' and 'sound artist' are somewhat different in nature. 'Sound art' begins in the art world, and if a person considers that, they could simply define a sound artist as a one who creates art in the 'sound art' genre. But I want to present it with an alternative nuance: a sound artist is 'one who does sound', meaning a person who works with sound. In this context, although they are sound artists, they do not engage in sound art. Hence, they emerge as people who can't be labelled or categorized easily such as the Tacit Group. It is the WeSA Festival where such artists can gather and loudly declare 'We are sound artists!'

Jaeho Chang   The festival was borne out of reactions to the preconceived notions that previously existed in the audiovisual sphere. When Tacit Group first formed, the environment was incredibly academic and somewhat myopic. Most of the interest came from groups and audiences composed of students who majored in computer music based in classical music, and the number of artists and size of audiences was very limited. However, beginning around 2010, those with somewhat avant-garde tastes in the club scene began to take notice. DJs began transforming into artists one by one. In fact, computer music and club music are similar in that both computers and other electronic equipment serve as creative tools. Witnessing this situation, I came to believe that an artist can traverse an audience, and that I could create a new chapter that crosses boundaries in both the academic computer music scene and club scene.

Gazaebal   WeSA aims to create a functioning ecosystem for sound artists. Artists themselves often endeavor to carve out a path guiding his or her music/art career. Wesa Festival is not held with the express purpose of exhibiting great performances for the sake of the audience, insomuch as providing opportunities for artists in a supportive and creative environment. Artists participating in the festival can receive inspiration for new work during their residency, or they can help mentor future artists by teaching at the academy. A number of projects are also being prepared to support artists' album releases and overseas expansion.

TACIT GROUP'S PRESENT ACTIVITIES

Gazaebal   As we stated in an interview for the 10th anniversary of the Tacit Group, we often feel that no one seems to be discussing our work. Few people talk about our work or us and we wonder whether it's because our endeavours are considered irrelevant or unenjoyable. Is it intermittently music? Is it art? We're not even sure about that myself, but we don't often have the opportunity to discuss with someone who may be asking these questions.

We have hosted and conducted seminars, and have also attended those of Park Young-wook, in addition to taking an aesthetic approach through fine art. Of course, people have a hard time with our work as it is not immediately or easily accessible. We met a curator once, and he asked, 'Why did you make this?' and we were immediately speechless. To explain the 'why', we had to explain in what context we created it, and in what chronological order and what the genesis of the idea was, and it was not easy to explain. It then occurred to us that we needed to be able to explain what I'm doing.

A lot of examples and explanations are still required in order to document exactly what 'audiovisual' entails. It is a genre that did not exist in the world until a relatively short time ago, and there are not many artists involved. We simply believe in just continuing what we want to do, what we have been doing up until this point in time. For example, what we were as a performing group is also reflected in our exhibits, creating something similar to an immersive experience. Performance is a process in which the artist draws an audience into the work. They enjoy and experience the same work in the same space. We feel that it is important to strive for this when we are doing exhibitions as well, even if the format and venue may differ.

Jaeho Chang   Gazaebal seems to have enjoyed a sense of immersion in the performance from the beginning due to his background as a techno artist. Initially, I didn't even know myself if I had that tendency. But repeatedly as an artist, I've come to know the joy experiencing our work as an artist and having to explore and confront my own being.

I sometimes say that Gazaebal was bullied in the techno scene and was bullied in the K-pop music scene, but these days I also seem to feel bullied in the world of classical music, and have grown apart from a group of composers based in classical music. I don't believe that they deliberately bullied me, it's just the way I position myself has changed.

Tacit Group is in an apparent state of limbo, being seemingly invisible to both the music and the art side. It is also a difficult situation in that there are not many theorists or researchers on our path who can criticize, analyze, and collaborate knowledgeably. So we always worry about exactly where we stand.

We believe that music and art are no longer exclusive or separate genres, as someone who has given music exhibits, and who draws pictures and produces records. Not only has the wall between genres crumbled, but also the methods through which fine and popular art are shared have become more unconventional. Just as there are musicians who compose and perform only with existing instruments, there are those creating and improving upon their own instruments, giving birth to their own genres in the process. We think the work of Tacit Group exists in that context. It is not music, it is not art, it is not technology. It balances in the ambiguous, yet with sharp, discernable edges that promote and allow creativity in any chosen direction. This may well be an intersection where many modern media artists will stand together.

태싯그룹의 게스트 멤버
N2(남상원): 2010년 – 2012년
GRAYCODE(조태복): 2012년 – 2014년
박규원: 2015년 – 2019년

태싯그룹의 테크니션
정창균: 2019년 – 2020년

태싯그룹 공연의 연주자
김광래, 김민강, 남상원, 박규원, 박성면,
박재록, 배미령, 백준태, 서혜민, 유태선,
윤소진, 윤제호, 윤지영, 이용현, 장순철,
정진희, 정창균, 조은희, 조태복, 최수환,
현종찬

태싯그룹의 시작을 함께 한 사람
박재록, 남상원, 윤제호, 김민강, 배미령,
이용현, 조은희, 최수환, 장한솔, 송현주

375

발행일 2021년 6월 10일

지은이 WeSA Studio
발행인 이진원
편집 신은진
디자인 홍은주 김형재
인쇄 으뜸프로세스
발행처 주식회사 위사
(제 2021-000028호)
서울특별시 용산구 서빙고로 67
103동 1107호
www.wesa.kr

이 책은 서울문화재단의 후원으로
발간됐습니다.

ISBN
979-11-974235-0-5 03680

First Published on the 10th of
June, 2021

Written by WeSA Studio
Publisher Jinwon Lee
Edited by Eunjin Regina Shin
Designed by Eunjoo Hong &
Hyungjae Kim
Published by WeSA Corp., LTD
(2021-000028)
#1107, Bldg 103, Seobinggo-ro 67,
Yongsan-gu, Seoul
www.wesa.kr

COLOPHON